Imaginal Worlds

Imaginal Worlds

Ibn al-'Arabī and the Problem of Religious Diversity

William C. Chittick

STATE UNIVERSITY OF NEW YORK PRESS

Published by
State University of New York Press, Albany

Printed in the United States of America

For information, address State University of New York Press,
State University Plaza, Albany, N.Y., 12246

Production by Marilyn P. Semerad
Marketing by Bernadette LaManna

Library of Congress Cataloging-in-Publication Data

Chittick, William C.
Imaginal worlds : Ibn al-'Arabī and the problem of religious diversity / by William C. Chittick.
p. cm.—(SUNY series in Islam.)
Includes bibliographical references and indexes.
ISBN 0-7914-2249-6 (alk. paper). — ISBN 0-7914-2250-X (pbk. : alk. paper)
1. Ibn al-'Arabī, 1165-1240. 2. Islam—Doctrines—History.
I. Title. II. Series.
BP80.I2C475 1994
297'.4'092—dc20 94-17044
CIP

10 9 8 7 6 5 4 3

Contents

Introduction

Muḥyī al-Dīn ibn al-ʻArabī, known as al-Shaykh al-Akbar or the "Greatest Master," is probably the most influential thinker of the second half of Islamic history. Born in Murcia in Muslim Spain in the year A.D. 1165, he exhibited his outstanding intellectual and spiritual gifts at an early age. In the year 1200, he was told in a vision to go to the East, and in 1202 he performed the pilgrimage to Mecca. From then on he traveled from city to city in the central Islamic lands, eventually settling in Damascus, where he died in 1240. He left behind some five hundred works. His *al-Futūḥāt al-makkiyya* or "Meccan Openings," which will fill more than 15,000 pages in its new edition, provides a few glimmers and flashes of the luminous sciences he acquired when God "opened" for him the doors to the "Treasuries of Unseen Generosity." He summarized his teachings in the most famous and often studied of his books, the *Fuṣūṣ al-ḥikam* or "Bezels of Wisdom." He synthesized Islamic law, theology, philosophy, mysticism, cosmology, psychology, and other sciences. His numerous students spread his teachings throughout the Islamic world, and within two centuries there were few expressions of Islamic intellectuality untouched by his genius. He has continued to inspire some Muslim intellectuals even in the present century, and his influence has permeated popular forms of Islam.[1]

The significance of Ibn al-ʻArabī's extraordinary influence on Islamic thinking is suggested by a frequently quoted passage in which he recalls his meeting, as a youth of perhaps fifteen, with the famous philosopher Averroes, when the latter would have been fifty-five. Averroes perceived in the young Ibn al-ʻArabī the wisdom for which he had been searching all his life. In cryptic language, the boy informed him that rational investigation was not sufficient to attain complete knowledge of God and the world.[2]

The different perspectives of the two thinkers suggest the differing destinies of Islam and the West. The philosophical works of Averroes were studied carefully by Western philosophers and theologians, helping them establish nature as an autonomous realm of intellectual endeavor. Under the discerning eye of reason, God was gradually abstracted from perceived reality, eventually becoming a hypothesis that could be dispensed with. The world of nature became the proper site for rational analysis and dissection, and the result has been the ever-increasing fragmentation of human knowledge, with a total divorce between science and ethics. In contrast, Averroes was largely forgotten in the Islamic world, but Ibn al-'Arabī's perspective was integrated into the mainstream of intellectual life. The result was a harmony between reason and spiritual perception. Muslim intellectuals were rarely able to conceive of nature without seeing its roots in God. If the natural world is rooted in God, it cannot be studied without an investigation of the moral and ethical demands that this rooting entails. Only in recent times, with the political and cultural domination of the West, have Muslim intellectuals been able to break out of their traditional worldview and look upon unrooted knowledge as an object worthy of pursuit.

Western scholars have offered differing judgments about Ibn al-'Arabī. During the first half of this century, most Orientalists ignored or dismissed him, while a small number of scholars, including H. S. Nyberg, Miguel Asin Palacios, and R. A. Nicholson, began the difficult task of studying and analyzing his works. In the 1950s and 1960s, Titus Burckhardt, Henry Corbin, and Toshihiko Izutsu recognized the intrinsic philosophical interest of Ibn al-'Arabī's extraordinary corpus. Instead of limiting their studies to his role within the Islamic intellectual tradition, they tried to suggest the general relevance of his writings for the history of human thought. More recently, interest in Ibn al-'Arabī has been increasing and other scholars have helped suggest the many facets of his personality and teachings. Especially worthy of mention among a large number of works are the thorough biography by Claude Addas, *Quest for the Red Sulphur*, and the two penetrating studies by Michel Chodkiewicz—*The Seal of the Saints* and *An Ocean Without Shore*.

The early Orientalists tended to neglect Ibn al-'Arabī for a number of reasons. One of the most important of these is that his works are far too voluminous and difficult to encourage anyone not willing to spend many years studying them. A second is that most Orientalists were supremely confident that modern scientific methods had given them a superior understanding of all things, so they felt free to dismiss as unorganized, incoherent, or superstitious anything that did not strike their fancy—and Ibn al-'Arabī seldom did. More recently, modern presuppositions about human nature have been called into question. The assorted intellectual and social movements that are lumped together as postmodernism, for all their excesses, give witness to the undermining of Western rationality. The dissolution of contemporary certainties has had a great deal to do with the eagerness of scholars to look at non-Western thinkers in a search for the constants of the human spirit. Within Islamic civilization Ibn al-'Arabī stands as a grand monument to the possibilities of preserving rationality while simultaneously transcending it, and he could not but act as a beacon for those looking for an exit from the impasses of modern and postmodern thought.

Ibn al-'Arabī has typically been recognized as a Sufi, and this is true enough if we understand the term *Sufism* to refer to a strand of Islamic thought and practice that emphasizes direct experience of the objects of faith. Like a number of other Sufis, he has often been cited in the West as a proponent of the "Unity of Religions."[3] Scholars have noted that Sufi Muslims in general have a more favorable attitude than non-Sufi Muslims toward religions other than Islam. A number of scholars have been attracted to the study of Sufism at least partly because of its liberal appraisal of human possibilities and its relatively nondogmatic approach to Islamic beliefs and practices. Certainly most Sufi masters who have acquired disciples in the West stress the universalistic side of the Sufi message.

It is not difficult to understand why Sufism should be seen as having a positive view of religious diversity. Speaking in a schematic and somewhat simplistic way, it is fair to say that the roots of the divergence between Sufi and non-Sufi Islam lie in different perceptions of the fundamental thrust of the Koran and the Sunnah of Muhammad. When Muslims understand religion to be something that pertains primarily to activity, they stress the Shariah—the revealed law of Islam—and they emphasize individual and social responsibilities toward God. Theologically, this leads to a vision of God that emphasizes His transcendence and rigor. Most non-Sufi Muslims fit into this category, and the general Western perception of Islam as rigid and severe is not unrelated to the exclusive focus of many Muslims on this domain of social and legal teachings.

In contrast, when Muslims see their religion as rooted in inner attitudes such as love and compassion, they place greater stress on the qualities that establish bonds between lovers. Theologically, this leads to an emphasis on the principle enunciated in the famous hadith, "God's mercy takes precedence over His wrath." The loving and gentle face of God is put forward rather than the stern and severe face. This softer and gentler form of Islam tends to be stressed by those Muslims who are inclined toward Sufi teachings.

Muslims who are aware of the issue of dialogue among religions have diverse opinions on how they should evaluate religions other than Islam. It is not too difficult to see that there are two extreme positions, with most people situated somewhere in between. On one extreme stand those who focus almost exclusively on the Shariah and the divine rigor. They tend to condemn non-Muslims as unbelievers, sometimes including in the category of non-Muslims any Muslims who do not agree with them. They support their position by citing Koranic verses that criticize specific practices and beliefs of unbelievers, polytheists, Jews, and Christians. On the other extreme are found those who see the human relationship with God almost completely in terms of love. Those who lean to this side of the spectrum like to give all those who follow a religion the benefit of the doubt. They support their position by citing Koranic verses that praise God's prophets and those who follow them. They assume that the good and the sincere among believers in other religions—like good Muslims—will reach salvation. And even the bad among them—like bad Muslims—will most likely be taken unawares by God's forgiveness and end up in a situation much more pleasant than they had any right to expect.

Many Sufi authorities who have looked positively on religious diversity have expressed opinions that focus on God's all-embracing mercy. Modern scholars who have discussed such teachings have usually done so by citing isolated passages from classical Sufis, or by reformulating the Sufi message in contemporary language without much attention to the actual words of the great representatives of the tradition.[4] In the chapters that follow, I take a third approach, which is to bring out in relatively detailed form a few specific Sufi teachings that have a bearing on the unity and diversity of the religious heritage of humanity.

That "religious diversity" is a "problem" may not be obvious to everyone. Certainly, it is not a problem for Ibn al-'Arabī himself or for the school of thought that he established. By and large, in fact, most Muslims have less difficulty accepting that there is something natural, normal, and providential about differences of religious opinion than, for example, most Christians. Appropriate proverbial sayings, typically attributed to the Prophet, are easy to find in Islamic literature: "The divergence of the religious scholars is a mercy." "There are as many paths to God as there are human souls."

Ibn al-'Arabī sometimes mentions the "problem of the diversity of opinion" (*mas'ala khilāf*), but usually he has in view differences among Islamic schools, and he typically wants to show that diversity has been established by God's wisdom and compassion. In one passage, he discusses this issue in his own typical fashion by pointing out that God Himself is the source of all diversity in the cosmos. Hence divergent beliefs stem from God.

> God Himself is the first problem of diversity that has become manifest in the cosmos. The first thing that each existent thing looks upon is the cause of its own existence. In itself each thing knows that it was not, and that it then came to be through temporal origination. However, in this coming to be, the dispositions of the existent things are diverse. Hence they have diverse opinions about the identity of the cause that brought them into existence. Therefore the Real is the first problem of diversity in the cosmos.

Ibn al-'Arabī does not see this diversity of opinion as a source of confusion or distress. On the contrary, he takes it as one of the many signs that God's mercy takes precedence over His wrath, leading to the ultimate happiness of all creatures. Hence he continues this passage by writing, "Since God is the root of all diversity of beliefs within the cosmos, and since it is He who has brought about the existence of everything in the cosmos in a constitution not possessed by anything else, everyone will end up with mercy" (III 465.23).[5]

Even though diversity is not a problem for Ibn al-'Arabī, it certainly is viewed as such by many people today, especially those who teach in the field of religious studies. In a long article discussing the challenges of this field, the president of the American Academy of Religion recently wrote, "There is a profound cultural need for more sophistication in understanding religious difference and negotiating a religiously diverse world. We live and work in cultures that are wrestling with a complex web of issues related to religious pluralism, religious freedom, and cultural diversity."[6]

This perception of difference, diversity, and even antagonism is only intensified by the academic study of religion. As scholarly activity increases, it becomes more and more obvious that few phenomena in human history are separable from religious beliefs and practices or, in more recent times, from reaction against these beliefs and practices. As Mircea Eliade has said, to be human is to be *homo religiosus*. As a result, even so-called nonreligious people think the way they do because of a certain interaction with religion.[7]

The bewildering diversity of religion's historical actuality is accentuated by the great variety of methodological approaches that are employed by specialists to study religion. Each of these approaches makes important contributions to our understanding of religion's nature, but most are firmly rooted in the experience of modernity undergone by the West. Even scholars who speak as Christian theologians tend to bow to the assumptions of modern thought. If they refuse to do so, they often assume the superiority or ultimacy of the Christian religion and devalue other religions appropriately, and of course they are likely to be ignored by the academy. Those Christian theologians who attempt to avoid exclusiveness often end up doing away with features that most Christians consider essential to their faith.

Ibn al-'Arabī's perspective on religion differs profoundly from that of contemporary Western methodologies in its assumptions about the role and function of human beings in the cosmos. Of course, most scholars of religion do not voice their assumptions on such matters, but it is precisely the unspoken assumptions that provide the greatest commonality among them. These assumptions are perhaps easier to express in negative than positive terms. For example, modern scholarship—in contrast to traditional Islamic scholarship—does not presuppose an ultimate reality that unifies all of existence, a clear purpose to human life, a moral dimension to both human activity and the natural world, the divine origin of religion, or the truth of scripture. One might reply that Christian fundamentalists, for example, do presuppose some or most of these things, and that they do not play an honored role in academic circles. I would add that they are also not known for the subtlety of their interpretative techniques or their positive evaluation of religious plurality.

Although Muslim authors have typically made certain assumptions about the nature of reality, they have not made them in exactly the same way. In fact, the Islamic tradition has witnessed a grand diversity over the ages, in spite of many points of commonality. On the issue of religious diversity, some Muslim scholars have tended toward exclusivism, some toward openness and inclusivism, and others toward a clear enunciation of the necessity of plurality. Ibn al-'Arabī represents probably the most sophisticated and profound thinker in the last category.

I do not mean to claim that the Shaykh al-Akbar set out to provide a theory of religion or a rationale for religious diversity. But he did aim to explain reality as such, and, as Michel Chodkiewicz rightly remarks, his great popularity over the centuries has to do with the fact that "He has an answer for everything."[8] Of course, the Shaykh addressed these answers to questions that had been posed by Muslim intellectuals, but the underlying issues are by no means unique to Islamic civilization. Once his overall worldview is grasped, it is easy to understand that his answers are utterly coherent with a certain view of reality, and that this view—whether or not we agree with it—leaves nothing out of account.

It is difficult to explain in a few words what is special about Ibn al-'Arabī's teachings. It is certainly tempting to simplify things by putting a label on him, but I am not aware that modern scholarship has devised a label that might be appropriate and not at the same time misleading. One way to suggest his unique accomplishments is to ask him to explain what exactly he thought he was doing, even though he provides several answers to this question in his works. In any case, it may be useful to reflect upon a title that he seems to have claimed for himself. This is *khātam al-awliyā' al-Muḥammadiyya*, which has usually been translated into English as the "Seal of the Muhammadan Saints," but which I prefer to translate as the "Seal of the Muhammadan Friends [of God]."[9]

The term *Seal of the Friends* derives from a title that the Koran gives to Muhammad, "Seal of the Prophets." This is typically understood to mean that Muhammad was the last of the 124,000 prophets that God sent to the world from the time of Adam. It is also understood to mean that Muhammad achieved in his own person all the human perfections possessed by all previous prophets, and that the revelation he received from God—the Koran—gathers together all the prophetic sciences in a single synthetic whole.

Like seal, the term *friend of God* is Koranic, and, by the time of Ibn al-'Arabī, it had become one of the standard expressions that was used to describe those Muslims who came close to embodying the model of human perfection established by Muhammad. Many Western scholars have translated this term as "saint," but "saint" has specific Christian connotations that do not apply in the Islamic context.

The idea of divine friendship is a major theme of Ibn al-'Arabī's writings. In brief, he follows the mainstream of the Islamic tradition by asserting that God chooses as His friends those people who embody the best qualities of the human race. These are first and foremost the prophets. Then God's revelations to the prophets make it possible for others to become His friends as well.

Each prophet is a source of guidance and a model of human perfection. Those who follow in the footsteps of any prophet may be given an "inheritance" (*wirātha*) from that prophet, and this inheritance has three basic dimensions: works, or activities that manifest noble character traits; states, or inner experiences of unseen realities; and knowledge, or the direct perception and understanding of various modalities of reality.

Ibn al-'Arabī considered the goal of religion to be the achievement of human perfection in the three modalities of works, states, and knowledge. The prophets are the models who establish the diverse paradigms of perfection. Knowledge is one dimension of perfection, and in many ways the most important and fundamental dimension. It demands discernment and putting things in their proper places. He writes, "As a person moves closer to perfection, God gives him discernment among affairs and verifies for him the realities" (II 525.2). The "realities" are the things of the universe as known by God Himself.

Each modality of human perfection that has been established by the prophets brings along with it knowledge of a certain configuration of the realities. The realities are infinite, so they can be known in their simultaneity only by God. Nevertheless, it is possible for human beings to know the principles of the manifest and nonmanifest realities, and these principles are typically understood to be denoted by the names of God. In many passages, Ibn al-'Arabī connects the modes of knowing the realities with the divine names. In his view, the great prophets, while knowing all God's names, have special insight into the manner in which certain specific divine names exercise their effects in the universe. In the *Fuṣūṣ al-ḥikam*, he associates each of twenty-seven prophets with a specific divine name.

Each prophet has left an inheritance, and Ibn al-'Arabī tells us that in every age there must be at least 124,000 friends of God—that is, one inheritor for each prophet of history (III 208.14). The prophetic inheritances define the various modes of authentic experience and knowledge of God. In other words, to attain to true knowledge, one must know God according to a certain paradigm of human perfection defined by a specific prophet.

The question of how people can gain the knowledge bestowed upon a prophet is central to Ibn al-'Arabī's writings. The simplest answer is that, to the extent human initiative plays a role, people must follow a given prophet's guidance. However, the guidance of most prophets has not come down to us. In the case of these prophets, the only way to receive an inheritance is to receive it by means of one of the later prophets. And since Muhammad's works, states, and knowledge comprise everything given to all previous prophets, the best way to receive a prophetic inheritance is to follow Muhammad. In any case, in the last analysis, it is God Himself who chooses to bestow a particular prophetic inheritance on a given individual.

Ibn al-'Arabī often says that human effort can take seekers only as far as the door. Having reached the door, they can knock as often as they like. But God must decide when and if He will open the door, and He alone decides what to give the seeker. Only after the door has been opened does prophetic inheritance in its full sense take place. This image of opening the door explains the meaning of the title of the Shaykh's magnum opus, *al-Futūḥāt al-makkiyya*, "The Meccan Openings." Ibn al-'Arabī did not acquire the sciences contained in this work by study or discursive reasoning. They were simply given to him when God opened the door. In a typical passage, he describes the process whereby one attains to opening: "When the aspiring traveler clings to retreat and invocation of God's name, when he empties his heart of reflective thoughts, and when he sits in poverty, having nothing, at the door of his Lord, then God will bestow upon him and give him something of knowledge of Him, of the divine mysteries, and of the lordly sciences. . . . That is why Abū Yazīd has said, 'You take your knowledge dead from the dead, but I take my knowledge from the Living One who does not die'" (I 31.4).

When the door was opened to him, Ibn al-'Arabī found that he had inherited all the sciences of Muhammad. Among these sciences was the knowledge that no one after him—except Jesus, at the end of time—would receive this inheritance in its fullness. Hence Ibn al-'Arabī saw himself as the Seal of Muhammadan Friendship, that is, the last person to actualize fully the specific mode of friendship that results from embodying the paradigm established by Muhammad.

Clearly, Ibn al-'Arabī's claim to be the Seal of God's Muhammadan Friends does not imply that there will be no friends of God after him. Rather, it means that no one after him, except Jesus, will inherit the totality of the prophetic works, states, and sciences, a totality realized by Muhammad alone among the prophets. Thus, Ibn al-'Arabī held that friends of God would continue to inherit from Muhammad, but from his time onward the Muhammadan inheritance would be partial, which is to say that the inheritors would inherit works, states, and sciences connected to specific prophets of previous eras. For example, the Shaykh writes, "Just as God sealed the prophecy of the revealed religions through Muhammad, so also God sealed, through the Muhammadan Seal, the friendship that is acquired through the Muhammadan inheritance, but not that which is acquired through the other prophets. For among God's friends are those who inherit from Abraham, Moses, and Jesus. These will continue to be found after this Muhammadan Seal. But after him, no friend will be found 'upon the heart of Muhammad'" (II 49.24).

If only the Muhammadan friends of God inherit all the sciences of Muhammad—which are equivalent to the sciences of all the prophets—the seal of these friends will be the person in his own time with the most knowledge of God. Thus Ibn al-'Arabī writes about the Seal, "There is no one who has more knowledge of God. . . . He and the Koran are siblings" (III 329.27).

Ibn al-ʻArabī's claim to be the Seal of the Muhammadan Friends is, of course, rather grandiose. Many scholars in both the pre-modern Islamic world and the modern West have dismissed it. Nevertheless, the fact remains that no one after Ibn al-ʻArabī has come close to matching the profundity, freshness, and detail of his vision. Whether or not we accept his claim, it is difficult to deny him the title of "Greatest Master."

The Shaykh considered it his function, as the Seal of the Muhammadan Friends, to explicate the primary modalities of human perfection embraced by the Muhammadan inheritance, which is identical with the inheritance of all the prophets. He considered every mode of existence accessible to human beings—each of which is defined by a specific constellation of works, states, and knowledges—to be a "station" (*maqām*) of knowledge. He saw each friend of God and each seeker of God as standing in a specific station. A person's station is determined by a host of factors, all of which go back ultimately to the nature of reality itself. But to the extent that these stations represent valid perspectives on the nature of reality, they derive from the inheritance of one or more of the prophets. Given that Muhammad's knowledge embraced the knowledge of all previous prophets, his station embraced all their stations, which is to say that he embodied every human perfection on the level of works, states, and knowledge.

To understand fully the nature of a station, a person must stand within it. Muhammad knew the station of all the prophets because he stood in all their stations, but they did not know the fullness of his station, because their standing in specific stations prevented them from standing in his universal station. Those who inherit fully from Muhammad inherit his knowledge of all the stations of the prophets. They stand with Muhammad in every station and in no station. This is to say that, by standing in all stations, they are able to situate each station in its proper place without being delimited and defined by it. Thus Ibn al-ʻArabī tells us that the "Muhammadan friends of God"—those who have inherited all the works, states, and knowledge of Muhammad—stand in "the Station of No Station." We will return to this concept several times in the course of this book.

One of the things that the Shaykh set out to do in the *Futūḥāt*, then, was to expose every mode of knowledge embraced by the Muhammadan inheritance. At the same time, he knew that this is an impossibility, because it would entail explaining every modality of knowledge available to the human species, and all the books in the universe could not contain that knowledge. Hence he repeatedly apologizes in the *Futūḥāt* for explaining things so briefly, and he often provides long lists of knowledges relevant to specific stations that he does not have the time to discuss.

In claiming to be a Muhammadan friend of God, Ibn al-ʻArabī could not identify himself with any single prophetic knowledge to the exclusion of other modes of knowledge. In effect, he laid claim to knowing all things, at least in their principles. But this claim means that he had to see the multiplicity of prophetic revelations as rooted in the nature of the cosmos. Moreover, as Addas's biography of the Shaykh has illustrated so well, his encounter with prophetic knowledge was by no means limited to the theoretical realm, since the "opening" of the door to specific prophetic knowledges often meant personal contact with the prophet in question in the visionary realm that he commonly calls the "World of Imagination." Especially significant is his account of how he met all the prophets in a single grand vision, a meeting that was no doubt demanded by his achieving the all-comprehensive knowledge of Muhammad and the Koran.[10]

With this brief explanation of what Ibn al-'Arabī thought he was doing, perhaps it becomes reasonable to claim that his perspective on things is unlike other perspectives in that he does not stand in a specific station. In other words, by situating himself in the Station of No Station, he is able to accept and reject every station. He acknowledges the validity of every mode of human knowing, and at the same time he recognizes the limitations of every mode. Thus he considers every perspective, every school of thought, and every religion as both true and false. He does not offer a single, overall system that would take everything or most things into account, but he does present us with a way of looking at things that allows us to understand why things must be the way they are.

Ibn al-'Arabī accepts the validity of the three basic modes of gaining knowledge: rational investigation; prophetic revelation; and "unveiling" (*kashf*), or the opening of the door to divine knowledge. Within the context of the first two modes, he follows the rules set down by the relevant authorities in such sciences as logic and jurisprudence, and he differentiates clearly between truth and falsehood. He recognizes that truth and falsehood can only be judged in terms of specific standpoints or stations. Thus, for example, in the case of prophetic knowledge, truth must be judged from within the context of the revelation in question. At the same time, within the perspective of the third type of knowledge, he recognizes the legitimacy of every perspective that exists. Thus, for example, he writes as follows:

> Revealed religion has a power whose reality does not allow it to be overstepped, just as reason has such a power. . . . I live with the present moment. With reason I deny what reason denies, since then my present moment is reason, but I do not deny it by unveiling or revealed religion. With revealed religion I deny what revealed religion denies, since my present moment is revealed religion, but I do not deny it by unveiling or reason. As for unveiling, it denies nothing. On the contrary, it establishes everything in its proper level. (II 605.13)

Not every unveiling, of course, allows for seeing everything in its proper level. Unveiling has its own dangers, some of which are discussed in Chapter 6.

What Ibn al-'Arabī is talking about here is the unveiling that is accorded to the Muhammadan inheritors, who stand in the Station of No Station and are given the ability to see the realities as they are known by God. It is they who have inherited the divine response that Muhammad received to his prayer, "O God, show us things as they are!"

One of the corollaries of Ibn al-'Arabī's acknowledgment of the legitimacy of revealed knowledge is that he sees it as correct in its perception of things and as justified in offering prescriptions for rectifying the human situation, even though he recognizes that the human situation is as it must be. In accepting the truth of the diverse perspectives on reality offered by human beings, the Shaykh announces the radical relativity of all things and all perceptions, even perceptions that are informed by prophetic wisdom. In this respect, his approach has a deep resonance with certain currents of postmodernism. However, he does not fall into doubt about the absolute demands made upon human beings by the nature of the Real. He affirms an ultimate ground that must present itself through relativity and, more important for human destiny, he stresses the personal dimension of this absolute ground, a dimension that is oriented toward human happiness. In short, the Shaykh provides a way of seeing religious teachings as both historically relative and as personally absolute. Despite the diversity of the demands that religions make, these specific demands, in their very specificity, are still absolutely necessary for the well-being of human beings and the cosmos as a whole.

Probably the most distinctive characteristic of Ibn al-'Arabī's teachings is the stress that he places upon imagination. Many contemporary scholars have taken fresh looks at the importance of imagination for religious expression, but they have usually done this within the perspective of a modern or postmodern sensitivity, with the result that imagination has been addressed largely in terms of its human subject. The Shaykh departs from contemporary views by giving imagination a grounding in objective reality. He makes imagination the fundamental constitutive element not only of the mind, but also of the cosmos at large. In his understanding, the forms that fill the cosmos—including us and our minds—are related to God as dream-images are related to a dreamer. Our own individual imaginations are so many streams in an infinite network of interlocking imagery. Here one can recognize a certain kinship with the Vedantic notion of Maya.[11]

In the introduction to my *Sufi Path of Knowledge*, I proposed that Ibn al-'Arabī's teachings on imagination may suggest that something was lost when the mainstream intellectual tradition in the West dismissed imagination as a faculty that can acquire real and significant knowledge. My attempt in the present book is to show how an understanding of the cosmic and even metacosmic role of imagination can help students of religion focus on issues that are central to the great commentarial traditions but tend to be pushed aside in modern studies because of disinterest in imaginal worlds. Ibn al-'Arabī goes so far as to claim that those who have not grasped the role of imagination have understood nothing at all. "He who does not know the status of imagination has no knowledge whatsoever" (II 313.2). This may sound extreme, but not if one understands what he means by imagination. In any case, he would certainly maintain—and I find it difficult to argue with him on this point—that only by placing imagination near the center of our concerns will we be able to grasp the significance not only of religion, but also of human existence.

The essays brought together in this book were originally written between 1984 and 1992 for specific conferences or collective works.[12] In all of them I attempted to address a relatively wide audience with the hope of making Ibn al-'Arabī's ideas more accessible to nonspecialists. After writing what is now Chapter 10 for a conference organized by John Hick on "Religious Models and Criteria," it occurred to me that all the essays could usefully be brought together under one cover, given that the coherence of the model I was proposing depended on Ibn al-'Arabī's overall view of things, a view that cannot possibly be presented in a single article. In the process of revising the articles for inclusion in the book, I changed most of them so drastically that they are, in effect, new compositions.

Much of what I have written in this book could be supported by citing passages translated in my *Sufi Path of Knowledge*.[13] For the most part, however, I have refrained from quoting the same material here, trusting that interested readers will be able to find more explanation there if so inclined. In their original form, the chapters of this book contained few citations from the sources, but in the process of revising them, I was not able to refrain from translating a few short selections to illustrate various points.

The chapters are arranged in three parts. The first outlines the Shaykh's basic understanding of the role of human beings in the universe. The second illustrates the fundamental role played by imagination in the cosmos, the human psyche, and language. The third brings out a few of Ibn al-'Arabī's teachings on the nature of belief and religious diversity. In the final chapter, I attempt to bring together the basic elements of Ibn al-'Arabī's theory of religion.

PART I

Human Perfection

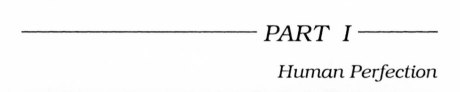

1

Oneness of Being

Ibn al-ʿArabī is most often characterized in Islamic texts as the originator of the doctrine of *waḥdat al-wujūd*, the "Oneness of Being" or "Unity of Existence." However, this expression is not found in his works. It was singled out to represent his point of view not so much because of the contents of his writings, but because of the concerns of his followers and the direction in which Islamic thought developed after him.[1] But even if the Shaykh al-Akbar never employs the expression *waḥdat al-wujūd*, he frequently makes statements that approximate it, and we are certainly justified in claiming that he supported *waḥdat al-wujūd* in the literal sense of the term. However, we cannot claim that "Oneness of Being" is a sufficient description of his ontology, since he affirms the "manyness of reality" with equal vigor. Hence we find that he often refers to *wujūd* in its fullness as the One/Many (*al-wāḥid al-kathīr*).

The term *wujūd* has typically been translated into English as "being" or "existence," and this often does justice to the way it is employed in Islamic philosophy and Kalām (dogmatic theology). However, the primary sense of the term is "finding" or "to be found," and Ibn al-ʿArabī never forgets this. The difficulty of providing an appropriate translation in English is compounded by the fact that terms such as *being* and *existence* have been understood by Western thinkers in a variety of ways. Because of these difficulties, I will usually refrain from translating *wujūd* in this book.[2]

Although the Shaykh employs the word *wujūd* in a variety of meanings, he understands the term in one fundamental sense, given the fact that *wujūd* is one. The different senses in which the term is employed have to do with the different modalities in which the single reality of *wujūd* manifests itself. On the highest level, *wujūd* is the absolute and nondelimited reality of God, the "Necessary Being" (*wājib al-wujūd*) that cannot not exist. In this sense, *wujūd* designates the Essence of God or of the Real (*dhāt al-ḥaqq*), the only reality that is real in every respect. On lower levels, *wujūd* is the underlying substance of "everything other than God" (*mā siwā Allāh*)—which is how Ibn al-'Arabī and others define the "cosmos" or "universe" (*al-'ālam*). Hence, in a secondary meaning, the term *wujūd* is used as shorthand to refer to the whole cosmos, to everything that exists. It can also be employed to refer to the existence of each and every thing that is found in the universe.

As the Essence of the Real, *wujūd* is the indefinable and unknowable ground of everything that is found in whatever mode it may be found. In this sense, the term is often employed more or less synonymously with "light" (*nūr*), a Koranic name of God. As the divine light, *wujūd* has certain characteristics in common with physical light, which is a single, invisible reality through which all colors, shapes, and objects are perceived. To the objection that light is not invisible but visible, one can reply that light in itself is invisible. Only when it is mixed with darkness can it be seen. Pure, unmixed light would annihilate the universe, just as the light of the sun would instantly blind us if we looked at it without the veil of the atmosphere, not to mention the veil of distance. In the same way, *wujūd* is invisible in itself, but nothing can be seen without *wujūd*; or rather, we see nothing but *wujūd*, made diffuse and visible by the veils that are the created things.

In short, the later Islamic tradition is correct to ascribe the doctrine of *waḥdat al-wujūd* to Ibn al-'Arabī, because he affirms that *wujūd* in its truest sense is a single reality and that there cannot be two *wujūd*s. Here he is following in the footsteps of a number of earlier thinkers, like the famous Ghazālī, who glossed the declaration of God's unity (*tawḥīd*)—the statement, "There is no god but God"—to mean, "There is nothing in *wujūd* but God." Nevertheless, Ibn al-'Arabī devotes most of his writings to explaining the reality of manyness (*kathra*) within the context of the divine oneness. It would be a great error to suppose—as some shortsighted critics have supposed—that he simply affirms the oneness of *wujūd* while ascribing the manyness of the cosmos to illusion or human ignorance.

In Ibn al-'Arabī's view, multiplicity is almost as real as unity, since it also has its roots in God, the Real. However, by affirming the reality of multiplicity, the Shaykh does not mean to imply that multiplicity "exists" in the same sense that God "exists," since there is only one *wujūd*, one true existence. To return to the example of light, we can affirm the reality of colors without claiming that each color is an independently existing thing. Red and green exist only through light; they are one in their luminous substance, but two in their specific realities.

If, on the one hand, the universe exists through God's *wujūd*, on the other hand the "things" (*shay'*) or "entities" (*'ayn*) that are found in the universe possess their own specific properties. These things are "other than God," and, as we have seen, God is *wujūd*. It follows that in themselves—without God—the things do not exist and cannot be found. The Shaykh maintains that everything we perceive in the cosmos is nonexistent in itself, but existent in some sense through the Real's *wujūd*. In the same way, every color we perceive is nonexistent in itself, but existent through the existence of light.

If we ignore the *wujūd* of the things for a moment, we can ask about the things "in themselves." What is an entity—a rock, a tree, a human being, a sun, a world—in itself, without reference to *wujūd*? The Shaykh tells us that no entity possesses real *wujūd*. Whether or not an entity is found in the cosmos, its reality or essence stays exactly the same. However, each entity has two states or situations. When an entity is found in the phenomenal world, it displays a certain borrowed existence, which it gives back to God when it disappears, as when a man dies or a stone turns to dust. Nevertheless, the reality of the entity never changes through its apparent existence. It did not possess existence in the first place—it only borrowed *wujūd* from God for a moment—so it does not cease to exist in the second place. It stays in its original state of "fixity" or "immutability" (*thubūt*) in nonexistence (*'adam*).

But what does it mean to say that a nonexistent entity is immutable? Briefly stated, Ibn al-'Arabī explains the "immutable entities" (*al-a'yān al-thābita*) as follows: God is not only infinite *wujūd*; He is also infinite and eternal knowledge. *God encompasses all things in knowledge* (65:12),[3] and it makes no difference whether or not the things that He knows are found in the cosmos. God knows all things forever, even before He creates them, and He knows them in all the characteristics that they will display during their sojourn in the universe. His knowledge of the things corresponds precisely to the nonexistent things in themselves. The "thing in itself" is called the "reality" (*ḥaqīqa*) or "immutable entity" of the thing, and these realities or immutable entities remain forever fixed in God's knowledge. The Shaykh sometimes calls them the "nonexistent objects of knowledge" (*al-ma'lūmāt al-ma'dūma*). Their plurality does not bring about plurality in *wujūd* any more than the plurality of our ideas causes our minds to have many parts.

No doubt the most puzzling aspect of this discussion is the nature of the "existent entities" (*al-a'yān al-mawjūda*). If the entities are nonexistent in their own essences, how is it that we see them in the cosmos and refer to them as "existent"? Ibn al-'Arabī answers this question in many ways. He tells us, for example, that we do not in fact see the things existing in the cosmos. The expression *existent entities* is employed conventionally. *Wujūd* is ascribed to the cosmos in a metaphorical sense (*majāz*), not in reality (*ḥaqīqa*). What we see is not the cosmos, but *wujūd* itself, the Real, since nothing else has existence to allow it to be seen. However, we see the Real only inasmuch as It is manifest (*ẓāhir*), not inasmuch as It is nonmanifest (*bāṭin*). Here the Shaykh typically cites the Koranic verse, *He is the First and the Last, the Manifest and the Nonmanifest* (57:3).

Ibn al-'Arabī explains that *wujūd* becomes manifest because God as Manifest displays Himself in a "locus of manifestation" (*maẓhar*), which is the cosmos itself. God cannot display Himself as the Nonmanifest, because, by definition, God as Nonmanifest is inaccessible and unknowable. Within the cosmos, many lesser loci of manifestation also appear, and these are known as "things" or "entities." These loci of manifestation are nonexistent in themselves, because only God has *wujūd*. Hence we do not perceive the entities themselves, but rather *wujūd* permeated by the "properties" (*aḥkām*) or "effects" (*āthār*) of the entities, while the entities remain immutably nonexistent.

Our perception of things in *wujūd* is analogous to what we perceive when light is passed through a prism: Although there are many different colors, we perceive only light, because only light exists. Hence, the Shaykh says, God's loci of manifestation are plural because of the multiplicity of properties and effects that they display, but they are one because of the oneness of the *wujūd* that is manifest within them. Unity lies in the things' manifestation—a manifestation that is *wujūd*—while multiplicity lies in their entities, which have no self-existence. Hence God in His oneness is identical with the *wujūd* of the things, but He is not identical with the things.

In several of the numerous passages in which he explains the relationship between *wujūd* and the entities, the Shaykh employs the example of colored light. For example, in describing the manner in which *wujūd* becomes manifest as the loci of manifestation without becoming sullied by the limitations of the possible things, he writes,

> The Real is identical with the locus of manifestation. That which is manifest is the properties of the possible entities, which are immutably fixed from eternity without beginning. *Wujūd* cannot belong to them. Thus the Real is declared too holy to be sullied by the changing properties of the possible things within the entity of the Real *Wujūd*. In other words, the Real in Himself is too holy and too sacred to change in Himself because of the changing of these properties.
>
> We say something similar in the case of a piece of glass colored by many colors when light is shone through it. The ray of light spreads out as diverse colors because of the properties of the glass's coloration. But we know that the light itself has not become colored by anything of those colors, even though sense perception witnesses the coloration of light in diverse colors. Hence that light is too holy in itself to accept coloration in its own essence. On the contrary, we bear witness that it is free of that. But we also know that it cannot be perceived in any other way. (IV 202.6)

Although all things are nonexistent in respect of themselves, they can be found in the cosmos inasmuch as they are given *wujūd* by the Real, or inasmuch as the Real is found through and in them. If, from one point of view, Ibn al-'Arabī insists that all things are nonexistent, from another point of view he affirms that they do indeed possess a certain mode of existence that allows us to speak appropriately of their being found. In this second perspective, he often explains the relationship between *wujūd* and the things in terms of the "Breath of the All-merciful" (*nafas al-raḥmān*). In Koranic language, God is the All-merciful, and His mercy *embraces all things* (7:156). This is the mercy that takes precedence over His wrath, so much so that wrath itself cannot exist without it.

The Shaykh points out that the only reality that embraces *all things* in the cosmos is *wujūd.* Hence *wujūd* is God's mercy. Through it He brings all things from the state of nonexistence within His knowledge, where they enjoy no bounties, to a state of existence in the cosmos, where they are able to perceive, enjoy, and experience their own specific realities. Building on hadiths in which the Prophet refers to the "breath" of the All-merciful and Koranic verses in which God's "breathing" is mentioned, the Shaykh compares the process of God's giving existence to the cosmos to the breathing of a breather. The All-merciful Breath is the substance underlying all things. Within it they assume their specific characteristics. Through it the "immutable entities" become "existent entities" (without losing their immutability in God's knowledge and without gaining true *wujūd*).

In the context of the All-merciful Breath, the Shaykh refers to many Koranic verses that mention the creative act of God in terms of His speech or that allude to the infinite "words of God." These infinite words are the individual entities or creatures. When the All-merciful exhales, He speaks, and within His Breath the whole cosmos takes form. Since God's words are individual and distinct realities, multiplicity is real. However, the Breath of God is the single reality of cosmic *wujūd.* All things share in this reality inasmuch as they are found within the cosmos. Words depend absolutely upon the Breath, but the Breath has no need for the words. God speaks not because some external factor forces Him to speak, but because He is merciful and generous by nature and wills to bring creatures into existence. Hence absolute and nondelimited *wujūd* displays God's innate qualities of mercy and compassion through overflowing and bringing the "other" (*ghayr*) into existence.

If we pursue the similarity of God's Breath with human breath a little further, we come across another primary teaching of Ibn al-'Arabī. Is breath the same as the human being or different? This question cannot be answered unequivocally. In one respect, a person's breath is not himself, since he is he and his breath is his breath. But a human being without breath is a corpse, and breath without a human being is moist air. So in fact, the two terms, *human being* and *breath*, are somehow inseparable. In the same way, the Breath of the All-merciful is the same as God, yet it is different from God. And the words that become articulated within the Breath are the same as the Breath, yet they are different. Hence there is no absolute identity between an existent entity and God, nor is there absolute difference. The exact relationship remains a mystery, even though we can understand something of it through rational investigation and God's help.

Divine Names and Human Perfection

What do we know about *wujūd* as *wujūd*? First, we know nothing. Or rather, we know that *wujūd* is indefinable and inaccessible, because we can know it only to the extent that we have it. But strictly speaking, we have nothing of *wujūd*, because we are nonexistent entities. Put otherwise, how can words encompass the speaker? How can a visible color comprehend the reality of invisible light? Or, as the Arabic proverb expresses it, "What does dust have to do with the Lord of lords?" Nevertheless, despite *wujūd*'s inaccessibility, we know something about it because we have a certain knowledge of ourselves and the cosmos around us, and this knowledge provides intimations of the Absolute Reality from which all things spring forth.

Analyzing the things of the cosmos in order to grasp the qualities and characteristics of *wujūd* corresponds to a certain methodological approach typically found among the Islamic philosophers. Although the Shaykh does not neglect this approach, he is far more concerned with investigating *wujūd*'s self-revelation through the prophets, that is, scripture. In practice, "scripture" is the Koran and the Hadith (though not in theory, since, like other Muslims, the Shaykh acknowledges the validity of the scriptures of other religions). Through scripture, *wujūd*—God Himself—reveals itself to human beings in a linguistic mode in order to inform them of its nature.

The message received through the scriptures is summarized in terms of the names of God, traditionally said to number ninety-nine. Each name of God mentioned in the Koran and the Hadith tells us something about the reality of *wujūd*, even if *wujūd*'s ultimate reality can never be known. Most of the Shaykh's writings deal with the explication of the Koran and Hadith. He is constantly concerned to find the "divine roots" or "divine supports" of all phenomena in the universe through scriptural help.[4]

God in Himself—the Essence of the Real—transcends phenomena absolutely, but the manner in which existent things are found in the cosmos tells us something about the Real and gives intimations of *wujūd*'s qualities. On the one hand, this something is expressed linguistically by the Koran through its verses, which are called "signs" (*āyāt*). On the other, it is expressed ontologically and epistemologically through the universe and our own self-knowledge. The Shaykh likes to quote the Koranic verse (41:53) that tells people to gaze upon the cosmos and within themselves in order to perceive the "signs" (*āyāt*) of God's Reality.

What then do human beings know about *wujūd*? They know what the Koran has told them, and they also know what they perceive in the cosmos and in themselves. Hence they know, for example, that *wujūd*—which is the Real—

is Alive, Knowing, Desiring, Powerful, Speaking, Generous, and Just. These seven Koranic names of God are frequently cited as the key attributes upon which all the other divine names and the cosmos depend. Through perceiving these and other divine names, people can grasp many of the characteristics that flow forth from *wujūd* and belong to *wujūd*, but they can never grasp *wujūd* itself, which transcends all its attributes while possessing each of them fully. These names and attributes, then, refer to God. But they also refer to the things or entities, since, in order to come into the world, the things must reflect *wujūd* in some manner, or else they could not be found.

For Ibn al-ʻArabī, the divine names and attributes are the bridge between the nonphenomenal and the phenomenal, both epistemologically and ontologically. In other words, without the divine names revealed in scripture, no one could gain full knowledge of *wujūd*'s modalities. The names denote the actual reality of *wujūd*, and hence they delineate the modes in which *wujūd* comes to manifest itself through its "signs," the things of the cosmos.

Only God possesses the attributes fully and truly. True life, knowledge, desire, and power belong to Him alone. But all things manifest certain aspects of God's life, knowledge, desire, and power by the fact of being found in the cosmos. However, their life is not true life, because true life belongs to God alone. Nevertheless, if their life were totally unreal, they would neither know nor perceive.

When God grants existence to the entities, they come into existence in keeping with what their realities demand. This means, for example, that God gives existence to a particular tree, and it enters into the cosmos exactly as He has known it for all eternity, with all the specific qualities of that particular tree in that time and place. This should make it clear that the immutable entities should not be referred to as "archetypes," since this term implies that a single reality gives rise to many things. But in the case of the immutable entities, each is utterly identical with its own, single, specific, existent entity, which, however, has been made manifest by the shining of *wujūd*'s light.

Although the Shaykh often refers to God's ninety-nine names and stresses the importance of having a scriptural basis for ascribing attributes to *wujūd*, he also declares that God's names cannot be enumerated, for each entity displays a property of *wujūd*, thereby signifying *wujūd* and "naming" it. Hence, each thing can be considered a name of God. Just as the things known by God are infinite, so also are the divine names.

These two views of the divine names led some of the Shaykh's followers to distinguish God's ninety-nine names from the immutable entities by calling the first God's "universal names" and the second His "particular names."

According to Ibn al-ʻArabī, each existent entity shares in all divine attributes, because each displays *wujūd*, and *wujūd* is God, the Essence named by all the names. But all entities do not *manifest* all attributes. Hence the whole cosmos is ranked in degrees of excellence (*tafāḍul*) depending on the degree to which the existent entities display the attributes of God. Some creatures possess life with a greater intensity and some with a lesser intensity, and some appear to have no life whatsoever—though the friends of God can perceive an invisible life even in stones, through the eye of unveiling.

Each and every attribute of God—knowledge, desire, power, speech, generosity, justice, mercy, forgiveness, and so on—manifests itself in varying intensities within the things of the cosmos. Each entity has a specific "preparedness" (*isti'dād*) that allows it to display the attributes of *wujūd* to a greater or lesser degree. A stone manifests power in a certain passive way. A plant shows traces of life, knowledge, desire, and active power. An animal displays all these attributes with much greater intensity. At the top of the visible hierarchy of *wujūd*, human beings have the potential to manifest every divine name.

All creatures are loci of manifestation for *wujūd*. As such, each is a "form" (*ṣūra*) of *wujūd*. "Nothing of the cosmos can have a *wujūd* that is not the form of the Real" (III 409.32). A famous hadith that echoes the Hebrew Bible tells us that God created Adam in His own "form." The Shaykh makes much of the fact that the hadith employs the name *God* (*Allāh*), which is the "all-comprehensive name" (*al-ism al-jāmi'*) to which all other divine names refer. Hence human beings were created with the potential of displaying God as God, that is, God as named by all His names, while other creatures in the cosmos are able to manifest only certain specific names of God, or certain specific and limited qualities of *wujūd*.

That human beings have a unique capacity to display the full range of divine names can easily be understood if we look again at the seven primary names of God mentioned above. Humans share with animals in possessing the attributes of life, knowledge, desire, and power. But these attributes can be found in human beings with much greater intensity than in animals. Who would compare the power of an elephant with that of a Genghis Khan, or the knowledge of a bee with that of the Buddha? Moreover, only humans can manifest the remaining three attributes within the sensory world. "Speech" is a specifically human quality, while "generosity" and "justice" cannot be ascribed to animals except metaphorically.

However, not all human beings employ their speech in a manner appropriate to the full perfection of *wujūd*. And few people are generous and just. Nor do they possess knowledge, desire, power, or any other divine attribute in equal measure. For the Shaykh—as for most other Muslim thinkers—fullness of humanity is rooted in the very nature of *wujūd*. In other words, human beings who want to actualize their true nature must bring out the divine qualities latent in themselves. The qualities of true humanity are God's qualities, which is to say that they belong to the Essence of the Real, *wujūd* itself. These divine qualities are in turn moral and ethical qualities, because they provide the model for every proper, compassionate, and humane act.

The Koran tells us that God is Generous, Just, Forgiving, Kind, Patient, Clement, and so on, and these are precisely the attributes that people must make manifest in order to reach moral and spiritual perfection. Hence the Shaykh refers to the Sufi path as the "assumption of the character traits of God" (*al-takhalluq bi akhlāq Allāh*) and he identifies these character traits with God's names. Thus he grounds ethics and social behavior in the same principles that govern the natural world.

Ibn al-'Arabī makes the clearest connection between the full manifestation of *wujūd* and the human role in the cosmos in his famous doctrine of the "perfect man" (*al-insān al-kāmil*), the complete and total human being who has actualized all the potentialities latent in the form of God. In one respect, perfect human beings—who are contrasted with "animal human beings" (*al-insān al-ḥayawān*)—embody every praiseworthy human quality. They are exemplars of human wisdom, compassion, and all moral and spiritual good. They guide individuals and society to optimum equilibrium with the ultimate Good. They act as the Real's representatives in society, leading people to supreme happiness in the next world. In their human manifestations they are found as the prophets and the great friends of God.

In another respect, perfect human beings are God's goal in creating the cosmos, since only through them does He manifest the totality of His attributes—in them alone does *wujūd* reach its full unfoldment. No creature other than a perfect human being possesses the requisite preparedness to display all God's attributes. If *wujūd* in its nonmanifest Essence is absolutely nonphenomenal, it attains to its full phenomenal manifestation only in perfect human beings, who display every name of God in complete harmony and equilibrium.

The Shaykh calls the most perfect of perfect human beings the "Muhammadan" friends of God. They have inherited the sciences and character traits of Muhammad and dwell in the highest of all human situations, the Station of No Station. This is to say that they have actualized all perfections of *wujūd*. As a result, no specific perfection dominates over them. Other friends of God are governed by specific divine names, or particular perfections of *wujūd*, such as knowledge, speech, generosity, justice, compassion, love, patience, gratitude, perseverance, and so on. But the Muhammadan friends of God actualize every divine name in perfect fullness and in keeping with a balance established by the unknowable Essence of *wujūd* itself. Hence no name, no perfection, "no station," determines their nature. On the contrary, they respond to every situation perfectly, because they manifest *wujūd*'s ultimate reality. Like God's Essence, they are unknowable and inaccessible in their innermost selves, yet they overflow with every imaginable good.

Incomparability and Similarity

Wujūd in itself is unknowable and transcends the entities absolutely. But *wujūd* shows itself through the things of the cosmos and scripture, and this self-showing allows human beings to acquire knowledge of its qualities. In the terminology of Kalām, God's unknowability and transcendence are referred to as *tanzīh*, or "incomparability." This is to say that God cannot be compared with anything. No existent thing stands on a par with *wujūd*. The only fully adequate knowledge of the Real is admission of ignorance.

The position of incomparability was affirmed by theologians long before Ibn al-'Arabī, and he accepts it as true. However, he points out that this description of the divine Reality does not provide a full picture of *wujūd*, because it does not account satisfactorily for the "signs" of God that appear in the cosmos and in scripture. In fact, says the Shaykh, the theologians based their analysis of the divine nature on rational analysis, and reason (*'aql*) understands only what God is not. Standing on its own legs, reason can acquire no positive knowledge of God's attributes. Hence it must seek help from scripture to gain knowledge of what God is. But most rational thinkers—the Kalām authorities in particular—insist upon interpreting (*ta'wīl*) scripture in accordance with their own understanding of what can properiy be attributed to God. As a result, they refuse to accept any description of God that suggests that He is somehow similar to the things in the cosmos. Hence they follow their own rational faculties, not the prophets.

If rational thought tends to negate attributes from God and affirm His incomparability, "imagination" (*khayāl*) has the power to grasp God's similarity (*tashbīh*). The Shaykh devotes hundreds of pages to contrasting these two ways of gaining knowledge. His constant theme is that perfect knowledge of God demands that He be recognized as both incomparable and similar: God in Himself—absolute *wujūd*—is incomparable with all existent things, but *wujūd* makes its properties manifest in the cosmos, and in this respect God is somehow similar to the created things.[5]

What then is the cosmos? It is the "other" (*ghayr*), since it is defined as "everything other than God." But it is not other in every respect, because it is the sum total of the words articulated in the Breath of the All-merciful, and the Breath is not completely different from the Breather. Or, the cosmos is God's "self-disclosure" (*tajallī*) within His loci of manifestation. Through the cosmos, *wujūd* displays its characteristics and properties, that is, its universal and particular names, both the ninety-nine names of God and the immutable entities. Hence the Breath of the All-merciful brings the invisible and nonexistent realities out to the visible and existent plane.

In one sense the universe is other than God, because God's Essence lies infinitely beyond it. In another sense the universe is identical with God, because nothing is found within it that does not name Him. The inexhaustible words spoken by God are the same as the Breath, and the Breath is the same as the All-merciful. Hence the words are the same as the All-merciful. The Shaykh constantly moves back and forth between the two points of view of identity and difference. He sums up his position with the deceptively simple statement

"He/not He" (*huwa lā huwa*). Each entity in the cosmos is identical with *wujūd* and different from *wujūd* at one and the same time.

The reality of He/not He can best be understood through the Shaykh's concept of imagination. An imaginal—not "imaginary"—reality is one that dwells in an intermediate domain between two other realities and shares in the attributes of both sides. An imaginal thing is both the same as and different from each of the two sides that define it. Hence we need to affirm both its identity with other things and its difference from them.

A commonly given example of an imaginal reality is a mirror image, which acts as a bridge or "isthmus" (*barzakh*) between the reflected object and the mirror. We have to affirm that the image is both the same as the mirror and different from it, or that it is identical neither with the object nor with the mirror. In a similar way, dreams are imaginal realities. If someone sees his father in a dream, he has seen his father and not his mother or his brother; at the same time, what he has seen is nothing but himself. The perceived imaginal reality is an isthmus between himself and his father. The most succinct statement that can be made about the dream image is "he/not he."

The Shaykh finds the properties of imagination on three basic levels within the cosmos. On the human level, imagination gives substance to inner experience. It is the domain of the "soul" (*nafs*), which dwells in an intermediate realm between the spirit and the body. "Imagination has no locus except the soul" (IV 393.11). The spirit, which according to Koran 32:9 derives from God's Breath, is a simple, noncompound reality that possesses innately all the divine attributes. Hence it is inherently luminous, alive, knowing, powerful, desiring, and so on. It represents a direct manifestation of God. In contrast, the body came to exist when God "kneaded it from clay." It has many parts and is overcome by darkness, inanimate matter, ignorance, and the lack of divine attributes. The soul is a mixture of the two sides. It is neither pure light nor pure darkness, but rather an intermediate stage between light and darkness. It possesses every divine attribute to a certain ambiguous degree.

For the Shaykh, as well as for many other Muslim sages, the terms *spirit* and *body* designate qualitative distinctions, not discrete entities. To speak of the "spirit" is to speak of a dimension of the human microcosm that is inherently luminous, alive, knowing, aware, and subtle, while to speak of the body is to refer to a dimension that is almost totally lacking in these same qualities. Hence in itself—without its connection to the spirit—the body is for all intents and purposes dark, dense, ignorant, unconscious, and dead. *Soul* or *imagination*, then, refers to an intermediate realm that is neither luminous nor dark, neither alive nor dead, neither subtle nor dense, neither conscious nor unconscious, but always somewhere between the two extremes. Through imagination, the high and the low interpenetrate, the bright and the dark unite. Imagination is neither high nor low, luminous nor dark, spirit nor body. It is defined by its in-betweenness. Each soul represents a unique mixture of qualities and a unique possibility of ascent toward the perfection of No Station, where all the divine attributes are made manifest in the fullest possible measure. But each soul may also descend toward multiplicity and darkness, thus becoming lost in dispersion and passing into an infrahuman state. The soul, then, is an intermediate realm of imagination and ambiguity, mixture and perplexity.

On a second level, the Shaykh employs the term *imagination* to refer to a semi-independent domain of the cosmos. Within the outside world or "macrocosm"—which is the mirror image of the human microcosm—there are two fundamental created worlds: the invisible world of spirits and the visible world of bodies, corresponding to spirit and body in the microcosm. The world of spirits is inhabited by angels, who are said in the traditional symbolism to be created from light, while the world of bodies is inhabited by the three kingdoms, whose visible parts are made of clay. Between these two worlds stand many other worlds that combine the qualities of spirit and body and are known collectively as the "World of Imagination." For example, the "jinn" are said to inhabit some of these intermediary worlds. They are made of "fire," which is a bridge between light and clay. Fire is luminous like light, yet it cannot dispense with fuel from the world of clay. It tries to ascend to light, yet it is attached by its root to the world of darkness. It illustrates its freedom from clay in the way it shoots up toward the sky, but it is bound to clay by the substance that burns. The Shaykh finds one proof for the existence of this macrocosmic World of Imagination in the correspondence between the microcosm and macrocosm. "Presence" (*ḥaḍra*) in his terminology refers to the world or realm wherein a reality—such as imagination—exercises its effects: "God placed sleep in the animate world only so that everyone might witness the Presence of Imagination and know that there is another world similar to the sensory world" (III 198.23).

In a third basic sense, the term *imagination* refers to the greatest of all intermediate realities, which is the whole cosmos, or the Breath of the All-merciful. The cosmos stands halfway between absolute *wujūd* and absolute nothingness. From one point of view it is identical with *wujūd*, from another it is identical with nonexistence. If its own immutable entity is taken into account, the cosmos has no *wujūd*. However, since the cosmos is found, it is a locus of manifestation for *wujūd*. The cosmos and everything within it are He/not He, themselves/not themselves, *wujūd*/not *wujūd*. Ibn al-ʿArabī finds a Koranic precedent for using the word *imagination* in this sense in a verse concerning Moses and the sorcerers. When the sorcerers threw down their staffs, Moses *was made to imagine, by their sorcery, that their ropes and their staffs were sliding* (20:66). So also, people are as if ensorceled, for they see the cosmos as existing independent of God.

> The cosmos stands between nature and the Real and between *wujūd* and nonexistence. It is neither pure *wujūd* nor pure nonexistence. Hence

> the cosmos is all sorcery, and you are made to imagine that it is the Real, but it is not the Real. And you are made to imagine that it is creation, but it is not creation. For the cosmos is not creation in every respect, nor is it the Real in every respect. . . . Hence it is known for certain that were creation to be disengaged from the Real, it would not be, and were it identical to the Real, it would not be creation. (IV 151.14)

The most common traditional text to which the Shaykh has recourse in order to support his contention that the cosmos is imagination is the saying attributed to the Prophet, "People are asleep, but when they die, they wake up." Thus, in the chapter on Joseph of the *Fuṣūṣ al-ḥikam*, which begins with a citation of this hadith, the Shaykh explains the relationship between *wujūd* and the entities with reference to light and shadow. Then he identifies the domain of shadow with that of imagination, since the shadow is defined by the two sides—light and the immutable entities.

> Hence everything that we perceive is the *wujūd* of the Real within the entities of the possible things. In respect of the He-ness of the Real, it is His *wujūd*, but in respect of the diversity of the forms within it, it is the entities of the possible things. . . . Since the situation is as we have mentioned to you, the cosmos is imaginal. It has no true *wujūd*, which is the meaning of "imagination." That is, you have been made to imagine that it is something extra, subsisting in itself outside of the Real, but in fact, it is not so. . . .
>
> Since the situation is as we have described, you should know that you are imagination, and that everything which you perceive and concerning which you say, "This is not I," is imagination, for *wujūd* is all imagination within imagination. (*Fuṣūṣ*, 103-4)

In other passages, the Shaykh stresses the fact that calling this world "dreamlike" can only mean that, like a dream, the world and everything within it need interpretation. It is utter folly to think that what we perceive, whether outside or inside ourselves, is anything but an image that reflects something else. These images, like dream-images, cannot be taken at face value.

> In this world, the human being dwells in a dream. That is why he has been commanded to interpret.[6] For the dream may be interpreted within sleep itself. "People are asleep, but when they die, they wake up." Since, according to this truthful tongue, both sense perception and sensory things are imagination, how can you have complete confidence in anything? You speak, but the intelligent and knowing person is confident that you, in your state of wakefulness, are the possessor of sense perception and sensory objects. And when you are asleep, you are the possessor

of imagination and imaginalization. But the Prophet, from whom you have taken the route of your felicity, has made you a dreamer in the state in which you believe that you are the possessor of wakefulness and awareness. Hence, since you dwell in a dream in your wakefulness in this world, everything within which you dwell is an imaginal affair and is sought for the sake of something else. That something else is not itself found in what you see. (IV 434.24)

Ambiguity and intermediateness are properties of cosmic things, which are nothing but imagination, not only in their present situation, but also in their temporal unfolding. Just as each thing is both identical with and different from *wujūd*, so also each moment of each thing is both identical with and different from the preceding and following moments. The Shaykh points to the infinity of *wujūd* and cites the axiom, "Self-disclosure never repeats itself." God in His infinite effusion is under no constraints. Hence no two things and no two instants are exactly the same. This is the Shaykh's famous doctrine of "the renewal of creation at each instant." As he writes concerning the cosmos, "Everything other than the Essence of God stands in the station of transmutation, speedy and slow. Everything other than the Essence of God is intervening imagination and vanishing shadow, . . . undergoing transformation from form to form constantly and forever. And imagination is nothing but this. . . . So the cosmos only becomes manifest within imagination" (II 313.17).[7]

The cosmos, then, is He/not He. It is both identical with *wujūd* and different from *wujūd*. Inasmuch as it is identical with *wujūd*, it manifests the oneness of *wujūd*'s Essence. Inasmuch as it is different, it manifests the multiple properties designated by *wujūd*'s names. As Ibn al-'Arabī often says, *wujūd* is one in its Essence and many through its self-disclosures. It is both incomparable with all entities and similar to every created thing. And the reality of *wujūd*, its simultaneous oneness and manyness, finds its most complete outward expression in perfect human beings, who manifest all the names of God in their fullness.

In its simultaneous oneness and manyness, *wujūd* can be said to have two perfections. The first is represented by the incomparability of the divine Essence, and the second by the similarity of the divine names. In the same way, perfect human beings have two perfections. The first is their essential reality as the form of God; the second, their accidental manifestations through which they display God's names in specific historical contexts. In respect of the first perfection, all perfect human beings are essentially one, and it is possible to speak of "*the* perfect human being" as a unique reality or as "the logos." In respect of the second perfection, each perfect human being has a specific role to play within the cosmos. Hence there are many such beings fulfilling the functions that God has given them. In respect of the essential perfection of perfect human beings, the Koran says that there is no distinction among God's messengers (2:285). In respect of their accidental perfection, it declares that God has ranked His messengers in degrees of excellence (2:253).

In short, perfect human beings are fixed in their essences, which are not other than the essence of *wujūd* itself. At the same time, they undergo constant transformation and transmutation by participating in the ceaseless self-disclosure of God and manifesting the properties of the divine names in a never-ending variety of cosmic situations. The heart (*qalb*) of perfect human beings experiences endless fluctuations (*qalb, taqallub*), since it is the locus within which they perceive God's self-disclosures, which never repeat themselves.

God created the universe to manifest the fullness of His own nature. As the famous *ḥadīth qudsī* expresses it, God says, "I was a hidden treasure, so I wanted to be known; hence I created the creatures in order that I might be known." In other words, through the cosmos, *wujūd* discloses the infinite possibilities latent within itself. Yet it reaches the fullness of its self-manifestation only through perfect human beings, since they alone actualize every ontological quality—every name and attribute of God. None other than perfect human beings have reached the goal for which people were created: to manifest the form of God Himself.

The Shaykh devotes most of his attention not to ontology but to anthropology, that is, to describing the nature of perfect human beings and the manner in which perfection can be achieved. The practical sides of his teachings—which are far more detailed than the theoretical side that we have been discussing—describe how people can discipline reason and imagination in order to combine the visions of incomparability and similarity. A mere rational understanding of the reality of He/not He will not help them ascend to the world of light. The inward world of imagination cannot be transformed into a place for witnessing the self-disclosures of *wujūd* without following the guidance of those human beings who have already reached perfection—the messengers, prophets, and friends of God.

In short, the ultimate reality of *wujūd* is both infinitely beyond and ever-present within. In its incomparability *wujūd* is one with an absolute oneness, but in its similarity it manifests itself through the real plurality perceived in the cosmos. The nonphenomenal remains forever incomparable, but it brings the phenomenal into existence through a mercy that is directed toward everything with the potential to exist. Perfect human beings return by way of their own selves to the nonphenomenal, thereby realizing their original state as nonexistent immutable entities. But, by realizing their essential nonexistence, they come to display the fullness of *wujūd*, since their nonexistent entities were made in the divine form, which is the form of *wujūd*. "No station" is at once every station. Not He is He. Oneness displays its infinity in the manyness of human perfections.

2

Microcosm, Macrocosm, and Perfect Man

When Ibn al-'Arabī discusses human beings, he usually has in view perfect human beings, not the forgetful and ignorant human beings of our own acquaintance. As already noted, he views these perfect human beings from two fundamentally different points of view, since he distinguishes between their nonmanifest reality in God's knowledge and their embodiments in clay. By the "reality" of the perfect human beings, he means the eternal and immutable archetype of all individual perfect human beings, and by their embodiments he means the prophets and the friends of God in their historical actualities. His discussion of the single reality of perfect human beings is complicated by the fact that he refers to it by many different names. For present purposes, we can simply say that he often calls it the "Muhammadan Reality."[1]

According to Islamic cosmology in general and the Shaykh's teachings in particular, God created the human being as the last creature, having employed all the other creatures to bring him into existence. As the final link in a great chain of being, people bring together and harmonize all previous links. Not only do they have mineral, vegetal, and animal components, they also replicate the invisible and visible cosmic hierarchy, beginning with the First Intellect and including the Universal Soul, Prime Matter, the Universal Body, the Throne of God, God's Footstool, the starless sphere, the sphere of the constellations, the seven planets, and the four elements. In some mysterious way, every human being contains everything in the cosmos.

The Goal of Creation

Ibn al-'Arabī discusses the cosmological links between human beings and the various strata and creatures of the macrocosm in many contexts. In a brief overview I can do no better than to discuss the most fundamental determinant of human existence: the fact of manifesting the divine form. It is important here to remember that in the hadith, "God created Adam in His own form," "God" translates the Arabic *Allāh*, which is known as the "all-comprehensive name," since every other name of God refers back to it. Thus, when one mentions "God," one mentions implicitly all divine names, including All-merciful, Forgiving, Just, Creator, Generous, Powerful, Exalter, Abaser, and so on. No other name includes in itself all names, since each of the other names has its own specific and limiting characteristics that sets it apart from the others.

God created human beings in His own form. Hence He created them in the form of all the divine names. This is one of the interpretations of the Koranic verse that says that God taught Adam *all the names* (2:30). As a result, human beings display an indefinite variety of divine aspects or "faces" (*wajh*). If all human attributes and activities for the whole of human history could be brought together in one time and place, we could begin to have an idea of what manifesting *all the names* implies. It is precisely this human all-comprehensiveness that allows for the existence of every sort of human possibility, every imaginable attribute, every conceivable act, whether good or evil, noble or base, just or unjust, compassionate or cruel.

If Adam had been created not in the form of God, but in the form of the All-compassionate, no human being could be angry or cruel. If he had been created in the form of the Vengeful, no one would ever forgive his enemy. If he had been created in the form of the Almighty or the Inaccessible, no one would ever obey God or anyone else. But since human beings were created in the form of all names, they can make manifest any conceivable attribute. The divine names, after all, are nothing but designations for the possible modalities of *wujūd*'s manifestation and nonmanifestation.

Again, since human beings comprehend *all* names, each human individual reflects every divine attribute to some degree. But during the course of a human life the divine names manifest themselves in all sorts of intensities, combinations, and interrelationships. The result may or may not be a harmonious and balanced personality. In the last analysis the mode in which the names display their properties determines human destinies in this world and the next. From the human point of view, this mode of display is completely unpredictable. As a result, the human situation stands in stark contrast with that of all other creatures, which are created within known and fixed stations (*maqām ma'lūm*).

Wujūd's attributes are disclosed in nonhuman realms in combinations that allow one or more attributes to dominate over others. But human beings concentrate and unify *wujūd*'s attributes such that, in the ideal situation, each attribute stands in perfect balance and equilibrium with every other. All things in the universe except human beings stand in known stations because each of them is colored by certain attributes of *wujūd* rather than others. Each animal or plant is fixed in its own identity, so carrots do not turn into peaches. In contrast, human beings are relatively fixed and stable in their outward forms, but infinitely diverse and ever-changing in their inward forms. In other words, they have no fixed stations in their souls, so they can become anything at all. Their stations do not become fixed until the moment of death. That is why the Shaykh generalizes the statement of the angels in the Koran, *None of us there is but has a known station* (37:164), to include all creatures, except human beings and jinn. A human being comes into the world as a potential divine form, but he or she may leave it as practically anything at all—an angel, a saint, a prophet, a devil, an animal, a vegetable. People reach their "known station" only at death. "Every existent thing other than [human beings and jinn]—whether angel, animal, plant, or mineral—is created in its station, so it does not descend from it, nor is it commanded to travel toward it, since it dwells within it" (I 259.4).

Only one creature other than human beings was created in the form of God as such—the cosmos in its entirety, which includes human beings. Together, God and the cosmos denote everything in reality, while each is the mirror image of the other. Hence every name of God finds loci of disclosure in the macrocosm. As the Shaykh puts it, the cosmos is the sum total of all the properties and effects of the divine names. The fundamental difference between God and the total universe is that God exists by His very Essence and has no need of the cosmos, while the universe has no existence in its essence and has every need for God. As we saw in the previous chapter, we can only speak of the *wujūd* of the cosmos in a certain sense, not in every sense. The cosmos exists only after a fashion, much as a reflection may be said to exist in a mirror. But God cannot not exist, which is to say that *wujūd* belongs to Him alone, or rather, *wujūd* is He and He is *wujūd.*

The human being and the cosmos are similar in that each was created in the form of God. However, the cosmos manifests the divine names in differentiated mode (*tafṣīl*). As a result, each and every divine name displays its properties and effects in the cosmos singly or in various combinations with other names or groups of names. Hence, in its spatial and temporal totality, the cosmos represents an infinitely vast panorama of existential possibilities. In contrast, human beings display the properties and effects of all the names in a relatively undifferentiated mode (*ijmāl*). The properties of all the divine names are drawn together and concentrated within each of them. God created the cosmos in respect of the multiplicity of His names, but He created human beings in respect of the unity of His names, the fact that each and every name refers to a single Reality. The Shaykh often expresses these ideas by employing the terms "small world" and "great world"—that is, microcosm and macrocosm. More commonly, he uses the expression "small human being" or "microanthropos" for human being and "great human being" or "macroanthropos" for the universe.

Since human beings are a part of the cosmos, the cosmos is not a complete divine form without them. Nevertheless, microcosm and macrocosm stand at opposite poles. The macrocosm, in its indefinite dispersion, is unconscious and passive. But the microcosm, through its intense concentration of all the divine attributes, is conscious and active. Human beings know the cosmos and can shape it to their own ends, but the cosmos does not know human beings and cannot shape them except to the extent that it is a passive instrument in the hand of God.

The fact that the microcosm dominates over the macrocosm leads the Shaykh to write at the beginning of the *Fuṣūṣ al-ḥikam* that the human being is the spirit of the cosmos, while the cosmos without the human being is like a proportioned and well-balanced body, ready and waiting for God to blow His spirit into it, but lifeless as long as the human being has not appeared. Similarly, he writes as follows in the *Futūḥāt*:

> The whole cosmos is the differentiation of Adam, while Adam is the all-comprehensive book. In relation to the cosmos he is like the spirit in relation to the body. Hence the human being is the spirit of the cosmos, and the cosmos is the body. Through bringing together all of this the cosmos is the "great human being," so long as the human being is within it. But if you look at the cosmos alone, without the human being, you will find it like a proportioned body without a spirit. The perfection of the cosmos through the human being is like the perfection of the body through the spirit. The human being is "blown into" the body of the cosmos, so he is the goal of the cosmos. (II 67.28)

In the same way, the Shaykh explains that the human being is the nonmanifest reality of the cosmos, while the cosmos is the manifest form of the human being: "Distinguish yourself from the cosmos and distinguish the cosmos from yourself. Distinguish the manifest from the nonmanifest and the nonmanifest from the manifest. For within the cosmos, you are the spirit of the cosmos, and the cosmos is your manifest form. The form has no meaning without a spirit. Hence the cosmos has no meaning without you" (III 363.2).

Because of the organic relationship between human beings and the cosmos, Ibn al-'Arabī calls perfect human beings the "Pillar" of the cosmos. Without them, the cosmos would collapse and die, which is precisely what will happen at the end of time when the last perfect human being departs from this world. Cosmologically speaking, the corruption and decay of the natural and social environments in modern times is one of the outward signs of the diminishing number of perfect human beings on the face of the earth.

That the universe is incomplete without human beings is a corollary of the common Islamic idea that the cosmos has no purpose in and of itself. Its only purpose is to bring human beings into existence. The perfect human being is the "Sought-after Entity" (*al-'ayn al-maqṣūda*), God's reason for creating the universe. The hadith of the Hidden Treasure tells us that God created the creatures in order to be known. He brought human beings into existence because they alone can truly know Him, even though their existence depends upon the prior existence of the cosmos. Every creature knows God after its own fashion, but only perfect human beings know Him as God, that is, in respect of His all-comprehensive name.

Ibn al-'Arabī frequently quotes the Koranic verses that tell us *Everything in the heavens and the earth glorifies God* (57:1, 59:1, etc.). This glorification, he says, is grounded in a knowledge of God possessed by each and every created thing. The creatures glorify God to the extent that they know Him. Flowers glorify Him as the Lord of the sun, the earth, and the rain, while bees glorify Him as the Lord of flowers. People glorify Him as the Lord of their goals and desires, whatever these may be. It is God who is Provider, Sustainer, Life-Giver, Beautiful, Merciful, and so on, and people call upon these names and glorify God by them when they utilize His bounties, whether or not they verbalize their glorification. But only perfect human beings glorify God as God, or—what amounts to the same thing—by mentioning all the divine names. This perfect glorification comprehends and includes the glorifications of all things. "The perfect human being glorifies God through all the glorifications in the cosmos" (III 77.24).

In short: The *microcosm* is the human being, created in the form of every divine name and containing within himself the realities that bring the cosmos into existence. The *macrocosm* is the whole cosmos, so long as perfect human beings exist within it, since without them it is incomplete, a body without a spirit. Both macrocosm and microcosm are forms of God, manifest (*ẓāhir*) within the created order. The *reality of the perfect human being*, also known as the "Muhammadan Reality," is then the nonmanifest form of God as known by God Himself, or the divine face turned toward the creation of both macrocosm and microcosm. Finally, the perfect human being in historical actuality is the "manifest side of the form of God" (III 109.13), God's sought-after entity whereby He actualizes His goal in creating the universe.

The Path to Perfection

Since perfect human beings embrace all the realities of both God and the cosmos, they recognize God in all things. They see with a vision that lifts all veils. For them the words of the Koran are concretely realized: *Wherever you turn, there is the face of God* (2:115). They see everything as a divine self-disclosure. They know God in respect of the knowledge possessed by everything in the cosmos, because, as microcosms, they embrace the reality of the macrocosm. And they worship God in a way that harmonizes with the teachings of every religion. But all this depends upon self-knowledge. "The perfect human being worships God through every revealed religion [*shar'*], glorifies Him with every tongue, and acts as a receptacle for His every self-disclosure—on condition that he fulfills the reality of his humanity and knows himself, for none knows his Lord but he who knows himself. If anything of himself veils him from perceiving his own totality, then he has committed a crime against himself and is not a perfect human being" (II 69.27).

By knowing themselves, perfect human beings know God, in keeping with the prophetic saying, "He who knows himself knows his Lord." In contrast, animal human beings have not achieved self-knowledge. And even though Adam was created perfect, imperfection and animality have gradually come to be the dominating characteristics of his children. However, the present animal state should not be taken as the defining characteristic of the human species. As the Shaykh remarks, it is incorrect to define human beings as "rational animals," since "The human being is defined specifically by the divine form" (III 154.19).

As already noted, the process whereby human beings come to actualize the divine form and manifest the divine names is often called "assuming the character traits of God." The cosmic role of the prophets is to provide people with the guidelines through which they can bring their beliefs, thoughts, and activities into conformity with the all-comprehensive name, in the form of which they were created. The Shaykh often calls the divine guidance that becomes embodied through the prophets "the Scale of the Shariah" (*al-mīzān al-shar'ī*). For Muslims, it is the law revealed by God in the Koran and exemplified by the Sunnah of Muhammad.

People cannot simply decide to assume the divine character traits on the basis of their own understanding of what these character traits might be. They cannot, for example, decide to be generous, just, and forgiving on the basis of what they understand from these qualities. For these are attributes of *wujūd* itself, and in their essence they are infinitely beyond human understanding. The problem of assuming God's character traits is made inconceivably complex because of the diversity and multiplicity of God's names. Moreover, the attempt to imitate God involves the danger of tremendous arrogance. Hence the goal of human endeavor must not be to acquire *divine* attributes. Rather, the immediate goal is to eliminate *human* attributes. The human attributes that need to be discarded grow up from self-will and caprice (*hawā*). Self-will must be abandoned and one's own likes and dislikes ignored. This, in short, is "surrender" or "submission" to God (*islām*), and its steps are defined by the Scale of the Shariah.

The path of "assuming the character traits of God" does not involve a gradual growth in stature until people become demigods rivaling God Himself. On the contrary, this path brings about a gradual decrease in stature until human attributes cease to exist, or until people become "nothing." But "nothing" is what belongs to them in the first place, because they are nonexistent entities. Once they eliminate their own attributes and efface their own selves, there remains only that which is truly found—the face of *wujūd* turned toward creation.

As full forms of God, human beings are He/not He. Inasmuch as they manifest *wujūd*, they are He, and *wujūd*'s attributes are displayed within them. But inasmuch as they are immutable entities, forever nonexistent, they are Not He, and none of these attributes belong to them. Hence the spiritual journey involves discarding the specifically human limitations that are called "not He" with the ultimate aim of identifying totally with the specifically divine self-disclosures that are called "He." In describing what takes place in the ascent to God, the Shaykh writes, "Since the servant is He/not He, he is carried up in respect of He—not in respect of Not He" (III 343.23).

But perfect human beings not only ascend; they also descend and play a role in the cosmos. They remain forever in the station of He/not He. Although they dwell in nonexistence by having negated every claim to *wujūd*, they also dwell in eternity, at ease in the *wujūd* and the bliss of God. "[Perfect human beings] are protected from the attribution of acts to themselves when the acts become manifest from them. They say, 'The acts belong to His names that become manifest within His loci of manifestation. How should we make any claims? We are no-thing [*lā shay'*] in the state of being loci of manifestation for Him, and in every other state.' This station is called 'the ease of eternity without end'" (II 96.33).

The Shaykh typically refers to the station of human perfection as "servanthood" (*'ubūdiyya*). As he often remarks, nearness (*qurb*) to God cannot be achieved unless one is first His servant. Perfect human beings are the utter and absolute servants of God. They do nothing on their own, for their separate existence has been negated. Whatever they do is done by God through them.

One more point needs to be brought out. By now it should be clear that according to Ibn al-'Arabī, being a perfect human being is not only the *highest* possible human aspiration; it is also, strictly speaking, the only properly *human* aspiration. Human beings who do not actualize their own divine form remain less than human, no matter what sort of great deeds they may accomplish in the present world. The station of perfection is the mark of true humanity, and it has been achieved only by a relatively small number of those whom we normally refer to as "human beings." By reaching perfection a person becomes the absolute servant of God, totally effaced as an independent individual but fully affirmed as a divine form. Perfect human beings live in every situation exactly as that situation demands according to the wisdom of God, not according to human norms. They are fully and completely merciful, compassionate, forgiving, loving, generous, just, and so on, exactly as demanded by the Divine Reality itself.

If the station of perfection is so exalted, would it not be better for everyone to give up the idea of being perfect and get back to "real life"? Certainly not, the Shaykh argues, since in any case people must strive to live up to the reality that is embodied within themselves. They owe it to their own selves to follow the Scale of the Shariah, which God revealed to guide their activity. And in any case God has guaranteed everlasting happiness to those who follow the Shariah to the extent of their capacities, whether or not they reach perfection. That is why Ibn al-'Arabī gives this advice to his readers:

> You should think about the degree of the animal human being in relation to the degree of the perfect human being, and then you should know which kind of human being you are yourself. For you have the preparedness to receive perfection, if you understand. That is why you have been admonished and notified by the whole world. If you did not have the preparedness to receive perfection, it would be incorrect to admonish you, and letting you know about perfection would be vain and useless. So blame only yourself if you do not receive that to which you have been called![2] (III 266.20)

3

Ethics and Antinomianism

Practically all spiritual masters looked back upon with reverence by the Sufi tradition have considered the Shariah the foundation of the path to God. But many of these same masters have been criticized by Muslim jurists and theologians for their antinomian views. In the case of Ibn al-ʻArabī and his followers, these criticisms often take the form of attacking the doctrine of *waḥdat al-wujūd.* According to the critics, supporters of *waḥdat al-wujūd* claim that understanding the oneness of all things makes them exceptional human beings. Hence they have a right to ignore the prescriptions of the Shariah, which are directed at the common people. They have understood that "All is He" (Persian *hama ūst*), so they have no need to distinguish between good and evil because, in truth, the two are the same.

The evidence presented by the actual texts of the Sufi masters in question suggests that practice of the Shariah has been the norm throughout Islamic history, whatever deviations may sometimes have occurred. And among Sufis, no one has proclaimed the absolute necessity of observing the Shariah with greater vigor than Ibn al-ʻArabī.

One of the many ways of approaching the Shaykh's understanding of the Shariah's role in human life is to ask how the domain of ethical and moral standards fits into the concept of *waḥdat al-wujūd.* This question seems to have special relevance in our own times, since traditional moral constraints do not usually receive much emphasis in the many forms of spirituality that are playing an ever more visible role in Western society. It seems not to matter whether these teachings and practices have roots in Eastern religions, Western religions, or the various currents of the New Age movement.

However we define morality, little of what the Shaykh has to say in his enormous corpus of writings is unrelated to it. It is impossible here even to begin to sort out the principles and details of his views on the nature and role of morality in human life. Instead I will attempt only to show what he understands by the single term *akhlāq*, a word normally translated as "ethics." Then I will suggest the manner in which he finds a grounding for *akhlāq* in *waḥdat al-wujūd* and what this has to do with the Shariah.

The Arabic word *akhlāq* is the plural of *khuluq*, which means both "character" and "character trait." The word *khuluq* is used twice in the Koran and repeatedly in the Hadith (often in the plural). It is separated only by pronunciation (not in the way it is written) from the term *khalq*, which is typically translated as "creation." Hence the very word *khuluq* is connected with *khalq*, which is to say that character is rooted in creation, or in the actual nature of things. For the Shaykh, the ontological side of character traits is fundamental.

Although Ibn al-'Arabī's views on ethics share a good deal with those of the Muslim philosophers (whose works are based largely on Greek sources), he finds his basic point of reference and the ultimate source for most of his key terminology in the Koran and the Hadith, especially the divine names. He frequently reminds his readers that these names are not concrete things, but providential designations for the relationships that exist between the Real and the cosmos. They provide human beings with knowledge of their own connection with the absolute and immutable ground of everything that exists. Without the names—or without the revelation that provides them—people would drown in a sea of uncertainties and relativities.

Noble Character Traits

In the general Islamic view, made completely explicit by Ibn al-'Arabī, noble character traits (*makārim al-akhlāq*) belong truly to God and only metaphorically to anything else. Everything good comes from God, and moral traits such as justice, generosity, patience, and forbearance are no exception. The Koran confirms this point by the divine names that it mentions—Just, Generous, Patient, Pardoner, Clement, Grateful, and so on.

When the Shaykh employs the terminology of Peripatetic philosophers such as Avicenna, he calls God the "Necessary Being." Everything else that can be said to exist is then a "possible thing" (*mumkin*). True *wujūd* belongs only to God, and at best the possible thing is said to have received *wujūd* on loan. But what is important in the present context is that the Shaykh prefers the religious to the philosophical terminology in explaining the characteristics of God's *wujūd*. He answers the question, "What are the attributes of *wujūd*?" by listing the divine names, which are intrinsic to *wujūd*.

Having been created in God's form, human beings are endowed with all His noble character traits. Their task is not to devise some ethical system or to debate about the meaning of morality, but simply "to be, to exist, to be found," and thereby to act as receptacles for the manifestation of *wujūd*'s inherent attributes. However, nobility of character is in practice not so easy to come by. Only perfect human beings fully actualize the noble divine traits. The Shaykh is of course aware that perfection is a relative situation, and he devotes a great deal of attention to the various kinds, levels, and degrees of perfection. Fully actualized perfection—absolute perfection (*al-kamāl al-muṭlaq*)—is found only in God. In contrast, human perfection always accepts increase, whether in this world or the next, since the finite can never attain to the Infinite. Hence, even in the case of the most perfect of perfect human beings, there is no question of a static situation.

Only those human beings who have attained to perfection can truly be said to be created in God's form. Within them the divine names display their full range of properties to the extent possible in the particular mode of manifestation actualized at the moment. The specific characteristic of human beings that sets them apart from other creatures can be explained by reference to this potentiality of manifesting all the names. The fact that each human individual brings together all ontological possibilities means that people can develop in any direction, whether this be perceived as "good" or "evil."

We can suggest some of the implications of this way of looking at things by taking the example of the divine quality of knowledge, which is God's awareness of Himself and all subsidiary realities. Having been created in God's form, human beings have the potential to know all things. Naturally there are fundamental differences between divine knowledge and human knowledge, but to the extent that human knowledge is not hindered by the limitations of contingent existence, it is infinitely expandable. Anything known by any human being at any time and place is, in principle, knowable by every human being, given a healthy mind and various other external conditions. Human beings forget, grow old, and die, but knowledge accepts only accidental limits. The underlying ethos and goals of modern science express a basic human intuition that everything can be known.

In a given human being, knowledge will be "perfected" to the extent that everything knowable comes to be known. In the context of Islam, what is knowable pertains to the principles (*uṣūl*) and ramifications (*furū'*) of the religion: God, His names, His angels, His scriptures, His prophets, the Last Day, and the various social, legal, and individual branches of this metacosmic and cosmic knowledge. Real knowledge is achieved when God is known and when the things of the cosmos are known with a view toward their roots in God.

In most people, knowledge is not brought to "perfection." At best, one or two possibilities or modes of knowing are developed to some degree. In the majority of cases knowledge remains a virtuality, even by contemporary standards. Formal education is not completed, the demands of social status prove more attractive than learning, the desire to have a comfortable livelihood overcomes intellectual potential. But contemporary ideas of knowledge are not too helpful in suggesting what perfected knowledge might entail. The Shaykh and other Sufis would consider most of what passes for knowledge in modern times as veils over real knowledge, because it has not been integrated into a wider view tying phenomena back to *wujūd*. Instead of devoting themselves to the roots of things, people become engrossed with the branches. Instead of searching out the First Cause, they dissect secondary causes (*asbāb*) with no sense of the ultimate significance of what they are doing. Instead of seeing inward meanings (*ma'ānī*), they fix their gaze on outward forms (*ṣuwar*).

In one of many passages where he sums up the various possibilities of human knowing, Ibn al-'Arabī explains the importance of avoiding the dispersion that is connected to the infinite proliferation of the possible objects of knowledge. If people simply set their hearts upon knowing, without focusing on the one source of all *wujūd*, they can know without end, but they will remain cut off from their own realities.

> In Himself, God is far beyond and far greater than that His servant should know Him. That is impossible. There remains no object of knowledge for us to pursue except relationships in particular, or the entities of the possible things and what is attributed to these entities. . . . The essences and entities you come to know innately, without reflection or consideration; the soul perceives them through what God has fixed within them. Then you come to know how things are related to them. This is the knowledge of what is reported concerning them, that is, their descriptions, the judgments made about them by logical proofs, and the reports given by revelation. There is no other way to reach knowledge of them.
>
> The judgments and reports are infinite in their multiplicity. Hence the person who considers them becomes dispersed and is not able to gather them together. The Real desires that His servant should gather them together in Him, not that the servant should follow up on this multiplicity in order to know it. Or rather, He has made permissible for some of His servants the knowledge of multiplicity that allows them to gather things together in Him. This is indicated by His words concerning the consideration of such things: *We shall show them Our signs upon the horizons and in themselves, until it is clear to them that He is the Real* [41:53].
>
> The one who becomes dispersed while gathering the sciences has failed to look at them in respect of the fact that they denote the Real. They veil him from the manner in which they denote the Real. Such, for example, are the sciences of calculation and geometry and the sciences of mathematics, logic, and natural science. But none of these is a science that does not have a denotation of God and a way leading to Him. (III 558.16)

For the Shaykh, to seek knowledge without the aim of finding the roots of one's knowledge in God is simply wrong-headed. The result is not knowledge at all. Rather, people end up being ignorant of the true nature of things. As he says, "Whenever one created thing is ascribed to another created thing, that is a metaphor, a form through which people are veiled" (III 386.30). Knowledge worthy of the human state is only knowledge of God. "The human being has no nobility save through his knowledge of God. As for his knowledge of what is other than God, that is a distraction through which the person who is veiled keeps himself distracted. The one who gives the situation its due has no aspiration but to know Him" (IV 129.5).

In present-day society, the result of seeking after knowledge without rooting it in the Real has been a tremendous accumulation of information. The human potential for unlimited knowledge is being actualized, but in a bewildering variety of peripheral modes. The fact that the fundamental reality of knowledge is awareness of the way things are is lost to sight. Instead, people tend to think of knowledge as facts that can be called up on a computer screen. They become more and more ignorant of the unity and undifferentiation of the microcosmic divine form and ever more engrossed in the indefinite differentiation and dispersion of macrocosmic reality. Proliferating specialization results in major increases in information, but it also brings about an increasing distance from all the human qualities that are rooted in oneness, harmony, wholeness, equilibrium, and integration. Dis-integration of the human microcosm leads to the decay and collapse of the macrocosm, of which human beings are the governing spirit. Through neglecting their divine form, human beings abdicate their responsibility of acting as God's vicegerents in the earth.

One could undertake a similar analysis of many other divine attributes. God is Desiring, Powerful, Speaking, Hearing, Seeing, Forgiving, Vengeful, Grateful, and so on. In the Shaykh's view, a perfect human being will have actualized all the divine names to the extent possible and in the appropriate manner—given individual limitations having to do with bodily constraints, time, place, environment, and so on, even though these limitations count for far less inwardly than they do outwardly.

The actualization of the divine names, it was just said, needs to take place in the "appropriate" manner. Appropriateness means harmony and equilibrium among all the divine attributes in a manner that corresponds with their situation in the Real Itself. The human task is to embody the divine attributes in a manner that does not allow any of them to play too great or too small a role. Actualizing the divine form in oneself results in nearness to God, whereas failing to keep the proper equilibrium among the names leads to imbalance, or a distorted divine form, and the result is distance from God. As Ibn al-'Arabī puts it in one of many passages where he discusses such issues, "God has attributes and names, and these have levels. The servant assumes them as his traits and becomes adorned by them in accordance with a specific limit, a revealed description, and a determined state. When the servant steps beyond that, then he falls into contention with the Real and becomes worthy of being driven away and banished from the nearness that establishes felicity" (IV 3.4).

One way to explain this idea of balance and harmony among the names is to return to the identification between *wujūd* and light. It was said earlier that *wujūd* can be compared to pure light, while the cosmos can be compared to the differentiation of this colorless light into an infinite number of colors. In the same way, the achievement of human perfection can be compared to the actualization of pure, colorless light through the unification and harmonization of an indefinite number of colored lights of varying intensities. The obvious problem connected with actualizing colorless light is how to prevent there being too much red, too much green, too much blue. How can the perfect balance of colors be achieved so that all colors return to the original light? What are the standards by which the different colors can be measured and integrated?

The divine names represent the primary colors found in *wujūd*'s infinite light. Many of these names are mutually contradictory. Just as light can be seen as appearing in various opposite hues such as red and green, so also *wujūd* manifests itself as Forgiver and Avenger, Merciful and Wrathful, Life-giver and Slayer, Abaser and Exalter. Given that human beings must actualize these qualities to reach perfection, how can their contradictory properties be harmonized in a single personality? According to the Shaykh, the highest stage of human perfection demands that the divine names reach an equilibrium such that human beings are uncolored and nondelimited by any name whatsoever, like *wujūd* itself. This is the Station of No Station, in which no specific quality dominates over any other.

Much of Ibn al-'Arabī's writing has to do with the manner in which human beings can become full and harmonious loci of manifestation for all the divine names and thereby display in the appropriate manner all the divine character traits. In every case his instructions are fundamentally the same: In order to attain the full perfection of human character, people must return to the right balance among the qualities as indicated by the divine names, and for practical purposes this balance is established by the Koran and the Hadith. In other words, the Shariah provides the necessary concrete guidelines for achieving equilibrium among the names and character traits. Having reached this equilibrium, human beings will have actualized the form in which they were created.

People have no recourse other than the Shariah because human perfection is inseparable from divine perfection. Hence it depends upon knowledge of God. But people cannot know God through their own powers, any more than a ray of light can know the sun. Hence God must provide the knowledge that escapes human nature in order to prepare the way for the achievement of perfection. This is one of the more common themes of the Shaykh's writings, a fact that suggests that even in his day, many intellectuals did not take divine revelation too seriously.

The process of actualizing the divine form is described in many ways. In the present context, I will refer only to a single term—*takhalluq*, the fifth verbal noun from the root *kh.l.q.*, from which we have *akhlāq*, "character traits." *Takhalluq* means to adopt a character trait as one's own, or to assume the character traits of something. The most famous use of the word in Sufi texts is the command, often attributed to the Prophet, "Assume the character traits of God!" The Shaykh quotes the following hadith: "God has three hundred character traits; he who assumes one of them as his own will enter paradise."

In the Shaykh's vocabulary "assuming the traits of the divine names" and "assuming the divine character traits" are synonymous expressions. He often reminds us of *takhalluq*'s connection with *khalq* or creation by giving the term a meaning that goes outside the ethical sphere altogether. For example, he writes that just as *To God belong the most beautiful names* (7:180), so also "To the cosmos belongs becoming manifest through them by *assuming their traits*" (II 438.23). In other words, all of manifest *wujūd* appears in conformity with God's attributes and character traits. But given the peculiar situation of human beings in the overall scheme of things—their quality of being God's vicegerents—they play a conscious role in bringing these character traits into manifestation. Hence to some degree they are responsible for the manner in which the divine qualities unfold. Unlike other creatures, they are able to manifest the divine qualities in modes that do not correspond to their own perfection. People need the Shariah because they do not and cannot know exactly how the divine attributes relate to God and to themselves. This is especially true of the many divine attributes mentioned in the Koran and the Hadith that refer to God in anthropomorphic terms.

> The servant has attributes and names that are worthy of him, and it may happen that the Real comes to be qualified by them in a manner that rational faculties consider absurd. . . . We do not know that these attributes are related to God except through God's giving knowledge. In the same way, the relationship to Him of every divine name by which we ourselves become adorned is unknown, unless God should give knowledge of it. . . .
>
> The human creature is created in the form of God. Hence, as vicegerent, he has no choice but to comprehend all the divine names and attributes that are demanded by the cosmos, of which the Real has put him in charge. Since the actual situation demands this, God sent down an affair from Himself that He named "the Shariah." Through it He explains how these divine names and attributes—which the vicegerent has no choice but to make manifest—are to be employed. (IV 3.7)

Blameworthy Character Traits

Much of the Shaykh's discussion of character traits as described to this point is implied if not stated explicitly by earlier authors. But we have not yet begun to investigate the second part of our topic, which is the relationship of character traits to *waḥdat al-wujūd*, an idea connected specifically to the works of the Shaykh and his followers. Here we will see the discussion given a new twist.

As explained in Chapter 1, *waḥdat al-wujūd* implies that every existing thing, by the fact of its existence, manifests absolute and nondelimited *wujūd*. In other terms, everything in the universe is a locus of manifestation for the divine names. There is only one *wujūd*, and anyone who supposes that each thing possesses its own *wujūd* has an imperfect perception of the nature of things. In the last analysis, *wujūd* in whatever form it appears is the nondelimited *wujūd* of God. That which delineates the specific properties of things described as possessing *wujūd* is the mode under which the *wujūd* of the Real manifests itself because of the laws of its own nature—laws that revelation summarizes as the divine names.

Such a perspective necessarily sees all experienced reality as stemming from the Real, even though many arguments are employed to avoid attributing evil directly to God. For example, the Shaykh devotes a good deal of space to discussing nonexistence and the manner in which it dilutes, as it were, the intensity of *wujūd*. Whatever defect is found in existence must be attributed to nonexistence, not to *wujūd* itself. Thus the Shaykh comments on a famous saying of the Prophet, "The good, all of it, is in Thy hands, but evil does not go back to Thee," as follows: "His words affirm the entity of evil but negate its attribution to the Real. This shows that evil is not a thing but rather a nonexistence. Were it a thing, it would be in the hand of the Real, for *In His hand is the dominion of each thing* [23:88] and *He is the Creator of each thing* [6:102]" (III 369.27).

The relationship of human acts to God has always been a central issue of theological debate in Islam, especially because it is bound up with the question of free will and predestination. Every human act must manifest an ontological quality, or else it could not occur. There is something positive and affirmative about action. Muslim theologians often call the creatures themselves God's "acts" (*af'āl*), and the Koran says explicitly, *God created you and what you do* (37:96). If character traits and activity are rooted in creation itself, what about the blameworthy character traits that give rise to blameworthy acts? Most theologians found ways to avoid attributing such character traits to God, but the Shaykh does not shy away from the demands of his own logic. Although he often says that blameworthiness pertains only to human beings and not to God, he admits that "All character traits are divine attributes, so all of them are noble, and all are in the innate disposition of the human being. . . . Human beings exist through their Lord, so they acquire *wujūd* from Him. Hence they acquire character traits from Him" (II 241.28).

This does not mean that the Shaykh ascribes blameworthy character traits directly to God, but it does mean that he reconsiders the blameworthiness of the base character traits that are attributed to human beings. In fact, he says, what we call base and blameworthy traits are really noble and praiseworthy. People speak of blameworthiness either because they misperceive the situation or because the character traits have been employed in an improper manner. Thus he shifts the focus of attention from the character trait that becomes manifest through human activity—a character trait that must be noble because it is rooted in *wujūd*—to the manner in which the character trait is perceived or employed (*maṣraf*). The issue becomes one of interpretation, or of human freedom and how it is used.

If people want to find the proper use for their own character traits as full manifestations of *wujūd*, they need the guidance of the prophets, who show them how to transform blameworthy traits into praiseworthy ones. In other words, if they follow the Shariah, this will ensure that they have made the right choices in employing the characteristics of *wujūd* that are inherent in their divine form. If they ignore or actively contravene the Shariah, they will be actively striving to contravene the laws of *wujūd*.[1]

The Shaykh's basic argument concerning prophetic guidance goes back to his position on the nature of existent things. All things in the cosmos are properties and effects of the divine names, while the names are providential designations for the relationships that can be discerned between nondelimited *wujūd* and the things. This means that in the last analysis nothing can be found but various modalities of *wujūd*, or various relationships and attributions. There is no plurality of existent things, but there is a plurality of relationships. Anything in the cosmos that we want to analyze is defined by its relationships with other things. There are no fixed entities, only the flux of changing attributions. All things are ambiguous, because they are embedded in imagination, the dance of He/not He. As the Shaykh puts it, "There is nothing in the cosmos that is absolutely blameworthy or absolutely praiseworthy, because aspects and contexts delimit each thing. For the root is delimitation, not nondelimitation, because existence is necessarily delimited, which is why proofs show that everything that enters into existence is finite" (III 472.23).

Human character traits are no different from anything else. They also can never be absolutely praiseworthy or absolutely blameworthy. Rather, they are conditioned by the situations within which people are placed. Hence, if the situations change in the appropriate way, character traits will no longer be called "base" but "noble," even though the exact same qualities are manifesting themselves. The Shaykh brings out the situational nature of ethics while explaining how the five rulings of the Shariah—obligatory, recommended, indifferent, reprehensible, and forbidden—come to be applied to things and activities. He points out that in itself nothing has any relationships with other things that could allow a ruling to apply to it; hence the thing itself is referred to as "indifferent." Only when it is contextualized and put into relationship with other things does the Shariah attach a command or prohibition to it.

> When a solid thing dissolves, the forms change, so the name changes, and hence the ruling changes. When a liquid thing becomes solidified, the form changes, so the name changes, and hence the ruling changes. The revealed religions were sent down addressing the entities in respect of their forms, states, and names. The entity is not addressed in terms of its essence, and no ruling applies to it in respect of its reality. That is why, among the rulings of the Shariah, "indifferent" pertains to the entity. As for doing the obligatory, the recommended, the forbidden, and the reprehensible, that pertains to extraneous matters that befall the entity in its existence. (III 390.30)

The Shaykh commonly explains how relationships determine character traits in connection with the prophetic saying, "I was sent to complete the noble character traits." Character traits were incomplete, he says, because many of the noble character traits had been left out when earlier prophets established guidelines for human character and conduct. Muhammad "completed" the noble traits by adding all the base character traits to them. His Shariah transforms blameworthy qualities into praiseworthy ones. It does this by changing the manner in which the so-called base character traits are employed. Thus, for example, attributes such as cowardice, avarice, envy, greed, talebearing, arrogance, and harshness are intrinsic to human nature, because they are intrinsic to *wujūd*. But if applied correctly, they become noble, as when the soul is cowardly toward breaking the Shariah or greedy toward performing the good.[2]

In a related discussion, the Shaykh sometimes looks at specific divine names as sources of blameworthy character traits. Although perfect human beings assume all the divine names, some of these—such as Magnificent, Inaccessible, Majestic, Slayer, Conqueror, Avenger, and Terrible in Punishment—conflict with nobility of character. How can people assume the traits demanded by these names without turning into monsters? The simple answer is that they have to assume the traits in proper measure, or in equilibrium with other divine character traits that neutralize the negative consequences, and that this equilibrium can only be achieved by following the guidance set down in the Shariah.

The fundamental function of divine guidance, which becomes manifest through the prophets, is to orient human beings toward establishing an all-inclusive character trait that is commonly called "servanthood." Although Islamic texts often describe this trait in exclusively legal terms, the Shaykh approaches it first as an ontological situation. The Koran provides ample basis for his understanding, as in the verse, *None is there in the heavens and the earth that does not come to the All-merciful as a servant* (19:93). In other terms, every created thing is a letter or word articulated within the Breath of the All-merciful. All things serve God by manifesting the qualities of *wujūd.*

In philosophical terminology, creaturely servanthood arises out of ontological possibility (*imkān*), the fact that things have received their existence and attributes on loan from God, the Necessary Being. The Shaykh equates this philosophical term with the Koranic expression "poverty" (*faqr*). By their very essences all existent things are poor toward God and in need of Him, while God needs nothing. *O people! You are the poor toward God, and God, He is the Independent, the Praiseworthy* (35:15).

The basic task for God's human servants is to understand fully the radical poverty of all things, especially themselves. Perfect action in accordance with this understanding is then called "servanthood," and a person can aspire to no higher station. Having utterly effaced themselves before the Real, perfect servants have nothing of their own and stand in the Station of No Station.

In order to establish their servanthood, human beings must recognize the proper relationships among things. They need to understand that *wujūd* and all its qualities belong to God alone. In everyday, practical terms, this means that they have to establish perfect humility. People cannot attribute any quality—except ignorance—to themselves, and hence they can find no reason to consider themselves superior to other human beings. The true significance of the fundamental human shortcoming—heedlessness of God (*ghafla*), which is the opposite of remembrance (*dhikr*)—is found in the necessity of establishing right relationships.

> It may happen that a person will become heedless and negligent of his own servanthood. Then he will see that he has a certain excellence [*faḍl*] over another servant like himself. This is especially likely to happen if this other servant is his slave, or if this negligent person is one of the possessors of authority, such as a king or a ruler. Then he sees a superiority [*maziyya*] over others in himself, but he fails to see that the superiority belongs to the position in which he has been placed—if he should be a possessor of authority—or it belongs to the attribute that subsists within him because he has been singled out for it by God, such as knowledge or nobility of character traits. Such a person does not distinguish between himself and his position, or between the attribute and that within which the attribute is found. He is the possessor of ignorance and ugly heedlessness. Because of his ignorance in this state, he says things like . . . "Who is so and so?" or "Of what worth is so and so?" or "Is he anything but my servant?" or "my subject?" or "He is such and such," mentioning every blameworthy thing. He declares himself purified of such things and ascribes them to the other.

> Such a person is totally different from the one who is not heedless of himself, for the latter places the excellence in the attribute and the position, not in himself. After all, he did not gain it through worthiness. On the contrary, he only gained it through God's favor toward him. (III 380.30)

Perfect human beings, then, have come with full consciousness into servanthood before the All-merciful. They recognize the source of every attribute found in themselves and others, and they witness the attribution of all character traits to God through tasting and unveiling, not just through rational understanding. They submit (*islām*) themselves utterly to *wujūd* and give up every specific trait that they used to call their own.

But perfect human beings do not thereby disappear from existence. Quite the contrary. It is they alone who are truly real among created things, since they alone know self and other for what they are. Having surrendered the illusion of selfhood, they have disappeared as limitations in *wujūd*, only to reappear at the next instant as *wujūd*'s self-disclosures. Having annihilated their human limitations, they subsist as faces of God turned toward creation. They act in every situation as the situation demands, according to the nature of *wujūd* itself. Standing in no specific station, they respond to each situation as the character traits of God demand. Dwelling in the perception of *waḥdat al-wujūd*, they represent the proper and appropriate human response to the nature of things.

4

Self-Knowledge and the Original Human Disposition

Ibn al-'Arabī frequently employs the term *fiṭra*, which can be translated as "original disposition." The basic meaning of the term's root is to split, break open, bring forth, create, make. The Koran employs various words derived from the root in twenty instances. Most significant is the single verse in which the word *fiṭra* itself, translated here as "bringing forth," is used along with its verbal form: *So turn thy face to the religion as one with primordial faith—the* bringing forth *of God in keeping with which He* brought forth *human beings. There is no changing God's creation. This is the right religion, but most people know not* (30:30).

Commentators typically understand this verse to mean that human beings were created worshiping God in the appropriate manner. To adhere to one's bringing forth or one's "original disposition" is then to follow God's right religion, understood by Muslims, naturally enough, as Islam. However, the Koran's use of the term *islām* involves several meanings, one of which is simply "revealed religion," and the passage suggests that this is what is meant here, given the mention of the term *ḥanīf* or "one with primordial faith," a term the Koran associates with Abraham, whom it considers the closest of the prophets to Muhammad.[1] The commentators also connect the *fiṭra* mentioned in this verse with the essential element of right religion, which is faith in God or *tawḥīd*, the assertion of God's unity that is defined by the first Shahadah: "There is no god but God." Ibn al-'Arabī identifies the primordial human disposition with the sum of the attributes of perfection possessed by the human spirit at its creation. He writes, "When God created the human spirit, He created it perfect, fully developed, rational, aware, having faith in God's *tawḥīd*, admitting His lordship. This is the original disposition according to which God created human beings" (II 690.30).[2]

A famous saying of the Prophet employs the term *fiṭra* in an especially suggestive way: "Every child is born with the original disposition, but then its parents turn it into a Christian, a Jew, or a Zoroastrian." The Prophet seems to be saying here that society's imperfections obscure the original human disposition and make it difficult for people to live in accordance with their own true nature.[3] In terms of the definition of *fiṭra* provided by the Shaykh, this is to say that people remain imperfect, undeveloped, irrational, and unaware; they deny *tawḥīd* and associate other gods with God (*shirk*).

In short, the Koran and the Hadith already contain the idea that human beings were created with an original disposition that allows them to understand things as they truly are. However, this disposition has been clouded by the human environment. The function of the prophets then is to "remind" (*dhikr*) people of what they already know, while the duty of human beings is simply to "remember" (*dhikr*).[4] Having remembered, they find the original disposition that they had never really lost, just as the sun is found when the clouds disperse.[5]

If the human spirit knows God and affirms *tawḥīd* at the moment of its creation, this has something to do with the fact that this spirit is not completely other than God. After all, the Koran tells us that it was blown into the body by God's own breath. Hence human beings are near to God through their spirits, but far from Him through their bodies made of clay.

As noted in Chapter 1, the qualities of spirit and body lie at opposite extremes. The spirit is luminous, alive, rational, aware, intelligent, powerful, desiring, speaking, and, in short, possesses all the attributes of God. But the body displays none of these qualities to any perceptible degree. It is merely earth and water, which represent the lowest of created things.[6]

When God blows the spirit into clay, this gives rise to the soul or self (*nafs*), which is an intermediate, imaginal reality that possesses qualities of both sides. Hence the soul—the level of ordinary awareness—lies between light and darkness, intelligence and ignorance, rationality and irrationality, awareness and unawareness, power and weakness, perfection and imperfection. Within the soul, the original disposition is represented by the luminous qualities of the spirit that are present only dimly. Actualizing the original disposition is then seen as the goal of human existence. The soul must be transmuted such that its darkness becomes fully infused with spiritual light. What this actualization entails for human consciousness is suggested in mythic fashion in a Koranic passage about Abraham, the prophet of "primordial faith" who is a model of actualized *fiṭra*:

> *We were showing Abraham the kingdom of the heavens and the earth, that he might be of those having certainty. When night outspread over him he saw a star and said, "This is my Lord." But when it set, he said, "I love not the setters."*

> *When he saw the moon rising, he said, "This is my Lord." But when it set he said, "If my Lord does not guide me I shall surely be one of the misguided."*
>
> *When he saw the sun rising, he said, "This is my Lord: this is greater!" But when it set he said, "O my people, surely I am quit of what you associate with God. I have turned my face to Him who brought forth* [faṭara] *the heavens and the earth, as one with primordial faith; I am not one of those who associate others with God."* [6:76-80]

The Nondelimitation of *Wujūd*

To understand Ibn al-'Arabī's concept of the original human disposition, we need to look more closely at the characteristics of *wujūd*, the unknowable and inaccessible ground of everything that exists. Just as God alone is true *wujūd*, while all things dwell in nonexistence, so also *wujūd* alone is nondelimited (*muṭlaq*), while everything else is constrained, confined, and constricted. *Wujūd* is the absolute, infinite, nondelimited reality of God, while all others remain relative, finite, and delimited.

Since *wujūd* is nondelimited, it is totally different from everything else. Whatever exists and can be known or grasped is a delimitation and definition, a constriction of the unlimited, a finite object accessible to a finite subject. In the same way, *wujūd*'s self-consciousness is nondelimited, while every other consciousness is constrained and confined. But we need to be careful in asserting *wujūd*'s nondelimitation. This must not be understood to mean that *wujūd* is different and only different from every delimitation. The Shaykh is quick to point out that *wujūd*'s nondelimitation demands that it be able to assume every delimitation. If *wujūd* could not become delimited, it would be limited by its own nondelimitation. Thus "He possesses nondelimitation in delimitation" (III 454.28). Or again, "God possesses nondelimited *wujūd*, but no delimitation prevents delimitation. Rather, He possesses all delimitations, so He is nondelimited delimitation, since no single delimitation rather than another rules over Him. . . . Hence nothing is to be attributed to Him in preference to anything else" (III 162.23). *Wujūd* must have the power of assuming every delimitation on pain of being limited by those delimitations that it cannot assume. At the same time, it transcends the forms by which it becomes delimited and remains untouched by their constraints.

Ibn al-'Arabī refers to the Real inasmuch as it is nondelimited, incomparable, and eternally unknowable as the Essence, while he refers to it inasmuch as it assumes all limitations and is similar to all things by such terms as the Real Through Which Creation Takes Place, the Cloud, or the Breath of the All-merciful. In function of the All-merciful Breath, the Real creates the universe, which is to say that *wujūd* manifests itself within the limitations of the others.

In its incomparability, *wujūd* stands beyond every limitation, but in its similarity, it discloses itself as every form in the external and internal worlds. Everything that "exists" or "is found" displays a modality of *wujūd*. Likewise, every finding—every mode of consciousness and awareness—is a mode of *wujūd*'s own self-finding.

Wujūd is unknowable in itself, yet it discloses itself through its self-manifestations. Just as light has modalities of self-disclosure that are called "colors," so *wujūd* has modalities of self-disclosure that are called "names" or "attributes" or "relationships." The Koranic names designate *wujūd*'s primary attributes. Wherever anything is found, these attributes are present, though not necessarily manifest. All colors are found in light, and the presence of light is sufficient to indicate that the colors are to be found in some way; but specific colors become manifest only through specific conditions.

When a positive quality appears, the statement of *tawḥīd*—"There is no god but God"—alerts us to the fact that the quality must belong to *wujūd*. If life is observed, we know that *wujūd* is alive and that "There is no life but real life," the unadulterated, pure, absolute, and eternal life of the Real. Life that is found among the creatures is ephemeral and unreal, while permanent and real life belongs exclusively to God. In short, when the Shaykh declares that *wujūd* is one, he is saying that reality is one, and by saying that reality is one, he is recognizing that all real qualities are found in their pure, absolute, and nondelimited form only in the Real.

Imaginal Consciousness

Ibn al-'Arabī expresses the basic intuition of *tawḥīd*—that all real qualities can be nothing but reflections of *wujūd*—in many ways, such as referring to the whole cosmos as "imagination." The universe and everything within it hang between sheer Reality and utter nonbeing; they are both God and not God, He/not He.

In the narrowest sense of the term, imagination refers to a specific faculty of the soul that brings together sensory things, which have shapes and forms, and consciousness, which has no shape or form. Thus dream images are perceived in sensory form, yet they are animated by a formless awareness, or, as the Shaykh often puts it, they manifest "meanings" (*ma'ānī*), which are suprasensory realities. "The dreamer sees meanings in the form of sensory objects, since the reality of imagination is to embody that which is not properly a body" (II 379.3). Every dream image brings together the multiplicity of the external world and the unity of the subject; each is an isthmus between the darkness of the bodily world and the luminosity of spirit.

In a slightly more extended sense, imagination refers to the realm of the soul, a level of being and consciousness that is situated between spirit and body. The soul is awareness and consciousness, but this consciousness cannot escape the ambiguity that is its very substance. If we ask the question, "Has so-and-so achieved consciousness?" the answer depends on the relationship we have in view. On one level, we may simply be asking if the chloroform has worn off. At the opposite extreme, we may be asking if the person has reached buddhahood. Consciousness, like all divine qualities, represents a continuum. It has degrees of intensity, and the difference between the highest and lowest created levels of consciousness is practically infinite. At the same time, the Real's consciousness is infinitely more real than the most intense consciousness possessed by the other, since nothing is real but the Real, and nothing is truly conscious but God.

Can human beings experience the consciousness of the Real, which alone can be called pure consciousness? The answer is always "Yes and no." *Tawḥīd* means that "There is no consciousness but God's own consciousness." Inasmuch as human consciousness is nothing but nondelimited *wujūd*'s finding of itself, the answer is yes. But inasmuch as a delimited reality—a human being—is involved in this finding, the answer is no. Every mode of consciousness accessible to anything other than the Essence of the Real is both identical with and different from the Real's own self-consciousness. Only nondelimited *wujūd* experiences identity without difference. As the theological axiom puts it, "None knows God but God."

Self-Knowledge

Wujūd in itself is the Real inasmuch as it is nondelimited, incomparable, and forever undisclosed, while *wujūd* in its self-disclosure is all the "others," all the things that find and are found. *Wujūd* as such cannot be found except by *wujūd*: "None knows God but God." But nothing other than the self-disclosures of *wujūd* can be found by anyone, since nothing else exists. Every "other" is simply a modality of *wujūd*.

The Shaykh employs a large number of terms to refer to different modes of awareness and consciousness, or different kinds of perception of and participation in *wujūd*'s self-disclosures. Most of these terms are rooted in Koranic names of God. The most general of these is Knowing (*'alīm*). Several other names represent specific modalities of divine knowledge, such as Aware, Seeing, Hearing, Encompassing, All-embracing, Witness, Subtle, Light, Examiner, Wise, and Guardian. Each mode of knowledge and consciousness represented by these names is accessible to human beings. The Shaykh discusses the divine and human implications of each in detail. *Tawḥīd* demands that in every case, the quality in its real and absolute sense belong only to *wujūd*, while in an unreal and relative sense it belong to the self-disclosures of *wujūd*—such as human beings.

Other terms that the Shaykh employs stress the human vision of *wujūd* disclosing itself in all things. Among these are gnosis (*ma'rifa*), unveiling (*kashf, mukāshafa*), tasting (*dhawq*), insight (*baṣīra*), and opening (*fatḥ, futūḥ*).[7] In the present context, it is impossible to provide more than the barest outline of what is implied in the most general of all these terms, that is, knowledge (*'ilm*), which is typically seen as the primary attribute of *wujūd* after life, upon which all other attributes depend. Although *wujūd* is nondelimited and unconstricted, it knows itself and every possible mode of its own self-disclosure. *Wujūd* is one, and *wujūd* is both knower and known.

On the basis of *wujūd*'s self-knowledge, it discloses itself according to the demands of its own attributes. The result is an infinitely diverse universe that externalizes the contents of *wujūd*'s self-knowledge. The creatures—the realities, entities, or things—are identical with the objects of this knowledge. Inasmuch as they are found in the universe, they have been given a trace of *wujūd*. Inasmuch as they are ephemeral and unreal, they reflect their own realities, which have no inherent claim to *wujūd*, any more than red and green, which are made manifest by light, have a claim upon light.

If we look at *wujūd* in terms of its own self-nature, we need to affirm that it is a single reality. But if we look at it in terms of its self-knowledge, then we must say that it knows every possibility of self-expression that it entails, which is to say that it knows the cosmos in all its infinite spatial and temporal expanse. Hence *wujūd* is one with a oneness that embraces potential manyness. God is One/Many, that is, One in terms of His Essence and many in terms of His names.

Ibn al-'Arabī and his followers distinguish between two categories of divine names in accordance with whether names stress the oneness of all things in respect of *wujūd* or the manyness of things in respect of the differentiation demanded by God's knowledge. Names that pertain mainly to oneness are called names of "mercy," "gentleness," or "beauty" and are closely associated with God's similarity. Names that pertain primarily to manyness are called names of "wrath," "severity," or "majesty" and are closely associated with God's incomparability.

The first category of names designates creaturely relationships with the Real that necessitate nearness, harmony, equilibrium, wholeness, sameness, and consciousness. The second category designates relationships that demand distance from God, disharmony with the Real, disequilibrium, partiality, difference, and ignorance. These are the "two hands" with which God molded the clay of Adam.[8]

The two categories of names—or the two hands of God—give rise to every polarity and complementarity in the universe, including spirit and body, which meet in imagination. If God's right hand dominates in the makeup of a human being, the qualities pertaining to unity and self-awareness—*wujūd*'s finding of itself—gain the upper hand. To the extent that God's left hand dominates, the human subject is overcome by dispersion, ignorance, and darkness.

When *wujūd* discloses itself, it does so in respect of both unity and diversity, both nearness and distance, both similarity and incomparability. Things that are more closely connected to *wujūd*'s oneness tend to manifest the qualities of unity, simplicity, harmony, equilibrium, and awareness. Salient examples are spirits, which are invisible, noncompound, and relatively everlasting. Those that are more closely connected to the diversity of the objects of *wujūd*'s knowledge display multiplicity, compoundness, disequilibrium, darkness, and unconsciousness. Examples are the bodily things that fill the visible cosmos.

The interrelationship between God's two hands is reflected in the relationship between the macrocosm and the microcosm. The universe as a whole, in all its spatial and temporal expanse, displays the infinite diversity of *wujūd*'s possible modes of manifestation. The predominant qualities are difference, lack of integration, dispersion, scatteredness, dimness of light, unconsciousness, ignorance, and passivity. In contrast, the human microcosm brings together and harmonizes all the diverse qualities of *wujūd* and manifests *wujūd*'s oneness and wholeness. To the extent that the microcosm represents a full and conscious self-disclosure of *wujūd*, the qualities that predominate are unity, harmony, concentration, luminosity, awareness, knowledge, and activity.

The Unknown Station

The Shaykh understands the hadith of God's creating Adam in His own form to mean that God brought human beings into existence possessing the inherent attributes of *wujūd*. Hence *wujūd* itself designates the original disposition of human beings. To be human is to manifest *wujūd* as *wujūd*, while to be anything else is to manifest certain qualities of *wujūd* rather than others. Notice, however, that "manifestation" is the issue here, not identity with *wujūd* in every respect. Although identity is desirable, it is, in a real sense, impossible, because *wujūd* belongs to God alone. Hence difference always remains. God's two hands retain their rights even in the experience of *waḥdat al-wujūd*.

In contrast to human beings, nonhuman things are innately ruled by certain specific attributes of *wujūd*. Hence they can never achieve an equilibrium of attributes or colors, a balance in which the colors cancel each other out, leaving only the pure, colorless light of *wujūd* itself. Human beings alone have the potential to manifest every color of light, every quality of *wujūd*.

If people develop in harmony with nondelimited *wujūd*, they will reach an unknown rather than a known station, what the Shaykh calls the "Station of No Station." A person who achieves this realization will display every quality of *wujūd* in perfect harmony and balance with every other. This is the actualization of the original human disposition, since it is a return to the divine form—or the manifestation of *wujūd* as such—from which the human being arose.

If people fail to develop in harmony with uncolored and nondelimited *wujūd*, their divine form will unfold in keeping with certain specific and determined qualities of *wujūd*. Hence they will enter into a known station like everything else in the universe. This may be a known luminous station like that of the angels, in which case they will dwell in paradise after death. But there are many other possible known stations, some of them dark, dense, and dispersed, corresponding to various hell worlds.

Human beings play a unique role in the cosmos because they alone allow for the full manifestation of those qualities of *wujūd* that bring about integration, harmony, and wholeness. This peculiar human characteristic is typically called *jam'iyya* or "all-comprehensiveness." Ontologically, all-comprehensiveness goes back to the fact that God gave human beings an original disposition that manifests the all-comprehensive name of God, a name that designates the formless form of *wujūd* and thereby signifies all realities. But the term *jam'iyya* is also employed to designate the fruit of meditation, concentration, and remembrance (*dhikr*). It is achieved through gathering together the dispersed powers of the soul and focusing them on the Real Himself, or actualizing to a significant degree *wujūd*'s own awareness of itself.

When discussed in positive terms, human perfection is viewed as the realization of every quality of *wujūd* latent in the divine/human form. Perfect human beings are looked upon as God's "vicegerents" (*khalīfa*), since they have brought together all His attributes in a conscious and active manner and rule the macrocosm in His stead. Their original disposition appears as the possibility to realize the qualities inherent in the divine/human form. Hence human perfection is seen as the full affirmation of divine similarity, such that all the qualities of *wujūd* are humanly embodied in perfect balance and harmony.

But human perfection is more often viewed in negative terms. Difference and incomparability are stressed, rather than sameness and similarity. Since there is nothing real but God, human beings are utterly unreal. Ignorance and deviation result from not recognizing this. From this point of view, human perfection is achieved by stripping away every claim to *wujūd*'s qualities. Human beings are the utter servants of God, since they have nothing of their own. The path of spiritual growth is pictured as abandoning the dark clouds that conceal the sun of *wujūd*. Only through achieving nothingness can people truly affirm the unique reality of the One. From this standpoint, the original human disposition is empty of created qualities, because created qualities are delimitations, and *wujūd* is nondelimited. Emptiness alone allows for the full self-disclosure of *wujūd*. But to be empty of created qualities is to be full of *wujūd*, which alone is uncreated.

The Shaykh's description of the Station of No Station combines the positive and negative perspectives. Since perfect human beings have abandoned all qualities, they stand in no quality. But standing in no quality can only mean standing in *wujūd*, which alone is nondelimited by any quality whatsoever.

Hence perfect human beings are *wujūd*'s full self-disclosures, unhampered by any quality or entity, yet in complete control of every quality and entity. As the Shaykh writes, "Correct nondelimitation goes back to the one who has the power of becoming delimited by every form without being touched by the harm of that delimitation" (III 472.25).

Annihilation and Subsistence

Ibn al-'Arabī and other Sufis employ many pairs of terms to explain the complementary functions of servanthood and vicegerency, that is, the human state of actualizing simultaneous incomparability and similarity. One of the most famous of these pairs is *fanā'* (annihilation) and *baqā'* (subsistence). Western scholars seem to have focused on the term *fanā'* because it is reminiscent of terms like *nirvana* and *moksha*. But in Sufi texts, *fanā'* is always contrasted with *baqā'*. The *locus classicus* for the two terms is Koran 55:27: *All that dwells on the earth is* annihilated, *and there* subsists *only the face of your Lord, the possessor of majesty and generosity.* For the Shaykh and many others, the term *earth* here can be understood to refer to the divine/human form in respect of incomparability, while the expression *face of your Lord* is the divine/human form in respect of similarity. Hence the verse can be read to mean that everything in the human being that dwells in the domain of distance from God will be annihilated and overcome by the attributes of nearness to God. Inasmuch as human beings are Not He, they are annihilated, but inasmuch as they are He, they subsist.

When human beings affirm God's incomparability, they negate reality from themselves. The goal of spiritual practice becomes the elimination of every claim to divine qualities. This is the station of "servanthood." Once all trace of self-affirmation has been erased, God's self-disclosure remains. God is experienced as disclosing Himself within the creature in order to bring it into existence. Creaturely attributes have been annihilated and divine attributes subsist. This is the station of "vicegerency," or acting as God's representative in the cosmos. But in truth it is God who acts, since the servant has been utterly effaced.

It should not be imagined that this negation of self and affirmation of God remain mental exercises. Quite the contrary, the experience of this reality preceded its formulation. Muslims who lived their faith to the fullest, having actually undergone the annihilation of their selfhood, were able, like al-Ḥallāj, to say "I am the Real," because the Real's consciousness of Itself became actualized within them. This at least is the constant claim of all the masters of Sufism, and Ibn al-'Arabī is no exception.

In a chapter of the *Futūḥāt* devoted to annihilation, the Shaykh points out that the term *fanā'* is used in its technical sense along with the pronoun *'an* (from). Thus the Sufis speak of annihilation *from* something. Likewise the term *baqā'* is employed with the pronoun *bi* (through). Hence one speaks of subsistence *through* something. In all cases, annihilation is lower and subsistence higher. "As for annihilation 'from the higher,' that is not a technical term of the Sufis, even though it is correct linguistically" (II 512.30).

The Shaykh does not provide an exact definition of the term *annihilation*, but rather examples of what Sufis before him have said about it. Thus he says that they have used it to mean "the annihilation of acts of disobedience, . . . the annihilation of the servant's vision of his own acts because God undertakes them, . . . and annihilation from creation" (II 512.27). He says that the Sufis consider *fanā'* to have seven levels, which he explains in some detail. Already at the third level seekers are so completely annihilated from the attributes of created things that they lose consciousness of their own attributes, since they perceive only God's attributes. The higher levels pertain to various modes of witnessing the Real.

The term *witnessing* (*shuhūd*) provides an important key to what is at issue when annihilation is mentioned. It always calls to mind the divine name Witness (*shahīd*), since "There is no witness but the Witness." In general, witnessing is synonymous with seeing, not only with the eyes, but also with the heart, the inner organ that is the locus of awareness and consciousness. Witnessing is often employed as a synonym for unveiling (*kashf*), the lifting of the veils between creation and the Real. It demands consciousness of what is witnessed, but it does not demand full self-consciousness.[9]

One of the Shaykh's students asked him why the mind does not stay the same after annihilation, given that annihilation erases the soul's faculties. If the faculties play no role, they should not be affected. In the process of answering the question, the Shaykh refers to the "witness" (*shāhid*), which he defines elsewhere as "the trace that witnessing leaves in the heart of the witnesser" (II 132.25).

> There is no instance of witnessing without a trace in the one who witnesses it. The trace is what is called the "witness." It brings about the increase that accrues to the rational and other faculties. If this witness is not found after the annihilation, then it was not an annihilation in *tawḥīd*. On the contrary, it was a sleep of the heart, since, in our view, annihilation is of two sorts: When we find the witness after it, then it is correct. When we do not find the witness after it, we call it a "sleep of the heart." It is like someone who sleeps and does not dream. (Ibn Sawdakīn, pp. 44-45)

Hence the Shaykh recognizes a loss of self-awareness in spiritual experience that has no benefit for those who undergo it, since they remain totally unaffected by it. In another passage, he explains that the annihilation of self occurs because the self is darkness, while what is witnessed is light. When the light shines, the soul disappears. "Shadows cannot be established when there is light. The cosmos is a shadow, and the Real is a light. That is why the cosmos is annihilated from itself when self-disclosure occurs. For the self-disclosure is light, and the soul's witnessing is a shadow. Hence the viewer for whom the self-disclosure occurs is annihilated from the witnessing of himself during the vision of God. When God lets down the veil, the shadow becomes manifest, and joy is experienced through the witness" (II 466.23).

The Shaykh seems to be saying that during the witnessing of the self-disclosure, there is no consciousness of self. It is only after the person returns to self-awareness that he or she experiences joy through the trace left in the soul by the witnessing. However, in another work he makes clear that the retention of a certain mode of self-consciousness during annihilation is a necessity of human perfection. Hence the annihilation of self that is experienced by perfect human beings is not absolute.

> True perfection is found only in the one who witnesses both his Lord and himself. . . . If someone were to witness his Lord while being completely free of witnessing himself—as some people have claimed—he would gain no benefit and be the possessor of imperfection. For then the Real would be the one who witnesses Himself through Himself, and that is the way things are in any case. So what benefit would accrue to the one who supposes that he was annihilated from himself and witnessed his Lord at the same time? (*Mawāqi'*, p. 27)

The Shaykh never lets his readers forget that annihilation is a relative term. Annihilation always means annihilation *from* some specific mode of lower consciousness and simultaneous subsistence *through* a specific mode of higher consciousness. One kind of awareness is given up to be replaced by a higher kind. Annihilation, in other words, is validated through the subsistence that accompanies it. That which subsists is the Real's self-disclosure, and that which is annihilated is the unreal—the limited self-awareness of the individual. "He" remains and "Not He" disappears. The Shaykh explains:

> Subsistence is your relationship with the Real. . . . But annihilation is your relationship with the engendered universe, since you say, "I have been annihilated from such and such." Your relationship to the Real is higher. Hence subsistence is a higher relationship, since the two are interrelated states.
>
> None subsists in this path except him who is annihilated, and none is annihilated except him who subsists. The one described by annihilation will always be in the state of subsistence, and the one described by subsistence will always be in the state of annihilation. In the relationship of

> subsistence is the witnessing of the Real, while in the relationship of annihilation is the witnessing of creation. You cannot say, "I was annihilated from such and such," without conceiving of what you were annihilated from. Your very conception of that is your witnessing it, since you cannot avoid making it present to yourself in order to conceive of the property of becoming annihilated from it.
>
> Subsistence is the same. You must witness the one through whom you subsist, and in this path, subsistence is only through the Real. Hence you have to witness the Real, since you must have made Him present in your heart and conceived of Him. Then you will say, "I subsist through the Real." This relationship is nobler and higher, because of the highness of the one with whom it is established. Hence the state of subsistence is higher than the state of annihilation, even if the two necessitate each other and are found in a single person at the same time. (II 515.24)

Human beings are forms of God. In other words, they epitomize the Real, in whom are found all the qualities of *wujūd*. However, "normal" people live in disequilibrium and dispersion. The divine attributes are actualized only partially and weakly, and certain attributes dominate over others. The dominant attributes most often pertain to qualities of *wujūd* that necessitate distance, differentiation, otherness, and darkness.

When incomparability is taken into account, the transformation that must take place as the divine form unfolds involves the affirmation of the exclusive reality of the Real and the negation of every human claim to selfhood. This negation is sometimes called "annihilation." But every annihilation demands a subsistence; incomparability cannot be viewed apart from similarity. Thus each of the Shaykh's seven levels of annihilation calls for an affirmation of *wujūd*'s self-disclosure and the reality of the human mode of consciousness that this self-disclosure brings about.

Becoming Human

In sum, the Shaykh holds that the original human disposition is established by the fact that people were created in the form of God, which is to say that they alone among all things in the cosmos have the potential to experience the full self-disclosure of *wujūd*. In order to actualize the divine form, they must abandon the limited consciousness that separates them from *wujūd*. Through "servanthood," they must surrender to God's will and return all things to their rightful owner, who is the Real. To be annihilated *from* the unreal is to subsist *through* the Real. This "Real" is precisely *wujūd* inasmuch as it discloses itself to the servant. It is the formless divine form in which human beings were created.

The famous ninth-century Sufi Abū Yazīd Basṭāmī reported that he did not reach God until God said to him, "Leave aside your self and come." Ibn al-'Arabī explains: "God invited him to come from the form of himself to the form of the Real in which God created Adam. The self is only able to assume that form when it departs from attachment to everything other than the Real" (Ibn Sawdakīn, pp. 38-39).

In a long account of a *mi'rāj* or spiritual ascent during which he was taken up through the celestial spheres into God's presence in the footsteps of Muhammad, Ibn al-'Arabī concludes by describing the final realization that was given to him.[10] He saw that he was none other than *wujūd*'s full self-disclosure: "Through this ascent I actualized the meanings of all the divine names. I saw how they all go back to a single Named Object [*musammā*] and a single Entity. That Named Object was the object of my witnessing, and that Entity was my *wujūd*. So my journey had been only in myself" (III 350.30).[11]

Consciousness represents one of the most salient qualities of *wujūd*. Hence, those who realize their own divine form actualize full human consciousness. When Abū Yazīd "left aside himself" and came to God, he left behind the constraints of ignorance and experienced himself as a face of God turned toward manifestation and undergoing endless and never-repeating self-disclosures. This station is achieved only by a small minority of human beings, those who attain to perfection, but it remains the original disposition of all human beings. In the Shaykh's view, only those who achieve it deserve the name *human* in the full sense. In other people, the dispersive qualities of the microcosm—represented most graphically by the diverse species of the animal kingdom—retain their ruling properties. Hence the self does not benefit fully from the integrating qualities of the undifferentiated divine form.

Having reached pure unity and integration, perfect human beings experience the self-manifestation of nondelimited *wujūd* on the level of delimitation. All qualities of *wujūd* are actualized within them exactly as they are found in the Real Itself. Hence no quality can be ascribed to them, since to say that they are *this* would mean that they are *not that*. But they are neither this nor that, or they are both this and that. Not only do they move beyond all created limitations, but they also move beyond domination by either of God's two hands—oneness and manyness, or mercy and wrath, or beauty and majesty, or similarity and incomparability. "The people of perfection have realized all stations and states and passed beyond these to the station above both majesty and beauty, so they have no attribute and no description" (II 133.19).

Frequently the Shaykh refers to the realization of the Station of No Station as the actualization of God's attribute of acting as a *coincidentia oppositorum* (*jam' al-aḍdād*). Only the perfect human beings deserve to be called the "Folk of God," because only they have actualized the form of this name fully.

They manifest every conflicting attribute, because they have realized the original disposition of *wujūd*, which is to be *the First and the Last, the Manifest and the Nonmanifest* (57:3).

> No one in the cosmos brings together opposites except the Folk of God specifically, because He whom they have realized is He who brings together opposites, and through Him the gnostics know. For *He is the First and the Last, the Manifest and the Nonmanifest* in respect of One Entity and one relationship, not in respect of two diverse relationships. Hence they have departed from rational categories, and rational faculties cannot delimit them. Or rather, they are the Divine Ones, the Verifiers, whom the Real has verified in what He has given them to witness. Hence, they are and they are not. *You did not throw when you threw, but God threw* [8:17], so God affirmed and He denied. (III 396.19)

The Station of No Station brings together every opposite quality in utter undifferentiation, pure unity, sheer consciousness, total freedom, complete lack of delimitation, and identity with the Real's self-disclosures. The nature of the consciousness experienced in this station can only be expressed through analogies and metaphors. It is utterly inaccessible to ordinary language, which is to say that people are blind to the shining of its light. In fact, of course, the light witnessed by perfect human beings is forever shining in the darkness of the cosmos; it is only human incapacity that prevents people from seeing it.

PART II

Worlds of Imagination

5

Revelation and Poetic Imagery

Ibn al-'Arabī wrote not only several hundred prose works, but also three divans of poetry and many thousands of additional verses scattered throughout his prose writings. As the greatest Muslim theoretician of imagination, he was able to utilize—with perfect awareness of what he was doing—the possibilities of poetical expression gained through imaginal perception.

So far as I know, the Shaykh did not explain systematically or in detail the relationship between cosmic imagination and the mode in which the poetic imagination makes use of the possibilities of language to express invisible realities. However, he alludes to this relationship in many passages and discusses it rather explicitly in *Dhakhā'ir al-a'lāq*, his own commentary on one of his divans, *Tarjumān al-ashwāq*. R. A. Nicholson realized the importance of these two works eighty years ago and published a complete translation of the *Tarjumān* with selections from the commentary. However, Nicholson provided no theoretical introduction to the translation, nor did he make any attempt to explain the technical nature of much of Ibn al-'Arabī's terminology. Without a detailed analysis of the Shaykh's concepts and worldview, it is impossible to grasp the world of meanings behind his literary forms.

The *Tarjumān al-Ashwāq*

Ibn al-'Arabī tells us that he wrote his commentary on the *Tarjumān al-ashwāq* to refute a certain jurist's claim that the work dealt with sensual love and not the divine mysteries. Nicholson, in contrast to some earlier scholars, had no doubt as to the Shaykh's sincerity, and he expresses his gratitude to the skeptic who caused him to write the commentary. As he remarks, "Without [Ibn al-'Arabī's] guidance the most sympathetic readers would seldom have hit upon the hidden meanings which his fantastic ingenuity elicits from the conventional phrases of an Arabic *qaṣīda*." Then Nicholson tells us that the Shaykh has "overshot the mark" and "take[s] refuge in far-fetched verbal analogies and . . . descend[s] with startling rapidity from the sublime to the ridiculous" (pp. 6-7).

While expressing our gratitude to Nicholson for his pioneering contribution to scholarship in translating the *Tarjumān al-ashwāq*, we may still be allowed to question his evaluation by asking how the Shaykh's commentary would have been perceived by intellectuals of his own day, and more particularly, by those familiar with his teachings. From this perspective, Ibn al-'Arabī's "ingenuity" does not seem nearly so "fantastic" as Nicholson believed, since, in the *Futūḥāt al-makkiyya* alone, he provides several thousand more pages of the same sort of "far-fetched verbal analogies." If one were to drop his commentary on the *Tarjumān al-ashwāq* into the middle of the *Futūḥāt*, no one would notice. The only thing "ridiculous" here is that Nicholson should have judged Ibn al-'Arabī from within the cognitive blinkers of British rationalism.

In providing selections from Ibn al-'Arabī's commentary, Nicholson leads us to believe that he has given us all the significant sections. He says, "I have rendered the interesting and important passages nearly word for word" (p. 9). But Nicholson's evaluation of the "interesting and important" rested on the concerns of the scholarship of his day. It is sufficient to read the Shaykh's commentary in relation to the *Futūḥāt* to see that in fact Nicholson left out most of what was "interesting and important" for the Shaykh and his followers and that much of what Nicholson no doubt considered as a "descent to the ridiculous" provides the key to situating the poetry within the context of Islamic thought. Everything that the Shaykh says about his *qaṣīda*s is firmly grounded in the Koran and the Hadith, Islamic theology and cosmology, and the Muslim experience of God.

The first line of the *Tarjumān* reads, "Would that I were aware whether they knew what heart they possessed!" The Shaykh's commentary tells us that the word *they* refers to *al-manāẓir al-'ulā*, a term that Nicholson translates as "the Divine Ideas," without any explanation as to what this expression might signify. Although called by various names, these "Divine Ideas" reappear in the commentary with frequency. Nicholson's first mistake, which precludes any real understanding of the rest of the work, is to translate *manāẓir* as "ideas" and *'ulā* as "divine."

Manāẓir is the plural of *manẓar*, from the root *n.ẓ.r.*, which means primarily "to look, to view, to perceive with the eyes."[1] The literal sense of the term *manẓar* is "a place in which a thing is looked upon" or a "locus of vision." *'Ulā* is the plural form of the adjective *a'lā*, meaning "higher." Hence, the *manāẓir al-'ulā* are the "higher loci of vision." As a technical term in cosmology, "higher" is contrasted with "lower" (*asfal*). The "higher world" is the invisible realm, inhabited by angels and spirits. The "lower world" is the visible realm, inhabited by bodies. Hence the "lower loci of vision" would be the things that we perceive with our sensory eyes, or our "sight" (*baṣar*), while the "higher loci of vision" are the things we perceive through the inward, spiritual faculty called by such names as "insight" (*baṣīra*), "unveiling" (*kashf*), and "tasting" (*dhawq*). The "organ" through which a human being perceives the invisible and higher things is the heart (*qalb*). Even God Himself may be seen with the heart, and in his commentary the Shaykh frequently reminds us of the famous *ḥadīth qudsī*, "Neither My heavens nor My earth encompass Me, but the heart of My servant with faith does encompass Me."

When the Shaykh refers to a *manẓar* or "locus of vision," he is indicating that a certain reality is seen at a specific level of existence. The ultimate object of vision is God. But God in Himself is absolutely invisible and indefinable, which is to say that He cannot be seen in His unknowable Essence. However, He can be seen in His self-disclosure, and this takes place within a form, which is the place or "locus" (*maḥall*) within which vision occurs. The form may be called by many names, such as "imaginal form" (*ṣūra khayāliyya* or *ṣūra mithāliyya*), "locus of witnessing" (*mashhad*), "locus of manifestation" (*maẓhar*), "locus of self-disclosure" (*majlā* or *mutajallā fīh*), and "spirituality" (*rūḥāniyya*). Each of these terms has special nuances and needs to be discussed in its own context. The present chapter can only touch on some of them.

The "higher loci of vision" that Ibn al-'Arabī mentions at the very beginning of his commentary provide the subject matter of the whole divan. In effect, each poem represents the description of God's self-disclosures as they appeared to the poet in the invisible worlds. By not providing an introduction and beginning the commentary with the term *Divine Ideas*, Nicholson makes it nearly impossible for anyone not thoroughly versed in Ibn al-'Arabī's world-view to realize what the commentary is all about, and thus Nicholson's claim that the interpretations are "far-fetched" seems plausible.

It was natural enough for Nicholson to talk of "ideas," given the context of Western intellectual history, where the mainstream tradition has until recently considered all significant thinking to be based on reason and ratiocination. Nor was it strange for him to translate "higher" as "divine," given the fact that the intermediate worlds have been all but banished from Western thought. As a result, we are left with only two levels of being, God and the physical realm. But now that the studies of Henry Corbin and others have appeared, it is generally known that Muslims never lost sight of the invisible worlds that separate the visible realm from God Himself. These worlds are basically two: that of spirits (or angels) and that of imagination. Ibn al-'Arabī's works have to be read with a clear understanding of the nature of these intermediate realms. Here I will concentrate on imagination, since it is closer to human perception and has a more immediate effect on poetic imagery.

One of the basic differences between "ideas" and "loci of vision" (or "images") is that the former are thought about, while the latter are seen, heard, touched, tasted, and smelled. The imaginal realm is a sensory realm, while the rational realm is disengaged (*mujarrad*) from sensory attributes. The rational faculty (*'aql*) works by a process of stringing concepts together and drawing conclusions, a process that the Shaykh typically calls "reflection" (*fikr*). In contrast, the imaginal faculty (*khayāl*) works by an inner perception that perceives ideas in sensory form. Hence imaginal perception may be visual, but this vision does not take place with the physical eyes; it may be auditory, but things are not heard with the physical ears. Again, dreams prove that everyone has nonphysical sense experience.

For the Shaykh, the subject matter of poetry is not something that one thinks about as one might think about a problem in dogmatic theology. Rather it is something that is seen with the inner eye and heard with the inner ear. Only then is it described.

Imagination

As already noted, imagination can be considered on three basic levels: as the cosmos itself, as an intermediate macrocosmic world, and as an intermediate microcosmic world. Its outstanding feature is its inherent ambiguity. On whatever level it is envisaged, it is always a *barzakh*—an isthmus or interworld—standing between two other realities or worlds and needing to be defined in terms of both. Thus a dream image needs to be described in terms of both subjective experience and objective content. We affirm the image as both true and untrue, since in one sense a specific thing is seen, and in another sense it is not.

On the level of the total cosmos, imagination's ambiguity pertains to everything other than God, because the universe—or what we commonly call "existence"—stands between absolute *wujūd* and absolute nothingness. If we say that God "exists," we cannot say the same thing in the same sense about the cosmos, so it must be considered "nonexistent." Yet we know that it does exist in some respect, or else we would not be here to speak about it. As a result, the universe is neither existent nor nonexistent; or it is both existent and nonexistent. Moreover, we know that the cosmos, while being "other than God," tells us something about God, since God's signs are displayed within it. In other words, the cosmos is in some sense the self-manifestation or self-disclosure of God. Hence, when the Shaykh calls the universe "imagination," he has in view the ambiguous status of all that exists apart from God and the fact that the cosmos displays God, just as an image in a mirror displays the reality of him who looks into the mirror.

In a second sense, imagination is the intermediate world between the two fundamental created worlds, the spiritual and corporeal worlds. These two worlds are contrasted in terms of opposite qualities, such as luminous and dark, unseen and visible, inward and outward, nonmanifest and manifest, high and low, subtle and dense. In every case imagination is an isthmus between the two sides, possessing attributes of both. Hence the macrocosmic "World of Imagination" needs to be described as "neither/nor" or "both/and." It is neither luminous nor dark, or both luminous and dark. It is neither unseen nor visible, or both unseen and visible. Or it is luminous and invisible in relation to bodies, but dark and visible in relation to spirits. The beings that inhabit the World of Imagination, such as jinn, are neither angels nor corporeal things, but they have qualities that are both spiritual and corporeal, luminous and dark. This is expressed mythically by the idea that the jinn are created of fire, which stands between angelic light and bodily clay. Hence they have bodily forms, so they are corporeal, yet they can change their forms at will, so they are free of many of the characteristics of corporeality.

The intrinsic ambiguity of the World of Imagination appears in the way in which it brings spiritual entities into relationship with corporeal entities. It does this by giving incorporeal realities the attributes of corporeal things. In other words, imagination brings about the embodiment (*tajassud*) of immaterial things, even though they do not gain all the attributes of corporeality, remaining "both/and." Thus, for example, dreams are the incorporeal reality of awareness embodied as images. Imagination allows unseen realities to be described as possessing attributes that pertain to the visible world, as when angels are said to have wings. And this description is not simply a figure of speech, because unseen things actually take on visible form in the imaginal realms.

When imagination is considered as a reality within the human microcosm, the term is used in two closely related meanings. In the first sense, imagination is the soul, and thus it corresponds to the World of Imagination in the microcosm. It is the human self, which acts as an intermediary between the luminous and immaterial divine spirit and the dark and dense body. Spirit and body—light and clay—have no common measure. The spirit is one, luminous, subtle, high, and invisible, while the body is many, dark, dense, low, and visible. But the soul is both one and many, luminous and dark, subtle and dense, high and low, invisible and visible. It is woven of imagination, which helps explain its affinity to the jinn—Satan in particular.

If the soul is both light and darkness, the human task is to strengthen the spiritual light and weaken the bodily darkness. The spirit is one reality while the body has many parts. Hence this strengthening of the soul's spiritual dimension amounts to a movement toward unity and integration. In contrast, the increasing domination of the soul's corporeal side represents a movement toward multiplicity and dispersion. In the next stage of life—the *barzakh* between death and resurrection—the happiness and wholeness of the human state depend upon the degree of integration that has been achieved in this world. We will return to this point in Chapter 7.

In a second microcosmic sense, imagination corresponds more or less to the faculty of the mind known by this name in English. It is a specific power of the soul that builds bridges between the spiritual and the corporeal. On the one hand, it "spiritualizes" corporeal things that are perceived by the senses and stores them in memory. On the other, it "corporealizes" the spiritual things known in the heart by giving them shape and form. The soul's "storehouse of imagination" (*khizānat al-khayāl*) is full of images derived from both the outward and the inward worlds. Each image is a mixture of subtlety and density, luminosity and darkness, clarity and murkiness.

Reason and Self-Disclosure

Whether imagination is considered as the whole universe, the domain between spirits and bodies, the human soul, or a specific faculty of the soul, its ultimate significance can only be understood in terms of its relationship with the Divine Reality from which it comes forth. One of the most important concepts through which the Shaykh describes the coming into existence of the cosmos and the soul is *tajallī*—self-disclosure. Both in the macrocosm and the microcosm, God discloses Himself by manifesting the properties of His names and attributes.

We have seen that Ibn al-'Arabī stresses both God's incomparability and His similarity. God is incomparable with all things because He stands infinitely beyond them, and He is similar to them because He manifests His own qualities through them. We noted that in the Shaykh's view, reason (*'aql*)—the primary tool of the theologians and philosophers—easily proves God's incomparability, but it cannot grasp His similarity. In contrast, imagination perceives His similarity, but knows nothing of His incomparability. Imagination is able to "see" God in His self-disclosure and similarity, while reason "knows" God in His incomparability. "The sensory and imaginative faculties demand by their essences to *see* Him who brought them into existence, while rational faculties demand by their essences and their proofs . . . to *know* Him who brought them into existence" (II 307.21).

Perfect knowledge demands knowing God through reason and seeing Him through imagination. The true nature of God's incomparability and similarity cannot be grasped unless both faculties are employed at once. Either faculty alone provides a distorted picture of reality. Exclusive stress upon incomparability cuts God off from the cosmos, while exclusive stress on similarity obscures the unity of the Real and leads to polytheism and "associationism" (*shirk*).

God's self-disclosure embraces everything that exists. From the human point of view, it has two dimensions, the manifest and the nonmanifest. The manifest is the visible world; the nonmanifest, the invisible world. Human beings are microcosms containing all worlds within themselves. Hence the body is a visible self-disclosure of God, the spirit an invisible self-disclosure, and the soul a self-disclosure that stands halfway between visibility and invisibility.

In the spiritual journey, Sufis strive to integrate body into soul and soul into spirit. The goal is for unity to dominate so that the human being becomes a perfect mirror reflecting the oneness of *wujūd*. The movement toward integration takes place within the imaginal world of the soul. The soul's psychological and spiritual states (*aḥwāl*), which are the self-disclosures of God to the human microcosm, cannot be satisfactorily described by rational categories, because reason's genius lies in abstraction. It isolates God from cosmic qualities by declaring that *Nothing is like Him* (42:11). But perfect knowledge also demands knowledge of His presence in the cosmos and the soul.

Through knowing their own souls, the Sufi adepts gain knowledge of God's similarity, or His self-disclosure within themselves. The Shaykh interprets the famous prophetic saying, "He who knows himself knows his Lord," to mean that through knowing oneself, one knows God's self-disclosures in one's body, soul, and spirit—even if God can never be known in Himself, in His very Essence, because of His incomparability. On the level of the soul, imagination comes to know God's self-disclosure by perceiving it concretely with an inward vision that combines the spiritual (or the suprasensory and the invisible) and the corporeal (or the sensory and visible).

The Revelation of Similitudes

The issues that arise in trying to grasp the nature of poetic imagery are intimately connected with those that arise in any attempt to understand Ibn al-'Arabī's concept of divine revelation (*waḥy*). In modern times, it is common to explain scripture almost entirely in terms of its human vehicles, who are typically looked upon as the authors of the texts. The Shaykh never ignores the human vehicle, but he also takes seriously the idea that revelation represents the actual spoken words of God. He explains in some detail the relationship between the divine Word, which is incomparable with human words and disengaged from any formal substratum, and the words of scripture, which take the form of human language. He describes the manner in which God's Word becomes pluralized as it enters the cosmos and descends into its many receptacles, who are the prophets. And he explains all this not through a theory that he has concocted, but on the basis of having seen the revelatory process in action and tasted it in himself. This tasting (*dhawq*) belongs to him not as a prophet, of course, but as an inheritor of the sciences revealed to the prophets. As he remarks about his knowledge in general, "I am not one to follow authority [*taqlīd*], thanks be to God. In my case, just as I have taken faith in the actual situation from my Lord, so I have witnessed the actual situation directly" (III 352.6).

Two of the many issues that the Shaykh discusses in connection with revelation seem particularly relevant to poetic imagery: the descent of meanings into imagination and the symbolism of language.

"Meaning" (*ma'nā*) is a key term in dogmatic theology, Sufism, and literary theory. The Sufis typically identify it with the inner, invisible reality of a thing, in contradistinction to its "form" (*ṣūra*), which is the thing's outer, apparent reality. Hence, the Shaykh often identifies a thing's meaning with its immutable entity, the thing as known by God. In this case the "form" that is contrasted with the meaning is the existent entity, or the thing inasmuch as it is found in the cosmos. More commonly, the Shaykh uses *meaning* as the opposite of *sense perception* (*ḥiss*). In this sense, the adjective *ma'nawī*, which is derived from *ma'nā*, can perhaps best be translated as "suprasensory." The Shaykh often makes this adjective synonymous with *spiritual* (*rūḥānī*), which is the opposite of *corporeal* (*jismānī*). But the lines separating the sensory from the suprasensory are ambiguous, especially because imagination—which is situated between spirit and body—has suprasensory as well as sensory characteristics. In some contexts, the Shaykh says that the adjective *suprasensory* pertains to everything that is not "elemental." Elementality—being composed of the four elements—is a characteristic of corporeal bodies, but not of imaginal bodies. Elsewhere he says that imagination includes the suprasensory because it combines sense perception and meaning. "The degree of imagination embraces that of sense perception and meaning. Hence it subtilizes the sensory object and densifies meaning" (III 451.2).

Meanings are "disengaged" (*mujarrad*), which is to say that they have no necessary connection to any locus of manifestation. They are essentially nonmanifest in relation to the external world or human knowledge. In contrast, all sensory things have a substratum or matter (*mādda*) that is part of their specific identity and allows them to become manifest in imagination or the physical world.

All this is to introduce the Shaykh's discussion of revelation, which has to do with the "sending down of meanings" by God. These meanings are present in God's knowledge, then enter the suprasensory or spiritual world, then become embodied through imagination in auditory or visual form. Meanings become manifest to prophets either in the Presence (*ḥaḍra*)—the world or level—of Imagination, or in the Presence of Sense Perception.

According to the Prophet's wife 'Ā'isha, "The first thing with which revelation began for the Messenger of God was the dream-vision [*ru'yā*]. He never saw any dream-vision without its coming forth like the breaking of dawn." This has been understood to mean that a few months before Gabriel appeared to reveal the Koran to Muhammad, he began seeing dreams that would then come true. The Shaykh sometimes refers to this hadith to explain what he calls the "beginning of revelation." Thus he writes that revelation begins with "the sending down of disengaged, intelligible meanings within delimited, sensory frames in the Presence of Imagination, whether this be in sleep or wakefulness. This [sending down] may be one of the objects of sense perception, in the Presence of Sense Perception, as in God's words, *[Gabriel] imaginalized himself to [Mary] as a man without fault* [19:17]. Or, it may take place in the Presence of Imagination, as when the Messenger of God perceived knowledge in the form of milk" (II 58.7).

Revelation takes sensory form when words are heard by a prophet or written down by him. But again, it begins in the imaginal realm.

> Revelation begins with dream-visions rather than sense perception because intelligible meanings are closer to imagination than they are to sense perception. Sense perception is the lower side, while meaning is the higher and subtler side. Imagination stands between the two.
>
> Revelation is a meaning. When God wants meaning to descend to sense perception, it has to pass through the Presence of Imagination before it reaches sense perception. The reality of imagination demands that it give sensory form to everything that becomes actualized within it. There is no escape from this. If the divine revelation arrives in the state of sleep, it is called a "dream-vision," but if it arrives at the time of wakefulness, it is called an "imaginalization" [*takhayyul*]. . . . That is why revelation begins with imagination. Then imagination is transferred to the angel in the outside world. The angel imaginalizes itself as a man, or as a person who is perceived through sense perception. It may happen that only the one who is the object of the revelation perceives the angel, or it may happen that those with him also perceive it. Then the angel casts the words of his Lord into the prophet's hearing, and this is "revelation." (II 375.32)

Note that the imaginalization of meanings through revelation demands that the prophet's message have more to do with God's similarity than His incomparability. This is because the prophet receives the images of God's attributes and qualities in sensory form, typically a linguistic form. Imagination and images function by bringing together two sides—in contrast to reason and abstraction, which separate and establish difference. Precisely because of the predominance of images in revelation, rational thinkers insist upon interpreting (*ta'wīl*) the sacred text to bring it into line with their own abstract understanding of things.[2]

Of course, Ibn al-'Arabī recognizes that there can be no pure imagination or reason, no pure similarity or incomparability, and that every revealed message combines the two modes of understanding. Nevertheless, when imagination predominates, similarity is perceived more clearly than difference. The predominance of similarity in the revealed text allows readers to sense the presence of God in a special way. Language itself pertains to the imaginal domain, given that it combines intelligible meanings with sounds, thus giving rise to meaningful speech. Our own experience of language is our most direct way of understanding the nature of the Breath of the All-merciful—also called Nondelimited Imagination—through which God creates the cosmos. The ambiguity of everything expressed in language, an idea dear to many contemporary thinkers, derives not only from the imaginal nature of language, but also from the imaginal nature of the cosmos itself and everything accessible to human understanding.

The second point about revelation that is relevant to the present discussion alerts us to one of its major differences with poetry. Both prophets and poets, to use Koranic terminology, "strike similitudes" (*ḍarb al-amthāl*). The word *mathal* or similitude derives from the same root as *mithāl* or image, and it is often used as its synonym. A speaker employs an appropriate similitude, image, or symbol to make a point. Striking appropriate similitudes is one of the outstanding characteristics of good poets. And naturally God Himself is more skilled than anyone else at striking similitudes. In the last analysis creation itself is a vast collection of similitudes that He has struck, just as it is a vast collection of words articulated within the Breath of the All-merciful. "God has intended to strike similitudes for people. He says, *Even so does God strike similitudes for those who answer their Lord* [13:18]. Hence the whole cosmos and everything within it is a striking of similitudes so that it may be known that He is He. He has made the cosmos a proof of Himself" (II 556.14).

Although the Koran often refers to similitudes that God has struck for Himself to bring about human understanding, it also forbids human beings from striking similitudes for God: *So strike not any similitudes for God; surely God knows, and you know not* (16:74). For the Shaykh, this means that human beings cannot devise symbols for God, because they do not know the object that is symbolized, for "None knows God but God." If people try to strike similitudes, the result will be inappropriate. Only the similitudes struck by God Himself can properly be applied to Him. The Shaykh explains:

> God strikes similitudes, but He forbids us from striking them for Him. He also provides us with a reason for that, saying, *Surely God knows, and you know not.* When God teaches someone to strike similitudes, that person strikes them on the basis of knowledge. Hence none strike similitudes but those who know God—those whom God has undertaken to teach. They are the prophets and the friends of God, and this is a stage beyond the stage of the rational faculty. In other words, reason cannot perceive this stage on its own in respect of its reflective faculty. This is because reason's knowledge of God is a knowledge of incomparability, while striking similitudes is a declaration of His similarity. (III 291.13)

Notice that the Shaykh understands the injunction not to strike similitudes as applying only to the common people, not to the prophets and their inheritors, the friends of God. Hence a poet may join the prophets, if he is a friend of God. This may explain why the Shaykh seems to have no fear of striking similitudes for God. Even so, he does not claim to strike them on his own, but rather in imitation of God's words. What he says in this regard helps explain his understanding of the imagery that he employs in his poetry:

> It is God who strikes similitudes for human beings because He knows where they apply. For God knows, and we know not. Hence the friend of God witnesses the similitudes struck by God. In that witnessing, he sees what it is that brings together the similitude and that for which it is struck. The similitude is identical with the object in respect of the factor that brings them together, but it is not identical in respect of the similitude. The friend of God does not strike similitudes for God. On the contrary, he knows the similitudes that God has struck for Himself. (III 345.3)

In sum, revelation has to do with the imaginal embodiment of meanings in language, but these embodiments are not haphazard. They take form on the basis of God's own knowledge of Himself. This helps explains both the necessity of revelation to establish human knowledge of God and the necessity of imaginalization for this knowledge to be complete. Rational operations have an indispensable function, because without them, God's incomparability cannot be understood; and indeed, the Koran frequently appeals to reason, as does the Shaykh. Tomes on philosophy and theology, which are rooted in the rational sciences, play useful and even necessary roles, so long as they do not become the exclusive source of knowledge. But imaginal understanding is also necessary, and revealed texts are full of images. Without images, God's similarity could never be grasped.

The positive role that poetry can play is to awaken the imaginal perception of God's self-disclosures. Ibn al-'Arabī, as an exponent of both reason and imagination—the "two eyes" with which God can be perceived—could hardly ignore poetry's teaching power. At the same time, he was perfectly aware that the true understanding of imagery demands a living vision, and that this is as difficult to come by as correct rational perception. Only the prophets and friends of God are given unveiling of the principles that rule the World of Imagination. Hence it is not surprising that the Shaykh should find it useful on occasion to provide rational explanations for his poetry, over and above any external reasons that may have motivated him.

Witnessing the Loci of Vision

Human beings have access to all the worlds. Through their external senses they perceive the visible world, and through their internal faculties they are able to perceive the whole microcosm, which includes body, soul, and spirit. God's self-disclosure may be perceived at any of these levels, but to the extent that this perception is expressible in human language, it must pertain to the imaginal realm of the soul. In other words, the adept may perceive God's self-manifestation at the level of the spirit, but if he is able to speak of this, he will do so through the imaginal effect that this perception leaves upon his soul. As we saw in the previous chapter, even the utter "annihilation" of the human subject leaves the "witness," and this takes imaginal form.

One question that the skeptical reader will immediately ask concerning Ibn al-'Arabī's use of imagery is why he does not say what he means in the first place. If his poetry refers to God and not to beautiful women, why does he disguise the fact? There are a number of answers to this question. One is that these are divine *self-disclosures*, not visions of God in Himself. By definition we are dealing not with God as God, but with God inasmuch as He shows Himself. Hence the adept speaks in terms of his perception of God's showings, and this perception takes place within a formal medium. This is the level of the divine similarity to the soul, and similarity can only be grasped in relation to created things. Hence creation and self-disclosure determine the points of reference.

Second, the poet wants to convey his vision to the reader in a language that the reader will be able to understand. He cannot use the rational and abstract language of dogmatic theology, since it is unable to express the divine self-disclosures. The perception of God's self-disclosures takes place within the imaginal realm in terms of the five senses. What has been perceived can only be expressed by language that describes concrete, sensory objects. Abstract explanation of the imagery would take the reader further away from the reality of the self-disclosure, not closer to it.

Third, the Shaykh felt that he had a message to deliver to his contemporaries concerning the spiritual life, so he tried to speak in a language that would attract his listeners and bring about some sort of awakening in those who had sufficient aptitude. As he remarks, "I allude [in the *Tarjumān al-ashwāq*] to lordly gnostic sciences, divine lights, spiritual mysteries, intellectual sciences, and Shari'ite admonishments. But I have expressed all this in the tongue of erotic love and amatory affairs, because souls are enamored of such expressions" (*Dhakhā'ir* 5).

A fourth important point has to do with "courtesy" (*adab*), which is one of the primary attributes of the perfect human being, an attribute that is intimately connected with "wisdom" (*ḥikma*), which puts everything in its proper place.[3] The Shaykh stresses the role of courtesy in speaking of God while discussing his words in the *Tarjumān*, "Her speech restores to life, as tho' she, in giving life thereby, were Jesus" (p. 49). He explains that this is a reference to the Koranic verse, *I breathed into him of My own spirit* (15:29), or, *Our only word when We desire a thing is to say to it, "Be!" and it is* (16:40). The reason "her speech" is compared to Jesus and not to the life-giving breath mentioned in these verses is "courtesy": "For we do not resort to declaring anything similar to the Divine Presence unless we find nothing in engendered existence to which similarity can be declared in what we intend" (*Dhakhā'ir* 13). In the same way, in discussing the striking of similitudes, he writes, "If we strike similitudes, let us look: If God has struck that as a similitude for the people, let us stop with that. This is the divine courtesy" (III 345.12).

Whatever the Shaykh's motivations for "not saying what he means," he frequently tells us in his commentary that his poems describe God's "self-disclosures," which he defines as "the lights of unseen things that are unveiled to hearts" (II 485.20). He often employs the term *mithāl* or "image" and its derivatives to refer to the World of Imagination within which the self-disclosures take place. For example, in explaining a verse that begins, "she said," he writes, "In other words, this divine reality within this imaginal form said" (*Dhakhā'ir* 27). Note here that grammatically, both "reality" and "form" are feminine, so the pronoun that refers to either of them must be she.[4] In commenting on another verse, the Shaykh writes, "Various sciences became manifest to me in corporealized form within the world of imaginalization" (*Dhakhā'ir* 204 [*Tarjumān* 124]). He speaks of the realities of the "high spirits" that enter the heart, while making reference to the hadith according to which Gabriel used to appear to the Prophet in the form of Diḥya Kalbī, the most beautiful man of the time: "The realities become manifest within imaginal bodies in the world of imaginalization—like the form of Gabriel within the form of Diḥya" (*Dhakhā'ir* 188 [*Tarjumān* 112]).

The imaginal loci of God's self-disclosures are often referred to as *mashhad*, "locus of witnessing." Explaining the significance of the word *moon* (*qamar*), the Shaykh writes, "The poet compares God to the *qamar*, which is a state between the full moon [*badr*] and the crescent moon [*hilāl*]. This is an isthmus-like, imaginal, formal locus of witnessing apprehended by the imagination" (*Dhakhā'ir* 143-44 [*Tarjumān* 98]).

Vision of the divine self-disclosures provides the spiritual traveler with knowledge of God. To support this claim, the Shaykh frequently refers to hadiths that speak of the visionary experiences of the Prophet and his Companions, as in his interpretation of these verses:

> [Boughs] trailing skirts of haughtiness;
> clad in embroidered garments of beauty;
> Which from modesty grudge to bestow their loveliness;
> which give old heirlooms and new gifts. (*Tarjumān* 107)

The Shaykh tells us that the imagery of these two verses represents the actual form in which he perceived the knowledge that was given to him through self-disclosure: "Since these gnostic sciences are provided from the Presence of

Imagination—just as knowledge was provided [to the Prophet] in the form of milk—the poet describes the sciences in the form in which they disclosed themselves to him" (*Dhakhā'ir* 169). He alludes to the same hadith in commenting on the verses,

> A woman slender, lissome, of fresh beauty,
> for whom the heart of the sad lover is longing.
> The assembly is filled with fragrance at the mention of her,
> and every tongue utters her name. (*Tarjumān* 117)

> The poet says: This knowledge [given by the vision being expressed in the poem] has as its object a [divine] attribute which, when it discloses itself in the world of imaginalization, is harmonious in character, inclining toward him who loves it, and fresh in beauty. Hearts in which the fire of uprooting has been kindled long for it. Whenever it is mentioned in an assembly, its mention fills the assembly with fragrance, because of the pleasantness of its aroma. Hence it is loved by every tongue, for each is refreshed by speaking about it.
>
> This is an attribute that can be grasped by verbal expression [*'ibāra*]. The reason for this is that it becomes manifest within the world of imaginalization and becomes delimited by description. However, the knowing listener recognizes that to which allusion is made through the description that is expressed, just as the reality of knowledge is recognized in "milk." (*Dhakhā'ir* 192)

In the *Futūḥāt*, the Shaykh makes an explicit connection between poets and the World of Imagination during a visionary description of the soul's ascent (*mi'rāj*) to the divine presence. Following the hadiths concerning the Prophet's *mi'rāj*, the Shaykh places a specific prophet in each of the celestial spheres, then discusses the sciences that pertain to each prophet and are acquired by the traveler who reaches the appropriate sphere. The third sphere, that of Venus, is inhabited by Joseph, the great dream interpreter. Hence at this level the spiritual traveler acquires knowledge of the World of Imagination and of how to interpret images, and it is from this sphere that poets gain their inspiration.

> When the traveler reaches the third heaven, Joseph casts to him the sciences that God had singled out for him, that is, those connected to the forms of imaginalization and imagination. For Joseph was one of the great masters of the science of dream interpretation, so God made present before him the earth that He created from the leftover of Adam's clay, the Market of the Garden, and the imaginal bodies of the spirits made of light and fire and of the high meanings.[5] He made known to

> him their yardsticks, measures, relationships, and lineages. He showed him years in the form of cows, the fertility of the years in the form of the cows' fatness, drought in the form of their leanness, knowledge in the form of milk, and firmness in religion in the form of a fetter.[6] God never ceased teaching him the corporealization of meanings within the forms of sense perception and sensory objects, and He gave him the knowledge of interpretation in all of that.
>
> This is the celestial sphere of complete form-giving and harmonious arrangement [*niẓām*].[7] From this sphere is derived assistance for poets. From it also arrive arrangement, proper fashioning, and geometrical forms within corporeal bodies. . . . From this sphere is known the meaning of proper fashioning, correct making, the beauty whose existence comprises wisdom, and the beauty that is desired by and is agreeable to a specific human constitution. (II 275.13)

Not every self-disclosure of God can enter into verbal expression, for self-disclosure may occur within the spirit beyond imagination and leave no expressible trace within the soul. The Shaykh often attributes this sort of self-disclosure to the Divine Essence, which is utterly incomparable and unknown. In both the *Tarjumān* and the *Futūḥāt*, he commonly compares this self-disclosure of the Essence to lightning. He explains the rationale for this by saying, "Flashes of lightning are compared to the loci of witnessing the Essence in that they have no subsistence" (II 98.21). In his commentary on the verse of the *Tarjumān*, "Thy lightning never breaks its promise of rain except with me," he writes,

> Here the poet alludes to the fact that he attained to a high station to which none of his peers had attained. "Lightning" is a locus of witnessing the Essence. The rains that come are the gnostic sciences that give fruit and are actualized in the heart of the witnesser. So the poet indicates that this is a locus of witnessing the Essence within an imaginal veil. In a similar way, God says concerning Gabriel: *He imaginalized himself to [Mary] as a man without fault* [19:17]. Through this imaginalization, God gave Jesus to her. In the same way, God gave various forms of gnostic sciences through "rain" within the locus of witnessing lightning to everyone but me.
>
> The poet says, "For thy lightning breaks its promise." In other words, no knowledge is actualized in the soul of the witnesser through this locus of witnessing the Essence, since it is a self-disclosure without material form. Hence imagination has nothing to retain and reason has nothing to understand, since this self-disclosure does not enter under how, how many, state, description, or attribute. (*Dhakhā'ir* 138 [*Tarjumān* 96])

The Shaykh adds more comments on the difference between "lightning" or the locus of witnessing the Essence and imaginal unveiling in explaining the line, "And when they promise you aught, you see that its lightning gives a false promise of rain" (*Tarjumān* 111). "They" are the "winds," which refer to different forms of self-disclosure that arise from the Breath of the All-merciful.

> The poet says, "When they make promises, it is like the lightning that breaks its promise," that is, the lightning that has neither thunder nor rain, so it produces no result, like the *barren wind* [51:41]. Here "their promise" comes through a locus of witnessing the Essence, which is why it is compared to lightning. The locus of witnessing the Essence yields no result in the heart of the servant, since it is not retained. Nothing is actualized through it except the heart's witnessing, while the heart beats wildly. For this locus of witnessing is exalted far above being constrained by any created thing. It contrasts with self-disclosure within a form in the world of imaginalization, since [in the latter case] the viewer retains the form of that which discloses itself to him and is able to interpret it—as shown by many examples in the hadith literature. (*Dhakhā'ir* 182-83)

In short, when the Shaykh says in the first line of the *Tarjumān al-ashwāq*, "Would that I were aware whether they knew what heart they possessed!" this is not some poetical conceit, but a description of an inward, imaginal experience. When he tells us that "they" refer to the "higher loci of vision," he is making this statement within the context of a metaphysical, cosmological, and psychological worldview that was developed by himself and earlier Muslim authorities to high degrees of sophistication. There is nothing "far-fetched" or "ridiculous" about his explanations, so long as one takes the trouble to study the experience and teaching within which they are grounded.

6

Meetings with Imaginal Men

Among the thousands of verses found in Ibn al-'Arabī's *Futūḥāt al-makkiyya* are the following. They describe some of his encounters with embodied spirits:

> One embodied himself to me in the earth,
> another in the air.
> One embodied himself wherever I was,
> another embodied himself in heaven.
> They gave knowledge to me, and I to them,
> though we were not equal,
> For I was unchanging in my entity,
> but they were not able to keep still.
> They assume the form of every shape,
> like water taking on the color of the cup.
> (I 755.7)

Spirits, as we know, embody themselves through imagination. To understand what this embodiment implies, we need to have a clear understanding of imagination's characteristics, the most outstanding of which is ambiguity, the fact that it escapes the logic of either/or.

The universe has three fundamental worlds. The highest is the world of the simple (or "noncompound") spirits, who are pure life, intelligence, and luminosity. The lowest is that of bodies, which are inanimate and compound, or made of parts. The middle domain is the world of imagination, whose inhabitants are both simple and compound at the same time. Hence they are not totally different from either spirits or bodies, and through them the two sides are able to interrelate.

Before we go further in this discussion, I need to remind the reader that we should not think of the basic characters in this drama—spirit and body—as discrete and autonomous things. Rather, the two terms designate configurations of certain tendencies found in existence, or certain divine qualities that are reflected in the created worlds. Both spirit and body are associated with a series of attributes, and no absolute distinction can be drawn between the two sides. The discussion of imagination itself alerts us to the fact that the qualities of spirit and body—which at first sight appear completely different—interpenetrate and intermingle. There can be no absolute differences, except when God as *wujūd* is contrasted with cosmos as nonexistence. Within the many worlds existentiated by the Breath of the All-merciful, things can be different only in a relative sense.

The World of Imagination allows spirits to become embodied and bodies to become spiritualized. On the microcosmic level, our minds spiritualize the objects of the outside world simply by perceiving them. The spiritualized nature of these objects becomes evident in the world of dreams, where we perceive sensory objects drawn from the outside world in a kind of never-never land between the inanimate matter of the corporeal world and the living and luminous substance of the spirit.[1]

The five senses remain active in imagination, but the five senses that perceive imagination are not necessarily identical with the five senses that function in the corporeal world. Hence the Shaykh distinguishes between the "eye of sense perception," which sees during wakefulness, and the "eye of imagination," which sees during sleep. However, the eye of imagination may also see during wakefulness (I 305.3). The Shaykh frequently tells us that "The person who undergoes unveiling sees while he is awake what the dreamer sees while he is asleep" (I 305.1). In other words, both the dreamer and the "unveiler" (*mukāshif*) perceive imaginalized objects (*mutakhayyalāt*), which are neither purely sensory nor purely spiritual.

Discerning Imaginal Realities

It is not always easy to tell the difference between an imaginal object and a sensory object. Although some people claim to experience the unveiling of luminous or fiery spirits—that is, angels or jinn—few of them know how they perceive what they perceive, nor do they know for certain the source of what they perceive. The Shaykh tells us that both the eye of imagination and the eye of sense perception function through the sense of sight, and the science of distinguishing between the perceptions of the two eyes is subtle (I 305.10). In fact, he says, this is one of the most difficult sciences to gain, and even many of the Folk of God do not have it. "Nothing causes greater obfuscation in engendered existence than imagination's becoming confused with sense perception. . . . If God gives a person the power of differentiation, then He clarifies affairs for him and shows him which eye he sees things with. Then he knows what they are—when he himself knows which eye he sees them with. The most necessary science for the Folk of God to obtain is this science, but many of them pay no attention to what we have mentioned" (III 507.30).

Even the Prophet's Companions, including 'Umar, did not possess the science of discerning between the vision of the eye of sense perception and the eye of imagination when Gabriel appeared in the form of a bedouin and asked several questions of the Prophet. And one of the most perfect of human beings, the Virgin Mary, did not possess this science at the time of the Annunciation, when Gabriel *imaginalized himself to her as a man without fault* (19:17). The Shaykh alludes to these two events while explaining the difficulty of discerning between the two kinds of perception:

> Not all those who witness imaginalized bodies discern between these bodies and bodies that are real in their view. That is why the Companions did not recognize Gabriel when he descended in the form of the bedouin. They did not know that the bedouin was an imaginalized body until the Prophet told them so when he said that it had been Gabriel. They had not doubted that he was a bedouin. The same was the situation with Mary when the angel *imaginalized himself to her as a man without fault*, because she had no mark by which to recognize spirits when they become embodied. (II 333.28)

The Shaykh tells us that this "mark" (*'alāma*) plays a fundamental role in discerning the nature of imaginal apparitions. Without it, people cannot even distinguish between the imaginal manifestation of spirits and that of God Himself. As the Shaykh notes, when people experience unveiling without possessing the mark, "The property of the divine and the spiritual sides is exactly the same [in their eyes]" (II 333.31). And without the mark, they have no way of discerning among the three types of created spirits that can manifest themselves in imaginal form—those of angels, jinn, and human beings.[2]

The Shaykh often employs the term *mark* in relation to a hadith that describes God's "self-transmutation" (*taḥawwul*) at the resurrection.[3] God reveals Himself to each group of people. But they keep on denying Him until He transmutes Himself into a form that has the mark that they recognize. In the context of the unveiling of imaginal realities, he apparently has something similar in view. He does not tell us what the mark is, because it is established between God and His servant and differs in each case, and perhaps also because he wants to prevent the unqualified from making false claims. Concerning a related mark, which is given to those adepts who become utterly disengaged from the natural world (*ṭabī'a*) and enter among the angels, he writes, "We know this mark, having tasted it. But we will not mention it to anyone, lest he make it manifest sometime, while being a liar in his claim. That is why God has commanded me and my peers to conceal it" (III 473.35).

Although Ibn al-'Arabī says nothing about the actual nature of marks, he does tell us something about their circumstances. For example, he says that God in His jealousy (*ghayra*) may decide that one of His lovers should love Him alone, even though the lover is still dominated by the natural world and has not yet escaped the constraints of imagination.

> God desires to deliver the soul from everything but Himself so that it will love nothing else. Hence He discloses Himself to it in a natural form and gives it a mark that it is not able to deny. This mark is what is called "incontrovertible knowledge" [*al-'ilm al-ḍarūrī*]. The soul comes to know that God is this form. Hence it inclines toward this form in spirit and bodily nature. When God comes to own the soul and teaches it that secondary causes[4] must have an effect upon it in respect of its nature, He gives it a mark whereby it will recognize Him. He discloses Himself to it through that mark in all secondary causes without exception. The soul recognizes Him and loves the secondary causes for His sake, not for their sake. (II 331.12)

Unless God has revealed the mark to spiritual seekers, they can always be deceived by visionary experiences. This is not only the case for beginners, but even for advanced adepts. Thus, for example, the Shaykh explains that a person can be deluded (*talbīs*) by the satans and evil jinn (*marada*) even during a spiritual ascent or *mi'rāj*, during which the traveler passes through the invisible worlds following the example of the Prophet. He writes that many Sufis have been mistaken on this point. Even Ghazālī was of the opinion that a person can only be deluded in the world of the elements; once the adept ascends beyond this world and the doors of heaven are opened for him, he will be protected against being deluded by the satans. The Shaykh, however, does not agree. He writes,

> Let us explain to you the truth in that: Some of the Sufis hold the view that [during a *mi'rāj*] all delusion in what is seen will be eliminated, because the travelers ascend into places where the satans cannot enter, places that are holy and pure, as described by God. This is correct. The situation is as they suppose. However, this is so only when the *mi'rāj* takes place in both body and spirit, as was the *mi'rāj* of the Messenger of God. Another person will ascend through his mind [*khāṭir*] or spiritual reality [*rūḥāniyya*] without the separation that occurs through death, but rather through an annihilation or a power of vision that has been given to him, while his body stays in his room. He may be absent from his body through annihilation, or present with it through a power he possesses. In

> this case, there must be delusion if this person does not possess the divine mark between him and God. Through that mark he stands *upon a clear sign from his Lord* [11:17] in what he sees and witnesses and in everything that is addressed to him. Hence, if he has a mark, he will stand *upon a clear sign from his Lord.* Otherwise, delusion will occur for him, and there will be a lack of certain knowledge in that, if he is just. (II 622.22)

For his part, the Shaykh makes clear that he possessed the mark that allows the gnostic to distinguish among the various kinds of imaginalized beings. He always knew if his imaginal eye was observing God, an angel, a jinn, or another human being. He writes,

> Some people distinguish the spiritual reality that becomes embodied in the outside world from a human being or whatever form in which it manifests itself, but not everyone distinguishes that. They also discern between a spiritual, supraformal, embodied form and an imaginal form within, by means of various marks that they recognize. I have come to know and realize these marks, for I distinguish the spirit when it becomes embodied in the outside or inside world from a true corporeal form. But the common people do not distinguish that. (III 44.12)

Note that by "common people" (*al-'āmma*) the Shaykh does not mean the man in the street, but rather the vast majority of Sufi adepts, the spiritual travelers who have experienced the unveilings of the imaginal world.[5]

It is perhaps worth remarking here that unveiling (*kashf*) is absolutely unreliable as a source of knowledge so long as people are unable to perceive the "marks" and thereby discern the true nature of the experience. As the Shaykh tells us, "Every unveiling that is not unmixed, completely untainted by anything of the bodily constitution, cannot be relied upon, unless the person already possesses the knowledge of the thing that takes form" (*Risāla*, p. 18). No one but the prophets and the greatest friends of God can know who or what becomes embodied to them in imaginal form during a visionary encounter.

The Shaykh reminds his readers that Satan and his followers among the jinn have a vested interest in leading people astray. This is their cosmic function, after all, just as the cosmic function of the prophets is to guide. The result of being led astray is to fall into "distance from God," which is the most concise definition of hell. In contrast, to follow guidance is to be brought near to God, that is, to end up in paradise.

This is not the place to go into detail concerning the Shaykh's views on the imaginal activity of satans, even though nowadays this is a topic that seems to have special relevance. It is worth noting, however, that he maintains that the jinn "play games with the rational faculties of certain people," making them think that they are receiving special knowledge (II 621.29). Thereby the jinn keep people confused in order to prevent them from finding the right path. The Shaykh even offers criteria for distinguishing whether or not a person's knowledge of invisible things comes from the jinn. He writes,

> Of all things in the natural world, the jinn are the most ignorant of God. Because of what they report to their [human] sitting companion, he has imaginings about the occurrence of events and what is happening in the cosmos, for they acquire that through listening to the Higher Plenum by stealth.[6] Then their sitting companion supposes that God has honored him. He should be careful in what he thinks!
>
> This is why you will never see any of those who sit with the jinn having actualized any knowledge of God whatsoever. The most that can happen is that the man who is provided for by the spirits of the jinn is given knowledge of the characteristics of plants, stones, names, and letters. This is the science of *sīmiyā'*.[7] Hence this person will acquire from the jinn nothing but a knowledge that is blamed by the tongues of the revealed religions. So, if someone claims to be their companion—and if he speaks the truth in his claim—ask him a question concerning divine knowledge. You will find that he has no tasting in that whatsoever. (I 273.35)

Varieties of Imaginal Perception

Given the fact that the Shaykh was able to recognize the distinguishing marks of imaginal phenomena, it is especially interesting to see how he describes his own perceptions. His writings are full of accounts of visionary experiences, and it would be possible to classify these into various types. Here, simply to suggest some of the range of the texts, I offer a preliminary and incomplete attempt at such a classification.

Visionary experience can be divided according to four basic criteria: (1) the state of the subject who observes the vision; (2) the reality of the object that undergoes imaginalization; (3) the form taken by the imaginalized object; (4) the cosmic "location" of the embodiment.

When Ibn al-'Arabī takes the observing subject into account, he usually distinguishes between visions that occur during normal, waking consciousness, and those that do not. Waking visions can be divided into two types according to the eye that perceives—the eye of sense perception or the eye of imagination. Nonwaking visions can also be divided into two types according to the mode of consciousness: The person may be asleep and perceive imaginal realities while dreaming, or he may have been overcome by a spiritual state (*ḥāl*), such as "absence" (*ghayba*) or "annihilation" (*fanā'*), which breaks his contact with the world of sense perception.

The realities that undergo imaginalization are the four things mentioned above: God, angels or luminous spirits, jinn or fiery spirits, and human beings. Each has the power—or may have the power—to manifest itself to others in imaginal forms. In the case of human beings, it is clear from the Shaykh's accounts that the person who imaginalizes himself may either be alive and present in this world or dead in this world but alive in the next.

The objects perceived can take any form whatsoever, with the sole qualification that the form must be sensory, like any imaginal phenomenon.

The cosmic location of the vision is often the most difficult of the four criteria to discern. I mean by "location" the world in which the embodiment occurs. On one level, this has to do with the distinction between the macrocosmic and microcosmic worlds of imagination, what the Shaykh refers to as "discontiguous imagination" and "contiguous imagination."[8] However, although he provides a theoretical distinction between these two worlds, he seldom draws the line in his writings. The difference between the two may be connected with the question of which eye perceives the imaginal apparition. If this is so, then the imaginal being perceived by the eye of sense perception would be located "out there" in the world of discontiguous imagination, while the being perceived by the eye of imagination would be "in here" in the world of contiguous imagination. However, I have not yet found a clear statement of these distinctions in the Shaykh's writings.

Also related to the question of cosmic location is the distinction between an imaginal embodiment that has the power to leave a concrete effect and one that has no such power. Here the Shaykh discerns between certain operations that sorcerers are able to perform through the science of *sīmiyā'* and the experience of the friends of God. For example, a sorcerer may provide food through *sīmiyā'*, but the person who eats the food will not become full. In contrast, when it is a question of the imaginalization experienced by the friends of God, "if you eat, you become full, and if you receive something in this station like gold or clothing or whatever, it stays with you in its state without changing. . . . We have found this station within ourselves. We experienced it through tasting with the spiritual reality of Jesus at the beginning of our wayfaring" (III 43.19).

Imaginal Men

If one were to employ the suggested criteria to classify all the accounts of imaginal perception that the Shaykh provides in the *Futūḥāt*—not to mention his other works—the result would be a major monograph. In some cases the Shaykh merely alludes to the visions, in others he provides many details. Usually he draws some conclusions relevant to his discussions. Here I will recount five instances of the Shaykh's visionary experience in which the second and third criteria are the same: The reality that undergoes imaginalization and the object that appears are both human beings. In two of the five accounts, the fourth criterion—that of location or world—seems to be different from that in the other three. As for the first criterion—the state of the observer—that also is not completely clear.

The Shaykh's imaginal visions often took place during dreams. He refers to many of them with the term *wāqi'a* or Incident (a word derived from the first verse of Koran 56). In defining Incidents, he tells us that they may be seen during sleep or wakefulness,[9] so it is rarely clear whether he himself was asleep or awake during the Incidents that he describes.

In the first account, the Shaykh was asleep during the vision, and hence the imaginalized man appeared to him within the World of Imagination. Nevertheless the Shaykh was certain of the authenticity of the vision, no doubt because of the marks that accompanied it. The person with whom he met had lived many thousands of years before. The subject of the chapter in which the vision is retold is time, and clearly the Shaykh recounts the vision in order to illustrate the fact that the mythic time in terms of which we commonly think comes nowhere near to exhausting the reality of cosmic time.

> Once God showed me, in the way in which a dreamer sees, that I was circumambulating the Kaabah with a group of people whose faces I did not recognize. They were reciting two lines of poetry, one line of which I remember and the other of which I have forgotten. The one which I remember is this:
>
> For years we have turned, as you have turned,
> around this House, all together, each of us. . . .
>
> One of them spoke to me, calling himself by a name that I did not recognize. He said, "I am one of your ancestors."
>
> I said to him, "How long ago did you die?"
>
> He replied, "Forty thousand and some years."
>
> I said to him, "But Adam himself did not live that long ago."
>
> He said, "Which Adam do you speak about? Are you speaking about the closest one to you, or about another?"
>
> Then I recalled a hadith in which the Prophet says, "God created one hundred thousand Adams." That ancestor to which I go back could have been one of those. (III 549.8)

In the second account, the Shaykh may have been awake during the apparition, and it seems clear that the imaginalized man was observed in the World of Imagination, because his physical body was dwelling in another country.

During the night when I was writing this chapter, the Real showed me through an Incident a light-complexioned man of medium height. He sat before me, but he did not speak. The Real said to me, "This is one of Our servants. Benefit him, so that this may be in your scales [on the day of resurrection]."

I said to Him, "Who is he?"

He said to me, "This is Abu'l-'Abbās ibn Jūdī, a resident of al-Bushārrāt [Alpujarras in Spain]."

At this time I was in Damascus. I said to Him, "O Lord, how will he take benefit from me? How do I relate to him?"

He replied, "Speak, for he will benefit from you. Just as I have shown him to you, so I am showing you to him. He sees you now just as you see him. Address him and he will hear you. He says the like of what you say. He says, 'I have been shown a man in Syria called Muḥammad ibn al-'Arabī. If he benefits me in a certain affair that I do not now possess, he will be my master.'"

I said to him, "O Abu'l-'Abbās! What is this affair?"

He said, "I was struggling in my search. I exerted the utmost efforts and struggled mightily. When I experienced unveiling, I came to know that I was desired. Hence I relaxed in that effort."

I said to him, "My brother, to a man who was better than you, more in union with the Real, more complete in witnessing, and more perfect in unveiling it was said, *And say: My Lord, increase me in knowledge'* [20:114]. So where is ease in the abode of religious prescription? You did not understand what was said to you. You said, 'I came to know that I was desired,' but you do not know *for* what. Yes, you are desired for your struggle and effort. This is not the abode of ease. When you are finished with the affair with which you are busy, exert yourself in the affair that comes to you with each breath. How can anyone be finished?"

He thanked me for what I said. Look at God's solicitude toward me and toward him! (III 431.20)

In three more visions, the Shaykh was unquestionably awake, and the visions seem to be of the type in which the imaginalized object is perceived in the external world. In the first of these, others were present but were unable to see the imaginal apparition. In the second, someone else may or may not have seen the visionary form. In the third, the imaginal apparition was perceived by at least one other person. The second and third of these accounts, like the first vision already discussed, have to do with the vision of human beings who existed in previous centuries.

The following apparition appears to pertain to the year 1194. Note that the imaginal form remained in the Shaykh's view until he turned away from it for a moment. The significance of this will become clear toward the end of this chapter.

> One day in Seville I was in the congregational mosque of al-'Adīs after the afternoon prayer. A person was telling me about a great man among the People of the Path, one of the truly greats, whom he had met in Khorasan. As he was describing his excellence to me, suddenly I was gazing upon a person near us, but the group with me did not see him. He said to me, "I am he—the person whom the man who met me in Khorasan is describing to you."
>
> I said to the man giving the account, "This man whom you saw in Khorasan—do you know his description?"
>
> He replied that he did. Then I began to describe the man's distinguishing features and the embellishments of his physical constitution.
>
> My speaking companion said, "By God, he does have the form that you have described. Have you seen him?"
>
> I said to him, "He is sitting right there, confirming to me the truth of the account you are giving of him. I described to you only what I saw as I was gazing upon him and he himself was making himself known to me." He did not cease to sit with me until I turned away. Then I sought for him, but I did not find him. (III 339.7)

Some years later, in 1200, the Shaykh was traveling in the Maghrib when he entered into the station of nearness to God (*maqām al-qurba*), the highest spiritual station that can be achieved by someone who is not a prophet. He found himself alone in the station and felt a terrible isolation. To "reach a station," it needs to be understood, does not imply any sort of absence from the world of everyday experience. In any event, at this time the Shaykh had already been living in the "Wide Earth of God" for seven years, and his universe was not one that any of us would necessarily recognize.[10] But he still walked and talked like other human beings. He interrelated with them, though they could have no idea of how he perceived the world. He tells us that on the day that he entered this new station, he happened to run into an amir with whom he was friendly, and the amir invited him to stay at the home of his secretary, who was also an old friend. To the secretary the Shaykh complained of his loneliness. But suddenly, he tells us, "While my friend was keeping me entertained, the shadow of a person appeared to me. I rose up from my seat, hoping to find relief in him. He embraced me, and I looked at him carefully. I saw that through him the spirit of Abū 'Abd al-Raḥmān Sulamī had embodied itself for me. God had sent him to me out of mercy" (II 261.9)[11]

Sulamī had died 170 years before this event. He was a great Sufi master and wrote many works, including one of the most famous collections of Sufi biographies. The Shaykh recounts their conversation, in which Sulamī explains to him certain aspects of the station of nearness.

The fifth encounter with an imaginal man took place two years later. This person, Aḥmad al-Sabtī, was a son of the famous Abbasid caliph Hārūn al-

Rashīd (d. 809) and had died some four hundred years earlier. He was well known in his own time for his piety. He used to fast six days a week and then work at a craft on Saturday, living on the proceeds for the rest of the week. This explains the name Sabtī, which means "[he who is connected] to the Sabbath." According to the Shaykh, he was the "Pole" (*quṭb*) of his time, the highest of the perfect human beings. In this meeting, the Shaykh's vision was shared at least by one other person. Hence he compares the meeting to the embodiment of Gabriel to the Prophet and the Companions.

> Among the Men [of God] are six souls in every time [who are given charge over the first six days of the week, during which God created the world]. They never increase or decrease in number. Sabtī, the son of Hārūn al-Rashīd, was one of them. I met him while circumambulating the Kaabah on Friday after the prayer in the year 599 [1202]. He was circumambulating. I asked him questions and he answered me while we continued to circumambulate. His spirit became embodied before me in sense perception during the circumambulation, just as Gabriel became embodied in the form of the bedouin. (II 15.27)

In another passage, the Shaykh provides a few more details about this event:

> I met him during the circumambulation after the prayer on Friday. I was circumambulating and did not recognize him. However, I saw that he and his state were strange during the circumambulation. For I did not see him pushing or being pushed. He would pass between two men without separating them. I said to myself, "This is a spirit that has become embodied, without doubt." I seized him and greeted him. He returned the greeting. I walked along with him and we spoke and conversed. . . .
>
> When I returned to the place where I was staying, one of my companions . . . said to me, "I saw a strange man whom we do not know in Mecca talking to you and conversing with you during the circumambulation. Who is he, and where does he come from?" So I told him the story. Those who were present were amazed. (I 638.32)

In a third passage the Shaykh provides a still more detailed account of his meeting with Sabtī:

> I had begun to circumambulate when I saw a man of beautiful mien who possessed gravity and dignity. He was circumambulating the House in front of me. I turned my gaze toward him thinking that I might recognize him. But I did not recognize him as one of those who live in the neighborhood, nor did I see upon him the mark of a newly arrived trav-

> eler, for he looked fresh and full of vigor. I saw that he was passing between two contiguous men during the circumambulation. He would pass between them without separating them, and they were not aware of him. I began to place my feet in the places where he left his footprints. He did not lift his foot without my putting my foot in its place. My mind was turned toward him and my eyes were upon him, lest he slip away. I would pass by the two contiguous men between whom he was passing and would pass by them in his tracks, just as he was passing them by, and I would not separate them. I was amazed at that. When he had completed his seven turns and wanted to leave, I seized hold of him and greeted him. He returned the greeting and smiled at me. All this time I did not take my gaze off him, fearing that he would slip away from me. For I had no doubt that he was an embodied spirit, and I knew that eyesight kept him fixed. (IV 12.1)[12]

Elsewhere the Shaykh explains what he means here by the fact that "eyesight kept him fixed" (*muqayyad*). Embodied spirits are controlled by human eyesight. As long as a person keeps such a spirit fixed in view, it cannot change its shape and slip away. The Shaykh refers to this in the midst of a discussion of the fact that spirits have the ability to assume any imaginal shape that they desire:

> When this spiritual world assumes a shape and becomes manifest in sensory form, eyesight fixes it so that it cannot leave that form so long as sight is gazing upon it with this characteristic—and here I mean the eyesight of the human being. When a person's sight fixes such a spiritual being and continues to gaze upon it, so that it has no place in which to hide, the spiritual being makes manifest a form to the person, and this form is like a covering over it. Then it makes him imagine that the form is going in a specific direction. His eyesight follows the form, and when this happens, the spiritual being emerges from fixation and disappears. When it disappears, that form also disappears from the gaze of the viewer who had been following it with his eyes.
>
> The form is related to the spiritual being just as a light that shines from a lamp into the corners of a room is related to the lamp. When the body of the lamp disappears, the light goes. So it is with the form. He who knows this and wants to fix the spiritual being does not follow the form with his eyes. This is one of the divine mysteries that is known only through God's giving knowledge. But the form is not other than the spiritual being itself; on the contrary, it is identical with it, even if it is found in a thousand places, or in all places, and is diverse in shape. (I 133.4)

This reminds us that imaginal men are one of the innumerable imaginal apparitions that can appear to the eye of imagination or to sight. As we saw at the beginning, the Shaykh writes about the inhabitants of the spiritual world,

> They assume the form of every shape,
> like water taking on the color of the cup.

But the beings that assume imaginal shape can be any sort of creature, good or evil, angel or jinn, prophet or demon. To return to what was said at the outset, the outstanding characteristic of imagination is its ambiguity, its uncertainty, its deceptive qualities. The Shaykh could live joyfully in the knowledge that he recognized the mark of every apparition. The rest of us, lacking in marks, had best be careful.

7

Death and the Afterlife

Teachings about death and the afterlife pertain to the "return" to God (*ma'ād*), the third principle of Islamic faith, after divine unity (*tawḥīd*) and prophecy (*nubuwwa*). Among the many topics that Muslim scholars discuss in this context are the "voluntary return" (*al-rujū' al-ikhtiyārī*) and the "compulsory return" (*al-rujū' al-iḍṭirārī*). The first deals with the path of attaining spiritual perfection in this life; the second, with the nature of physical death and bodily resurrection. Ibn al-'Arabī discusses both these topics voluminously and sets the stage for most subsequent treatments by Sufis, philosophers, and theologians. In the present chapter I will outline a few of his teachings on the compulsory return and suggest how they fit into his overall worldview.

Revelation and Reason

Sufi teachings are often looked upon as a departure from "orthodox" Islam, but this view typically rests upon a misuse of the term *orthodox* and an ignorance of the exact contents of the teachings in question. More careful examination suggests that the specifically Sufi explanations of Islamic teachings are not made to subvert the dogma but to support it and to open the way to faith for those individuals who find the unidimensional explanations offered by theologians and jurists intellectually and spiritually stultifying. The Shaykh would not dream of rejecting such articles of faith as the two angels who question the soul in the grave, the blast on Seraphiel's trumpet that awakens the dead, the scales that are set up to weigh human deeds at the resurrection, and the division of human beings into the inhabitants of paradise and hell. On the contrary, he maintains that anyone who attempts to turn these doctrines into metaphors or allegories through "rational interpretation" (*al-ta'wīl al-'aqlī*) only proves that his intelligence is corrupt and his faith is imperfect. In his view, there is no rational reason to reject the literal meaning of such Koranic verses and hadiths—so long as one understands the ontological referents of the passages in question.

From early times theologians discussed the problem of how to understand the revealed accounts in terms of *tashbīh* and *tanzīh*, similarity and incomparability. The general tenor of earlier Islamic thought as developed by the theologians and philosophers was to negate any sort of similarity between God and the creatures and to affirm God's incomparability. Hence it was held that when the Koran and Hadith speak of God's hand, face, eye, foot, speech, and laughter, these terms need to be interpreted in such a way that God's incomparability is not affected. For his part, Ibn al-'Arabī contends that such hermeneutical efforts are based upon ignorance of the nature of reality, disrespect for the revealed character of the Koran and the Hadith, and discourtesy toward God. In a typical passage, he identifies the theologians with those people who are stigmatized in various Koranic verses for having faith in part of the Book and disbelieving in other parts.[1] "It is the greatest discourtesy toward God to take what He has ascribed to Himself and use it to declare Him incomparable with what He has ascribed to Himself. Such a person *has faith in part*—that is, His words *Nothing is like Him* (42:11)—and *disbelieves in part; . . . those in truth are the disbelievers* (4:150), for the servant has appointed himself more knowledgeable of God than God is of Himself. There can be no greater ignorance" (III 375.10).

The Isthmus after Death

The hadith literature establishes the *barzakh* or isthmus as a realm of after-death experience. According to the Koran commentators, the isthmus is the object of reference in the verse, *Beyond them is a* barzakh *until the day they are raised up* (23:100). Typically, this *barzakh* is identified with what the Prophet most often called the "grave," where all sorts of events take place after death and before the resurrection. Like others, Ibn al-'Arabī makes an explicit connection between the *barzakh* and imagination. Thus he often cites another Koranic mention of the *barzakh* as referring to the properties of imagination in a general sense: *God let forth the two seas that meet together, between them an isthmus that they do not overpass* (55:20). "If it were not for the isthmus," says the Shaykh, "the two seas would not become distinct" (III 47.26). This isthmus is the reality of imagination, and the "two seas" may be *wujūd* and nonexistence, or the spiritual world and the corporeal world, or the spirit and the body, or this world and the next world, depending on how the verse needs to be applied in a given context.

The connection between the *barzakh* and imagination is well attested in the early sources, especially when they are read with the hindsight of the later tradition. The Koran establishes a clear relationship between sleep and death (39:42), while the Prophet called sleep "death's brother." It was only a short step from such traditional data to the suggestion that dreams provide the living with perceptions that are somehow similar to those of the dead. Moreover, many of the descriptions of after-death experience found in the Hadith are totally explicit in speaking of the "embodiment" of works and meanings. For example, the Prophet said that negligent prayers will be rolled up like shabby clothes and thrown in the sinner's face; good deeds will appear as lovely people and evil deeds as ugly hags; and evil works will turn into dogs or pigs.[2] By Ibn al-'Arabī's time the imaginal nature of experiences in the *barzakh* had long been accepted by many philosophers, theologians, and Sufis. His task was only to explain how this took place within the context of his own metaphysical and cosmological teachings.

As microcosms, human beings contain the three created worlds: spiritual, imaginal, and corporeal. The spirit derives from the divine Breath, while the body is made of clay. The soul stands between the two and shares in qualities of both sides. Hence it is one like the spirit through its essence, but many like the body through its faculties. The soul's ambiguous nature comes out clearly in the general categories of soul that can be distinguished on the basis of people's moral and spiritual maturity. Three of these are typically described by the Sufis, employing Koranic terminology: *the soul that commands to evil* (12:53), *the soul that blames* (76:2) itself for its own shortcomings, and *the soul at peace* (89:27) with God. For the Sufis, these are three successive levels of the soul's development. The important point here is that what needs to go beyond the stage of commanding to evil and become perfected through peace with God is the soul. In contrast, the spirit, as the breath of God, already possesses the perfection of the *fiṭra*, the original human disposition.[3]

In this scheme, the body provides a vehicle for the soul's development and unfolding. Without the body, the divine spirit could not manifest itself in the form of a particular human individual. The Shaykh compares God's spirit to the sun and the individual spirit to sunlight entering the windows of houses. He explains that God's wisdom requires these individual lights to continue in existence. Hence He created bodies for them at every stage of their development, including the *barzakh* after death. "Since God wants those lights to preserve the distinctness they have received, He creates for them *barzakh* bodies, within which these spirits remain distinct when they leave their this-worldly bodies in sleep or after death. . . . They never cease to be distinct for all eternity. They never return to their original state of being one entity" (III 188.1).

The experiences of the "grave" that are detailed in the Hadith take place while the human spirit is connected to the imaginal body in the *barzakh*. In a long passage that throws a good deal of light on how he understands such experiences, the Shaykh describes twelve categories of things that can be embodied as imaginal forms and seen by the friends of God during the process of the soul's becoming separated from the corporeal body at death. These include works, knowledge, belief, a station (*maqām*), a state (*ḥāl*), a prophet, an angel, and divine names that denote God's acts, attributes, descriptions, incomparability, or Essence. The images in which these realities appear provide a foretaste of paradise. The Shaykh says that each of the twelve kinds of form represents an experience of supraformal realities or meanings, for, in the isthmus after death, "Meanings become embodied and manifested in shapes and sizes, so they take on forms" (II 295.30). His explanation of the embodiment of "knowledge" and a "prophet" can suffice to demonstrate the tenor of the passage.

If the dead man's knowledge of God is derived from unveiling, then the embodiment of knowledge perceived at death will be more complete than if it is derived from rational proofs. "The form of unveiling is more complete and more beautiful in self-disclosure, because unveiling and its attainment are the results of god-wariness and wholesome works; it is referred to in God's words, *Be wary of God, and God will teach you* [2:282]. This person's knowledge will make manifest to him at death a beautiful form or a light that he wears and enjoys" (II 296.10).

In describing the appearance of the "form of a prophet," the Shaykh alludes to the teaching that helps structure the *Futūḥāt* and more particularly his short classic, *Fuṣūṣ al-ḥikam*—that the Muslim friends of God inherit their sciences, states, and stations not only from the prophet Muhammad but also from other prophets. Thus an individual may have a spiritual connection to one of the pre-Islamic prophets.

> Sometimes, as death approaches, the prophet from whom the person has inherited will be disclosed to him, for [as the Prophet said], "The possessors of knowledge are the heirs to the prophets." Hence as death approaches, he will see Jesus, Moses, Abraham, Muhammad, or some other prophet. Some of them may pronounce the name of the prophet from whom they have inherited in joy when he comes to them, for the messengers are all among the felicitous. While dying, such a person will say "Jesus," or he will call him "Messiah," as God Himself has done—this is what usually happens. Those present will hear the friend of God speak words of this sort and become suspicious, saying that at death he became a Christian and Islam was negated from him. Or he will name Moses or one of the Israelite prophets, and they will say that he became a Jew. But this person is one of the greatest possessors of felicity in God's eyes, for the common people never know this locus of witnessing, only the Folk of God, the possessors of unveilings. (II 296.27)

"Felicity" (*sa'āda*), it should be noted, is the most common Islamic expression for the experience of nearness to God and paradise. Its opposite is "wretchedness" (*shaqā'*), which is the pain and torment of hell brought about by distance from God.

The Unfolding of the Soul

The examples just cited illustrate the general principle that the human situation in the *barzakh* is determined by life in this world. Life in turn is the process whereby the attributes latent within the spirit's *fiṭra* come to be manifest, whether harmoniously or disharmoniously. The soul grows and develops in accordance with the relationship it establishes between the two sides of its own reality, the spirit and the body. Gradually, its imaginal nature becomes strengthened, and eventually it has no more need for the physical body to experience the corporeal world.

No doubt there is a certain natural development of the soul that is especially obvious in the early stages, that is, during infancy and childhood. But even here "environment" plays an important role in determining how the soul will grow. Thus the hadith of *fiṭra* says that "Every child is born with the original disposition, but then its parents make it into a Christian, a Jew, or a Zoroastrian." The Shariah makes the practice of religion incumbent from the age of puberty, when reason—the soul's power to discern between true and false, right and wrong—begins to manifest itself. To the extent that the rational faculty is present, people assume responsibility for their own development, whether they want to or not. If they follow the Scale of the Shariah, that is, the guidelines for moral, spiritual, and intellectual development revealed through the Koran and the Hadith, they develop in harmony with the divine form in which they were originally created. To the extent that a human life entails the assumption of God's character traits—the noble traits that define the divine form and make a person good and virtuous—the person will gain nearness to God and enter into a happy and harmonious state of being.

As the Scale of the Shariah gradually brings the soul into equilibrium and integrates it into the proper relationship between spirit and body, the human being develops in an "ascending" direction. In other words, through the guidance provided by revelation, the soul conforms more and more with the attributes of the divine spirit that was blown into the body, such as luminosity and knowledge. Without the Scale, people fall away from the vertical axis and sink down to the *lowest of the low* (95:5). Hence they come to be dominated by bodily attributes such as darkness and ignorance. Or they waver in between and gradually stray into horizontal dispersion. Harmony, completion, and totality depend both on *tawḥīd* or the declaration of God's unity and on faith (*īmān*), which, in the standard theological definition that Ibn al-'Arabī adheres to, includes works (that is, observance of the Shariah). "Complete souls are those that declare God's unity and have faith. *Tawḥīd* and faith prevent them from becoming the locus of pain and chastisement" (III 175.21).

In short, life is a process whereby human beings shape their own souls. When the body is discarded at death, the soul becomes embodied in imaginal forms suitable to its attributes. All its works, character traits, states, stations, knowledge, and aspirations appear in appropriate forms. "In the *barzakh*, all human beings are pawns to what they have earned and imprisoned in the forms of their works until the day of resurrection. Then they are raised up from those forms and given over to the configuration of the next world" (I 307.22).

The period in the *barzakh* prepares people for the resurrection, just as the time spent in the womb prepared them for birth into this world. "In relation to the configuration of the next world, the period in the *barzakh* is like the time the embryo spends in its mother's womb. God configures people in one configuration after another. Their stages of configuration are diverse until they are born on the day of resurrection" (III 250.19).

During and after the resurrection, the soul undergoes further transformations, until it assumes its place in the Garden or the Fire. But even at these stages, it is not attached to a fixed form similar to its corporeal body in this world. To clarify this point we need to look more closely at the ontological situation of the resurrection.

The Next World

The *barzakh* is called by this name because it is an isthmus between this world (*al-dunyā*) and the next world (*al-ākhira*). However, the Shaykh uses the term *barzakh* in many ways, since it can apply to any intermediate situation, and all situations are intermediate. Thus he writes, "The resurrection is a *barzakh*. There is nothing in existence but *barzakh*s, since a *barzakh* is the arrangement of one thing between two other things, like the present moment [between the past and the future]" (III 156.27).

The Shaykh does not always situate the isthmus after death between this world and the next. Sometimes he includes it in the next world as, for example, when he refers to it as "the first waystation [*manzil*] of the next world" (IV 282.13). However, in other passages he draws a clear distinction between the *barzakh* and the next world. For example, he writes that the *barzakh* is different from the next world, because the next world is sensory and nonimaginal. Thus the resurrection, the stage of existence that follows the *barzakh*, is "something verified, existent, and sensory, similar to human beings in this world" (I 311.21). Elsewhere he interprets a Koranic verse in a similar vein. The Koran tells us that the people of Pharaoh *will be exposed to the Fire, morning and evening; and on the day when the Hour has come: "Admit the people of*

Pharaoh into the most terrible chastisement!" (40:45-46). The exposure to the Fire mentioned here refers to the period in the *barzakh*, when the people of Pharaoh will be tormented at the imaginal level; but in the next world they will be admitted to the sensory fire of hell (I 299.9, 307.17).

These passages suggest that the basic difference between the *barzakh* and the next world lies in the distinction between imaginal and sensory existence. However, imagination is by definition sensory, as was mentioned earlier. Part of the solution to this problem may lie in a distinction that the Shaykh draws between the ontological status of the Garden and the Fire, the latter being denser and darker than the former. In the same way, the *barzakh* is less luminous than the resurrection. Certainly both the *barzakh* and the resurrection display the characteristics of imaginal existence. As the Shaykh writes, "The configuration of the next world is similar to the *barzakh* and to the inner dimension of the human being in respect of possessing imagination" (III 435.16). But the next world is more real than the *barzakh*, because it lies closer to the spiritual side of things and is therefore subtler and more luminous.

The Shaykh makes clear that the "body" that is resurrected in the next world is not similar to the this-worldly body in every respect: "Although the substances are exactly the same—for it is they that are poured forth from the graves and raised up—the composition and constitution differ because of accidents and attributes that are proper to the next abode, but not to this" (I 207.14).

One of the similarities between the resurrection and the *barzakh* is that in both of them, the realities of things shine forth more clearly than they do in this world. Thus, when the soul enters the *barzakh*, it grasps its own situation and comes to understand that the body it has discarded was but a veil. Speaking of death, the Koran says: *We have removed from you your covering, so your sight today is piercing* (50:22). In this context the Shaykh likes to quote the famous saying attributed to the Prophet: "People are asleep, but when they die they wake up." However, the awakening through death is only the first awakening. At the resurrection, people will wake up once more.

> Your awakening through death is like someone who sees that he wakes up in the midst of his dream. While dreaming he says to himself, "I saw this and that," and he supposes that he is awake. (II 313.6)

> [Then, on the day of resurrection] God comes to judge and decree. Hence He only comes within His name Light, so *the earth will shine with the light of its Lord.* Then each *soul will know* through that light *what it has sent before and left behind* [82:5], since it will see it all made present, unveiled for it by that light. (II 485.33)

One of the results of the vision of things under the radiance of the eternal light will be that everything is known for what it is. Intentions and motivations can no longer be hidden. Servanthood, which in this world is utter abasement before the Lord, will appear there as elevation. Having effaced themselves before God in this world, in the next world the servants will display nothing but the attributes of God, since no human limitations will remain to block the divine light. "Not He" has gone and "He" remains.

> In the next world, people will be ranked in the measure of their states in this world. He who was a sheer servant in this world will be a sheer king in the next world. He who was qualified by the attribute of kingship in this world—even if it be only [the fact that he considered] his bodily members his own kingdom—will have his kingdom in the next world decreased precisely in the measure that he took his share of it in this world. . . .
>
> Hence there is none more exalted in the next world than he who, in this world, reached the extremity of abasement before the Real and the Reality. And there is none more abased in the next world than he who reached the extremity of exaltation in his own soul in this world, even if he was slapped down here. I do not mean by "exaltation in this world" that a person should have been a king, only that the attribute of his soul should be exaltation—and the same goes for abasement.
>
> As for the person who is a king or something else in his outward situation, I do not care in which station or state God has placed His servant outwardly. The only thing that can be taken into account is the state of his soul. (I 221.18)

In short, people's outward situations in the next world depend upon their inward situations in this world. After all, the divine form that they embody pertains primarily to their inward attributes, their character traits. To the extent that people actualize the divine form, they acquire the noble character traits of God, and to the extent that they fail to actualize the form, they remain distant from God's traits. These traits are the qualities of *wujūd* itself, the human *fiṭra*. In the *barzakh* and to a greater degree at the resurrection, a person's nature is revealed for what it is, which is to say that it becomes embodied in appropriate forms.

Inside/Outside

The macrocosm, like the microcosm, is God's form. God discloses Himself in keeping with His name Manifest, while He keeps Himself hidden in keeping with His name Nonmanifest. Because of God's infinity, His self-disclosure never repeats itself. In other words, *wujūd* reveals its qualities in ever-changing patterns and modalities within the cosmos. Hence the things of the cosmos undergo constant transformation.

Both macrocosm and microcosm were created in God's form, and both display the properties of the name Manifest. In the case of the macrocosm, the divine attributes become infinitely differentiated into all things in all times and all worlds. This differentiation appears outwardly and concretely. The form of each individual thing at each moment manifests certain specific qualities of *wujūd* to the exclusion of other qualities, and these qualities change moment by moment.

The microcosm corresponds to the macrocosm in the sense that all divine attributes are present. But the microcosm differs from the macrocosm in that its unity appears in the outward human form. The diverse divine qualities that are displayed outwardly in the macrocosm appear on the microcosmic level in the diversity of human souls and the fact that each soul, as a divine image, is a unique self-disclosure of God. Hence the macrocosm is infinitely diverse in its manifest dimension, while microcosms are infinitely diverse in their nonmanifest dimensions.

The things of the macrocosm are dominated by partiality and specificity, which is to say that each is part of the whole. Hence each thing has a "known station." In contrast, human beings are themselves wholes, so they cannot be pinned down to specific attributes before death, if ever. In this world, they dwell in unknown stations, and, if they reach perfection, their stations remain unknown in the next world. In this world, this human unknowability pertains to inward attributes, since outwardly they all appear in human bodies.

God as Manifest discloses Himself in the infinite diversity of both macrocosm and microcosm, and His self-disclosure never repeats itself, whether in time or space. But God as Nonmanifest is fixed and immutable. The Essence of God does not change, whereas the properties of His attributes are reflected in the infinite diversity and constantly renewed self-disclosures that make up the cosmos. Human beings are comparable to mirror images of this divine reality. Hence a reversal occurs between outward and inward. People are relatively fixed and unchanging in their outward forms, but they undergo an indefinite variety of changes moment by moment on the level of their thoughts and awareness. The Shaykh explains this as follows:

> The Prophet said, "God created Adam in His own form." The human being undergoes variation in his nonmanifest dimension, while he is fixed in his manifest dimension. No organ is ever added to his manifest dimension, but he does not remain in a single state in his nonmanifest dimension, so he possesses both variation and fixity. But the Real is described as the Manifest and the Nonmanifest. The Manifest possesses variation, while the Nonmanifest possesses fixity. So the Nonmanifest Real is the same as the manifest dimension of the human being, and the

> Manifest Real is the same as the nonmanifest dimension of the human being.
>
> Hence the human being is like an ordinary mirror: When you lift up your right hand as you look at your form in a mirror, your form lifts up its left hand. Hence your right hand is its left hand, and your left hand is its right hand. Hence, O created thing, your manifest dimension is the form of His name the Nonmanifest, while your nonmanifest dimension is His name Manifest. (IV 135.33)

Human beings are God's mirror images in this world, but these images cease to be reversed after death. What had been inside here becomes outside there, and what had been outside here becomes inside there. As one of the Shaykh's disciples puts it, "The *barzakh* is a world where the outward becomes inward, and the inward outward."[4]

If the human situation in this world can be compared to a mirror image, in the world after death it can be compared to rays of light in the midst of the air before they are reflected and reversed. In the next world the manifest dimension of human beings will reflect God as Manifest, while the nonmanifest dimension will coincide with God as Nonmanifest. Hence the inner reality of each individual will be fixed, while the outward dimension of each will undergo constant transmutation and change. The Shaykh explains:

> The Real never ceases disclosing Himself constantly to hearts in this world. Hence human thoughts undergo variation because of the divine self-disclosure, and no one is aware of how this happens except the Folk of God. They also know that the diversity of forms manifest in this world and the next in all existent things is nothing other than His variation, for He is the Manifest, because He is identical with each thing.
>
> In the next world, the nonmanifest dimension of the human being will be fixed, for it is identical with his manifest dimension in this world, which undergoes continual change in a manner that is hidden, for this is its new creation at each moment, about which *They are in confusion* [50:15]. But in the next world, the manifest dimension of the human being will be like his nonmanifest dimension in this world: The divine self-disclosure will come to it constantly in actuality. Hence in the next world his manifest dimension will undergo variation, just as in this world his nonmanifest dimension undergoes variation in the forms taken by the divine self-disclosure, so that he becomes colored by their coloration.
>
> This is the imaginal conformity with God. However, in the next world this conformity will be manifest, while in this world it is nonmanifest. Hence the property of imagination accompanies the human being in the next world, and also the Real, in whose case it is called a "task": *Each day He is upon some task* [55:29]. (III 470.16)

> The next world is a domain that is quickly and immediately receptive to activity, just like the nonmanifest dimension of the configuration of this world at the level of thoughts. Hence in the next world the human being is reversed in configuration, since his nonmanifest dimension is fixed in a single form, like his manifest dimension here, while his manifest dimension undergoes quick transmutation within forms, like his nonmanifest dimension here. (III 223.31)

> The nonmanifest dimension of the human being in this world is the manifest dimension in the next world. It had been unseen here, but it becomes visible there. The entity remains unseen as the nonmanifest dimension of these shapes and forms. It does not change or undergo transmutation. So there are only forms and shapes that are taken away from it and placed upon it continuously and forever, ad infinitum, without end. (III 441.14)

The Shaykh often quotes a Koranic verse in which the people of paradise are addressed as follows: *Therein you shall have all that your souls desire, all that you call for* (41:31). Likewise he refers to a hadith in which the Prophet describes how God will send a letter to the people of paradise in which it is written, "From the Living, the Everlasting, who never dies, to the living, the everlasting, who will never die: I say to a thing 'Be!' and it is. I give to you to say to a thing 'Be!' and it will be" (III 295.16).

In the Shaykh's view, such traditional reports can be understood only in the context of the imaginal nature of paradisial existence, the fact that the outward plane of the next world corresponds to the mental and imaginal plane in this world. Hence, just as in this world God gives form to thoughts and imaginings in our minds, so also He will give form to thoughts and imaginings in the next world. However, in the next world this will be experienced concretely and "outside" of ourselves at a level of reality that is far more intense than the corporeal level. The Shaykh explains these points as follows:

> In this world the Real is the locus in which the servant engenders things within the Presence of Imagination. No thought occurs to the servant without God's engendering it within imagination, just as He engenders [within the corporeal world] the possible things that He wills when He wills. But within the Presence of Imagination the servant's will derives from the Real's will, because the servant wills nothing unless God wills it. Hence in this world God never wills without the servant willing. Some of what the servant wills in this world occurs in the sensory domain. But in imagination, his will's influence is like that of the Real. Hence the Real is with the servant within imagination in everything that the servant wills, just as He is [with him] in the next

> world in respect of the all-inclusive controlling property of the will. The reason for this is that the nonmanifest dimension of the human being [in this world] is his manifest dimension in the next world. Therefore everything comes to be in accordance with his own will when he desires it. . . .
>
> Hence, the Real follows the servant's desire at the level of imagination and in the next world, just as the servant's will follows God's will. So God's task is to keep watch over the servant by bringing into existence for him everything he desires in this world at the level of imagination and likewise [everything that he desires] in the next world. But the servant follows the Real in the forms of self-disclosure. The Real does not disclose Himself within a form without the servant's becoming colored by it. Hence the servant undergoes transmutation in forms because the Real transmutes Himself, while the Real undergoes transmutation in bestowing *wujūd* because of the transmutation of the servant's will specifically within the Presence of Imagination in this world, and generally in the Garden in the next world. (III 509.32)

In another passage, the Shaykh makes the main point of this passage more clearly and succinctly: "In this world, the Real is the locus of your engendering things, because He undergoes variation according to the variations you undergo. But in the next world, you undergo variations according to His variations. Hence, in this world, He wears your form, but in the next world, you wear His form" (III 502.24).

The fact that the next world is the reversal of this world helps explain the function of the Shariah in this world, given that there is no Shariah to follow in the next world.

> God created the human being in a configuration that is reversed. Hence his next world lies in his nonmanifest dimension, while his this world lies in his manifest dimension. His manifest dimension is delimited by the [divine] form. Hence God delimited him by prescribing the Shariah. Just as the form does not change, so also the prescription does not change. However, in his nonmanifest dimension, the human being undergoes constant variation. He fluctuates in his thoughts according to the forms in which thoughts occur to him. So also is the situation in the next world. Hence his nonmanifest dimension in this world is his manifest form in the next world's configuration, and his manifest dimension in this world is his nonmanifest dimension in the next world's configuration. That is why God says, *As He originated you, so you shall return* [7:29], for the next world is the reversal of this world's configuration, and this world is the reversal of the next world's configuration. But the human being [here] is identical with the human being [there]. Hence you should

> strive here so that your thoughts may be praiseworthy according to the Shariah, and then your form in the next world will be beautiful. (IV 420.1)

Having reached the Garden, people determine their situation through their own desires. Whatever they imagine comes to be. God's words become their own: *Our only speech to a thing, when We desire it, is to say to it "Be!" and it is* (16:40). In effect, human beings construct their own paradises.

The Shaykh often cites the following hadith: "There is a market in the Garden wherein is no selling or buying, only the forms of men and women. When a person desires a form, he enters into it." In his view, this saying illustrates the fact that the inhabitants of paradise "continue to be gathered from one form to another, ad infinitum, so that they may come to know the divine vastness" (II 628.4). Moreover, the paradisial state is of such subtlety that people can exist in one form without this preventing them from existing in other forms as well.

> We enter into any of the Market's forms that we will, even though we remain in our own form, and none of our family or acquaintances would fail to recognize us. Yet we know that we have put on a newly engendered form, while we remain in our old form. (II 183.22)

> The human configuration in the next world is not similar to the configuration of this world, even if the two come together in names and in the form of the person. Within the configuration of the next world, spiritual reality dominates over sensory reality. We have tasted this within the abode of this life, in spite of the density of its configuration. Thus a person can be in several places at once, though the common people perceive this only in dreams. (I 318.26)

Not only do people construct their own paradises; they also construct their own hells. The Shaykh writes, "The People of the Fire conceive no dreadful thought of a chastisement greater than what they are experiencing without that chastisement coming into existence within them and for them; the chastisement is identical with the actualization of the thought" (I 259.30). More generally, he writes that the Fire is in fact nothing but the embodiment of works and thoughts. These works and thoughts represent the specific human limitations that constrict the divine form and prevent it from becoming fully manifest. "The Fire seeks only those human beings whose divine form has not become manifest, outwardly and inwardly" (III 387.10). This helps explain why the Shaykh says repeatedly that even the Fire is rooted in God's mercy, and its goal is to purify (*taṭhīr*) those who fall into it. Purification of human beings amounts to burning away from them everything opposed to their *fiṭra*.

In one passage Ibn al-'Arabī explains the ontological roots of the reversal that occurs between this world and the next. God created the cosmos to make Himself manifest. In other terms, the Real *Wujūd* by its very nature gives rise to a manifest dimension that is known as creation or cosmos. The full perfection of *wujūd* cannot become manifest in the present world because of the peculiar sorts of limitations that rule over it. However, human beings, made in the divine form, gradually strengthen the character traits and qualities that pertain to that form and gain the power to make manifest many of the divine attributes in this world. But in order for the full range of divine attributes to become manifest, another mode of existence is necessary that allows human beings to exercise control over the whole of manifest existence. This occurs in the next world, where *wujūd*'s perfection reaches its full manifestation.

> God did not create creation for the sake of creation itself. Rather, He created it as a similitude struck for Himself—glory be to Him, and high indeed is He exalted! Hence God brought creation into existence in His own form. Thus, creation is tremendous because of God's design, but it is insignificant because it has been put in place.
>
> There must be a knower and a known. Hence there must be a creation and a Real. *Wujūd* does not reach its perfection without both. *Wujūd*'s perfection becomes manifest in this world. Then the situation is transferred to the next world in the most complete manner and in the most perfect inclusiveness in the manifest domain. Just as the mode of manifestation in this world was all-inclusive in the nonmanifest domain, so it is all-inclusive in the next world in both the manifest and the nonmanifest domains. Hence the next world demands the resurrection of bodies and their manifestation, and the property of engendering things must be put into effect through them.
>
> In this world, everyone says to a thing "Be," and it comes to be in their conceptualization and imagination, because, in some constitutions, this world's homestead falls short of engendering the entities of things in the manifest domain. But in the next world, they will say that word to whatever they desire to engender. "Be!" and it will come to be in its own entity in the external domain, just as engendered things come to exist here, with their secondary causes, from the divine "Be!" Hence the next world is more tremendous in perfection [than this world] in this respect, because the word "Be" embraces the two presences of imagination and sense perception. (IV 252.2)

The Garden and the Fire

Heaven and hell are similar in certain respects, but different in others. Both pertain to the next world and involve a double level of experience: outward and inward, or corporeal and spiritual. In insisting on the bodily resurrection, Ibn al-'Arabī distances himself from those philosophers who held that the souls of the blessed survive only in an "intellectual configuration" (*nash'a 'aqliyya*). Such thinkers, says the Shaykh, "ignore the fact that there are two configurations: one for the bodies and one for the spirits, the latter being suprasensory. Hence they affirmed the suprasensory configuration, but not the sensory" (I 311.23). In brief, "The soul is resurrected in the form of its knowledge, and the body in the form of its works" (I 99.20).

The difference between heaven and hell goes back to their divine roots, which are the two hands of God, or the names of mercy and wrath. Only through understanding the contradictory properties of these opposing names can one grasp the ontological difference between the Garden and the Fire. In order to do this, we need to look at the Shaykh's cosmological scheme.

Ibn al-'Arabī describes various stages of creation in many different passages.[5] Briefly, the picture he draws is as follows: Within the Breath of the All-merciful, God creates a supreme spirit, known as the "First Intellect" or the "Supreme Pen." By means of this first spirit, He then creates a second spirit, known as the "Universal Soul" or the "Guarded Tablet." These two mark the boundaries of the world of disengaged spirits. On the spiritual plane, they are the active and receptive principles of all creation, or yang and yin.[6]

Several levels of creation separate the Universal Soul from the Throne of God, which is the sphere that lies at the outermost limit of the corporeal world. The Koran tells us that *The All-merciful sat upon the Throne* (20:5), and hadiths tell us that the precedence of God's mercy over His wrath is inscribed on the Throne itself. The Shaykh concludes that the Throne is sheer mercy and has nothing to do with wrath. Wrath enters the picture only at the second level of sensory existence, the Footstool, which *embraces the heavens and the earth* (2:256). Upon the Footstool God places His "two feet," which are pure mercy and mercy mixed with wrath (III 432.14). In other words, above the Footstool, nothing exists except the precedent and prior mercy, so only the beautiful and gentle names of God manifest their properties. Below it, the wrathful and severe names show their effects.

This scheme is built upon the understanding that the more real attributes of God are those that begin displaying their traces in creatures near Him, such as angels. God manifests His severe attributes only toward those creatures who are far from Him. As the Shaykh remarks, "Nothing makes the Real wrathful except what He has created. Were it not for the creatures, the Real would not have become wrathful" (III 386.1). In Himself, God is sheer mercy and love, which is to say that He is sheer *wujūd* and sheer reality. When "others" appear, they are deprived to some degree of *wujūd*, and hence they are deprived to some degree of God's precedent attributes. But in the Shaykh's cosmological scheme, wrath can only manifest itself in the Footstool and what lies below it.

The descending levels of the cosmos below the Footstool (also known as the "tenth sphere") represent a progressive "solidification" and "densification" of the cosmos. As the various kinds of created things move farther from the Real, their luminosity decreases. The four natures produce the four elements—fire, air, water, and earth—in their simple, intelligible form (*al-basīṭ al-ma'qūl*). In the earth, the elements come to exist in their compound forms, that is, as they appear in the corporeal world. Finally, from the combination of the elements, the elemental creatures come into existence: minerals, plants, and animals (I 293-94). Hence the three kingdoms are the most dense (*kathīf*) and least subtle (*laṭīf*) of all sensory beings.

The first thing to come into existence in the sensory world is the Throne. However, a distinction needs to be drawn between the sensory things of imagination and those of the corporeal world. Part of this distinction has to do with the difference between "natural" and "elemental." The Throne, for example, is natural, but not elemental. Nature (*ṭabī'a*) has no existence in itself, yet its properties become manifest throughout the sensory world, from the Throne down to the earth. Below the Throne, relatively few things are made of elements—only the three kingdoms. Everything else is natural, but not elemental. Exclusively natural things include the eleven spheres, the lower angels, the mental faculties, the particular spirits,[7] and the simple elements themselves. When the Shaykh calls certain angels and the mental faculties "corporeal bodies" (*ajsām*), he is referring to subtle or imaginal bodies, not to elemental bodies.[8] In short, every elemental thing is also natural, but every natural thing is not elemental.

The Shaykh locates the various levels of paradise between the starless sphere and the sphere of the fixed stars. Paradise is natural but not elemental. In contrast, he places the hells below the sphere of the fixed stars and tells us that they are elemental and extend down to the "lowest of the low." Hence the substance of hell is similar to that of the present world, which is to say that hell is neither pure chastisement nor pure bliss. That is why the Koran says about hell, *Therein they neither die nor live* (20:73).[9]

The similarity between this world and hell goes back to the fact that the attributes of wrath become fully manifest in both, but these attributes have only limited access to paradise. At the elemental level mercy and wrath are mixed, but not at the level of those natural corporeal bodies that dwell above the seventh sphere.[10]

Hell exists for the same reason that paradise and this world exist: to make manifest the properties of the divine names. But in this world, the attributes of mercy and wrath are relatively balanced. In paradise, mercy predominates to such a degree that wrath is totally hidden. And in hell, wrath predominates. However, the Shaykh insists that even the people of wretchedness are not cut off from God's mercy, because pure wrath cannot exist.

The Cooling of the Fire

Ibn al-'Arabī provides numerous arguments based on various texts from the Koran and the Hadith to prove that hell's chastisement cannot last forever.[11] He does not dispute the Koranic verses that say that the *sinners*[12] will remain *forever within it*, but he points out that the pronoun in the phrase *within it* is always feminine. In other words, it refers to "Fire," not to "chastisement." Nothing was revealed in the Koran and the Hadith that would indicate that chastisement lasts forever, although this is hardly the case with the bliss of the Garden. Moreover *God forgives all sins* (39:53), so nothing can make the chastisement eternal. In addition punishment can only be *an appropriate recompense* (78:26), so a limited sin cannot warrant unlimited punishment.

Hell's chastisement must disappear because in the end (*bi'l-ma'āl*) mercy will show its precedence and priority. "Wretchedness derives from the divine wrath, while felicity derives from the divine good-pleasure [*riḍā*]. Good-pleasure is the unfolding of mercy without end, but wrath will be cut off" (III 382.35).

The predominant, merciful attributes of *wujūd* are those that pertain to the very substance of the Breath of the All-merciful. The human "assumption of the divine character traits" involves gaining greater harmony with *wujūd* itself, greater nearness with God. The divine form in which human beings were created is governed by mercy, because mercy pertains to the essential nature of the Real, while wrath is a secondary quality. All this means that reality—which is fundamentally mercy, love, and bliss—must show itself, and what keeps human beings away from reality is simply unreality. The unreal is annihilated and the Real subsists. These ideas are implicit if not explicit in the following passage, which points to the ontological roots of hell's impermanence.

> God made [human] hearts loci for the real and the unreal, faith and unbelief, knowledge and ignorance. The eventual outcome of unreality, unbelief, and ignorance will be dissolution and disappearance, because these are properties that have no entity in *wujūd*. They are a nonexistence that has a manifest property and a known form. This property and form seek an ontological something by which they can be supported, but they do not find it, so they dissolve and become nothing. Hence the final end will be felicity.
>
> In contrast, faith, reality, and knowledge are supported by something that has existence in entity, and that is God. Hence their properties are fixed in entity, that is, in the entity to which they are ascribed, because that which preserves the existence of this property exists. Or rather, it is identical with *wujūd* itself, which is God, who is named by these names and described by these descriptions—He is the Real, the Knowing, the Faithful. Hence faith is supported by the Faithful, knowledge by the

> Knowing, and the real by the Real. God is not named by unreality, because He is *wujūd*; nor is He called "ignorant" and "unbeliever"—high exalted is He above these names!
>
> Hence the divine books and the scriptures descended upon the hearts of the faithful, the vicegerents, the subjects, and the inheritors, and their profit pervaded every heart that was a locus for every good.
>
> As for accidental affairs that are not sent down by a divine command of the Shariah, these are capricious winds [*ahwā'*][13] that occur as accidents to the deputies and subjects and are called "deviation." But accidents have no fixity, so their properties disappear when they disappear. In contrast, the entity that was engendered before them and became described by them is an existent thing; it must have some state by which to be described. Since its wretchedness has disappeared with the disappearance of its cause—since its cause was an accident that occurred—there must be its contrary, and that is called "felicity." If anyone enters the Fire, it will only be so that his loathsomeness can be annihilated and his goodness subsist. Once the loathsomeness has gone and the goodness subsists, that is what is referred to as "the felicitous one whose felicity had been consumed by his loathsomeness." (III 417.35)

The cosmos, in short, grows up from the Breath of the All-merciful, and the All-merciful is sheer good. Everything that exists must return to its root, so everything will go back to sheer good. The sheer good of a thing demands that the thing be felicitous.[14] The "evil" that creatures meet derives from their possibility (*imkān*)—their ambiguous ontological situation halfway between the necessity of nondelimited *wujūd* and the impossibility of nothingness—or the fact that everything other than God is He/not He. If evil enters the cosmos, "It becomes manifest from the direction of the possible thing, not from the direction of God" (III 389.25). The side pertaining to evil and wretchedness will eventually disappear, since it derives from nonexistence; yet the creatures themselves will never disappear, because they partake of *wujūd*: "The entities of the essences that enter into *wujūd* from nonexistence will never cease to exist after their *wujūd*" (I 312.34). In sum, "The cosmos is the object of mercy in its very essence; it experiences pain only in what occurs to it accidentally" (III 207.28).[15]

Ibn al-'Arabī does not have too much patience with the juridical and theological minds that would insist on the eternal chastisement of those whom they perceive as sinners. He criticizes such misunderstandings of God's motives in many contexts. Typical is the following:

> [When you reach this understanding] you will come to know the difference between him who desires the spreading of God's mercy among His servants—whether they be obedient or disobedient—and

> him who desires to take God's mercy away from some of His servants. This second person is the one who prohibits the mercy of God that embraces all things, but he does not prohibit it to himself. Were it not for the fact that God's mercy takes precedence over His wrath, the possessor of this attribute would never attain to God's mercy. (III 370.15)

The fact that mercy will eventually prevail might suggest that God ceases to have the attribute of wrath. But God, after all, has "two hands," and His reality does not change. Cosmologically, the subsistence of God's wrath is indicated by the fact that hell is located in the heavens and the earth, which are the domain within which wrath has some effect, and hell never ceases to exist. But wrath is experienced by human beings as chastisement, and this chastisement does come to an end. The Shaykh explains, however, that chastisement will continue to be accessible to imagination, since experiencing bliss demands the understanding of its opposite.

> No chastisement will remain in the Fire except imaginal chastisement within the presence of imagination, in order that the properties of the divine names may subsist. A name necessitates only the manifestation of the property that its reality demands. It does not specify the presence nor the individual, since that is a property of the names Knowing and Desiring.
>
> Hence, whenever the property of the Avenger becomes manifest within an imaginal body or a corporeal body or in anything else, its rights are fulfilled through the manifestation of its property and effectivity. So the divine names continue to exercise effectivity and determine properties for all eternity in the two abodes, and the inhabitants of the two abodes never leave them. (III 119.2)

In another passage, the Shaykh takes a slightly different approach to the question of the properties of the divine names and illustrates how they exercise their effects after God ceases to be wrathful toward the creatures. This occurs at the end of the day of resurrection, which, the Shaykh is reasonably sure, lasts fifty thousand years—like the angelic day mentioned in Koran 70:4.[16] He is referring to some of the wrathful attributes of God mentioned in the Koran: vengeance, severity in assault, abasing, and holding back.

> After the expiration of this time period, the ruling property returns to the All-merciful, the All-compassionate. To the All-merciful belong *the most beautiful names* [17:110], and they are "most beautiful" to the one toward whom their ruling properties are directed. So the All-compassionate takes *vengeance* upon wrath through His mercy, and the All-

> compassionate is *severe in assault*. Through mercy He *abases* wrath and *holds back* its reality. Hence the property of the mutual contradictoriness of the names subsists in the relationships, but the creatures are drowned in mercy. The property of mutual contradictoriness remains forever in the names, but not in us. (III 346.14)

In still another passage, the Shaykh looks not at the divine names themselves but rather at the practical result of the fact that the names of wrath cease to exercise effects that lead to pain and suffering. In the process, he alludes to various accounts in the Koran and the Hadith about the fierce angels who watch over hell and the animals that inflict pain on those who suffer there. At the beginning of the passage, he alludes to the Koranic verse, *Wherever you turn, there is the face of God* (2:115), suggesting that this is a universal rule of existence and that hell is not excluded. In personifying hell, he is following Koran 50:30: *Upon the day We shall say unto hell, "Art thou filled?" And it shall say, "Are there any more?"*

> After the expiration of this time period, there will be a bliss in every face toward which [the sinner] turns. There will be no difference between him and those who populate hell—the guards and the animals. The latter strike and sting because of the bliss and ease that serpents and scorpions find in striking and stinging. And the one who is struck and stung finds a pleasure in that along with a dullness of the limbs and a numbness of the organs that he enjoys exceedingly. This continues forever, for mercy has now taken precedence over wrath. As long as the Real is described by wrath, sufferings remain for the people of hell, those who are its inhabitants. When the divine wrath disappears—as explained earlier—and when the Fire is filled with it, then sufferings cease. The wrath is spread among the harmful animals who are in the Fire. They seek to achieve their own ease, because of the duty they have against the People of the Fire. But the People of the Fire find pleasure in that, just as the serpent and the Fire find pleasure in taking vengeance for God, because of the divine wrath that is in the Fire. But neither the Fire nor those within it know that its inhabitants are finding pleasure in that, because they do not know that ease has reached them and mercy has exercised its ruling property over them. (III 411.15)

Although the sinners will reach felicity in the Fire, one factor continues to differentiate their felicity from that of the inhabitants of the Garden: They will always remain veiled (*maḥjūb*) from God, while the felicitous in the Garden will be given a vision (*ru'ya*) of Him. Hence the Shaykh can write, "The next world has two abodes: vision and veil" (II 335.18).

The tradition speaks of the eight gates of paradise and the seven gates of hell. According to the Shaykh, hell's seven gates will eventually be opened. "But Gehenna has an eighth gate that is locked and will never be opened: the gate of being veiled from the vision of God" (I 299.5). So long as the inhabitants of hell experience chastisement, the veil will be hung down so that the vision of God will not increase their chastisement, for if they were to see God, they would have a better idea of the depths of their own deprivation. And when the chastisement comes to an end, the veil will stay in place so that they can experience bliss.

> Were God to disclose Himself to them in the Fire, given their precedent evildoing and their worthiness for punishment, that benevolent self-disclosure would yield nothing but shame before God for what they had done, and shame is chastisement—but chastisement's period has come to an end. Hence they will not know the joy of witnessing and vision, so they will have bliss while being veiled. The goal is bliss, and it has been achieved with the veil—but for whom? How can the bliss of the vision of God be compared to bliss with the veil! *For on that day they are veiled from their Lord* [83:15]. (III 119.7)

In the last analysis, felicity is that which is agreeable (*mulā'im*) with a person's constitution (*mizāj*). This explains why the people of hell will rest in ease. The Shaykh explains this in a long discussion of the nature of the wall between paradise and hell mentioned in Koran 57:13: *And a wall will be set up between them, having a door on the nonmanifest side of which is mercy, and on the manifest side of which is chastisement.* In fact, he says, the wall itself is essentially mercy, for if there had been chastisement on the nonmanifest side of the wall, the chastisement in hell would be eternal, like the bliss in paradise. He goes on to tell us that whenever the people of the Garden desire to do so, they climb the wall and enjoy the vision of the people in the Fire. On the wall they are immersed in mercy, and while gazing on the people of the Fire they find a bliss that they do not find in the Garden, since the security that comes over a frightened person is a greater joy than being constantly secure. For their part, after having been included in mercy, the people of the Fire gaze from the wall upon the people of the Garden.

> After mercy has embraced them, the people of the Fire will find their joy from being in the Fire, and they will praise God for their not being in the Garden. That is because of what is demanded by their constitution in that state: If they were to enter the Garden with that constitution, pain would overcome them and they would suffer. So—if you have understood—bliss is nothing but the agreeable, and chastisement is nothing but the disagreeable, whatever it might be. So be wherever you are! If

that which is agreeable with your constitution strikes you, you will be in bliss, and if that which is disagreeable with your constitution strikes you, you will be in chastisement.

The abodes have been made lovable to their inhabitants. The Fire is the abode of the people of the Fire, those who are its inhabitants. From it they were created and to it they will be returned. And the people of the Garden, those who are its inhabitants, were created from the Garden, and to it they will be returned.

The abode's joy is an intrinsic attribute of its inhabitants. However, they may be veiled by an accidental falling short or a going too far that arises from their works. This causes their situation to change. The diseases they bring about within themselves veil them from the joy of the abode.

For example, if the people of the Fire did not perform works that demand the existence of pains and illnesses for them and if they were resurrected from their graves in the constitution of their own abode and were given a choice between the Garden and the Fire, they would choose the Fire, just as a fish chooses water and flees from the air through which the inhabitants of the earth have life. (IV 14.34)[17]

To bring this brief summary of Ibn al-'Arabī's extensive eschatological teachings to a close, let me recall the point with which I began: In the Shaykh's view, all the traditional descriptions of the afterlife, no matter how strange they may appear to the rational mind, can be explained by reference to the power of imaginalization possessed by *wujūd*. The Koran and Hadith are full of statements about God and the next world that most people have either accepted on faith or interpreted in accordance with the dictates of reason and logic. But the Shaykh objects to any interpretation that strays from the literal meaning, especially by a person claiming faith in Islam. Anyone who interprets the text demonstrates that "He has faith in his interpretation, not in the revealed report" (I 218.26).[18]

In our eyes this is one of the most wondrous of things—that a person should follow the authority of his reflection and consideration, whereas these are temporally originated things like himself, faculties created by God within him. God appointed these faculties as servants of reason. Yet reason follows their authority in that which they give to it! At the same time, reason knows that these faculties do not pass beyond their own levels and that, in themselves, they are incapable of having the property of any of the other faculties, such as memory, form-giving, and imagination, or the properties that belong to the sense faculties—touch, taste, smell, hearing, and sight. Yet, with all this incapacity, the rational faculty follows their authority in knowledge of its Lord. At the same

> time, it does not follow the authority of its Lord in what He reports concerning Himself in His Book and upon the tongue of His Prophet. This is one of the most wondrous errors that occur in the cosmos! (I 288.27)

All rational interpretation of the type the Shaykh criticizes ignores the approach that, in his eyes, leads to true knowledge: What appears as impossible to reason in fact occurs exactly as it is described by scripture through the power of imagination.

PART III

Religious Diversity

8

A Myth of Origins

Ibn al-'Arabī was thoroughly versed in the dry ratiocination of the contemporary doctors of theology, but he avoided their methodological approach. He was more likely to rely on images, symbols, analogies, and allegories derived primarily from "openings" and "tastings" and deeply rooted in the Koran and the sayings of Muhammad. He constantly returns to one basic theme: All things are intimately interrelated through their common roots in the Divine Reality. The universe in its indefinite multiplicity is nothing but the outward manifestation of God's names, which are the faces that God turns toward creation. The revealed names provide keys that unlock the door to the invisible world. Everywhere we look we see the properties and traces of the names within the created things.

Unique among creatures, human beings display the properties of every name of God, because they alone were created in God's form and given dominion over all creatures, each of which manifests only some of God's names. But people cannot actualize the divine names unless they follow the guidance revealed through the prophets. Reason, even in the best of circumstances, provides insufficient knowledge of God. It allows people to understand that God is incomparable and forever unknowable, but it can never tell them anything about His similarity and self-disclosure in the macrocosm and microcosm. In contrast, revelation provides a balanced knowledge of God, for it combines the declaration of incomparability that is grasped by reason with the similarity that answers to imagination. Only when reason works harmoniously with imagination on the basis of the prophetic message can people reach perfection. Those who are able to combine reason and imagination in proper balance are those who have truly witnessed the lifting of the veils between themselves and God—the People of Unveiling. "The common people stand in the station of declaring similarity, the People of Unveiling declare both similarity and incomparability, and the rational thinkers declare incomparability alone. Hence, God combined the two sides in His elect" (II 116.7).

The Koranic View of Revelation

The Koran pictures revelation as a message sent by God to human beings by means of a "prophet" (*nabī*) or "messenger" (*rasūl*). Revelation is a universal phenomenon, since *Every nation has its messenger* (10:47). It has two complementary dimensions that correspond to the two Shahadahs, the Islamic testimonies of faith: "There is no god but God" and "Muhammad is the messenger of God."

All prophets are given a message of *tawḥīd*, which declares that experienced reality comes from the One and returns to the One: *And We never sent a messenger before thee save that We revealed to him, saying, "There is no god but I, so serve Me"* (21:25). Muslims must have faith in every messenger of God, because each confirms the truth (*taṣdīq*) of the messages that went before. *And when Jesus son of Mary said, "Children of Israel, I am indeed God's messenger to you, confirming the Torah that has gone before me"* (61:6).

Although the basic message of all the messengers is the same, each messenger also brings unique teachings that define the particularities of his message. Thus, if "Muhammad is the messenger of God," Jesus, for his part, is *the messenger of God and His word that He committed to Mary, and a spirit from Him* (4:171). Other divine messengers also have specific functions and teachings. *We have sent no messenger save with the tongue of his people* (14:4).

The general function of the prophets is to guide people to felicity. God sent them to remind people that they were created to be His servants and vicegerents and to warn them of the consequences of shirking their responsibilities. The Koran makes clear that ignoring guidance will lead to wretchedness and prevent felicity. Quoting as it were from the primordial revelation given to human beings, the Koran says that when God sent Adam down from paradise, He said to him, *When there comes to you from Me guidance, then whosoever follows My guidance shall not go astray, neither shall he be wretched; but whosoever turns away from My remembrance, his life shall be a life of narrowness, and on the day of resurrection, We shall raise him blind* (20:123-24).

In short, the Koran declares that the essential message of every prophet is the same, while the details of each message are unique. Hence the universality of religious truth is an article of Islamic faith. It is true that many Muslims believe that the universality of guidance pertains only to pre-Koranic times, but others disagree; there is no "orthodox" interpretation here that Muslims must accept.

One would expect to find among Sufis a clear exposition of the universality of revealed truth without the reservations expressed by most other Muslims. But the Sufis had to take into account the beliefs of their contemporaries. Even Ibn al-'Arabī, who was not afraid to attack the limitations of the juridical and theological mentalities, often defends a literal reading of the Koranic criticisms of the People of the Book, without suggesting that by "Christians" or "Jews" the Koran means anyone other than the contemporary practitioners of those religions.

The Koran never criticizes the prophetic messages as such, but it often condemns misunderstandings or distortions by those who follow the prophets. The Shaykh sometimes criticizes specific distortions or misunderstandings in the Koranic vein, but he does not draw the conclusion that many Muslims have drawn—that the coming of Islam abrogated (*naskh*) previous revealed religions. Rather, he says, Islam is like the sun and other religions like the stars. Just as the stars remain when the sun rises, so also the other religions remain valid when Islam appears. One can add a point that perhaps Ibn al-'Arabī would also accept: What appears as a sun from one point of view may be seen as a star from another point of view. Concerning abrogation, the Shaykh writes,

> All the revealed religions [*sharā'i'*] are lights. Among these religions, the revealed religion of Muhammad is like the light of the sun among the lights of the stars. When the sun appears, the lights of the stars are hidden, and their lights are included in the light of the sun. Their being hidden is like the abrogation of the other revealed religions that takes place through Muhammad's revealed religion. Nevertheless, they do in fact exist, just as the existence of the light of the stars is actualized. This explains why we have been required in our all-inclusive religion to have faith in the truth of all the messengers and all the revealed religions. They are not rendered null [*bāṭil*] by abrogation—that is the opinion of the ignorant. (III 153.12)

If the Shaykh's pronouncements on other religions sometimes fail to recognize their validity in his own time, one reason may be that, like most other Muslims living in the western Islamic lands, he had little real contact with the Christians or Jews in his environment, not to speak of followers of religions farther afield. He had probably never met a saintly representative of either of these traditions, and he almost certainly had never read anything about these two religions except what was written in Islamic sources. Hence there is no reason that he should have accepted the validity of these religions except *in principle*. But this is an important qualification. To maintain the particular excellence of the Koran and the superiority of Muhammad over all other prophets is not to deny the universal validity of revelation nor the necessity of revelation's appearing in particularized expressions. Since all revealed religions are true in principle, the particular circumstances that lead one to suspect that they have been corrupted may change. This is what happened when Sufis like Dārā Shikōh in India met Hindu saints.[1]

The Divine Names and the Origins of Religion

In Chapter 66 of the *Futūḥāt*, the Shaykh provides a highly original account of God's creating the universe and sending the prophets. He focuses on the divine roots of revelation, which is to say that he sets out to explain what it is in *wujūd* that results in the appearance of prophets in the cosmos. Instead of answering in the usual fashion that prophecy is rooted in mercy and guidance, he looks deeper into the Divine Reality. In the process he shows that man-made law—and here he uses the Arabic word *nāmūs*, which is derived from Greek *nomos*—manifests the same divine motivations that establish revealed religions.

Ibn al-'Arabī frequently discusses divine roots by explaining the implications of the divine names in the rational mode of the theologians. But in Chapter 66, he provides an imaginal, even mythic, account of how the divine names exercise their effects in the world. In the process, he personifies the names in a manner that is probably unprecedented in Islamic sources, not least because, if the names of the names were changed, we would have a polytheistic myth. He is completely aware of what he is doing, of course, and he warns the reader at the beginning not to imagine "manyness or an ontological gathering." He gives the narrative an imaginal slant so that people will be able to grasp in concrete terms the principles that function within the divine things (*ilāhiyyāt*). Otherwise, they would be forced to fall back on the abstract theorizing of the theologians.

What the Shaykh explains in his account should by now be more or less familiar. He states, in brief, that the immutable entities are known by God, but in order to become existent entities, they need both God's desire to give them existence and His power to do so. Thus he is explaining in mythic fashion the hierarchy of attributes that are found in *wujūd*. Creation of the universe depends upon God's power; His power comes into play on the basis of His desire; His desire depends upon His knowledge of the possible things; and His knowledge depends upon His *wujūd*, which the Shaykh sometimes identifies with the divine life. Thus we have the four basic names that are embraced by the name God: Living, Knowing, Desiring, and Powerful. Their order is not haphazard, but depends upon the intrinsic characteristics of *wujūd*.

The mythic form of the Shaykh's account suggests one of several resources that Muslims have for bridging the gaps between Semitic monotheism and various forms of polytheism. Are the gods properly to be understood as independent beings, or as personifications of what Muslims know as "divine names"? Certainly Ibn al-'Arabī would choose the latter alternative—there can be no "ontological gathering." He would maintain that any attempt to consider the gods as independent entities represents a human opinion or a distortion of an original prophetic message.

After explaining how the divine names meet together and decide among themselves to bring the cosmos into existence, the Shaykh imagines that God gives them free rein to exercise their effects. The result verges on chaos, for the entities that manifest the effects of the Exalter disagree with those who manifest the Abaser, those who display the Forgiver argue with those who reflect the Avenger, and those who represent the Withholder dispute with those who act on behalf of the Bestower. Hence the creatures have recourse to the names, asking them to establish norms of order. The names in turn refer back to the divine Essence, who appoints the name Lord (*rabb*) to give order to their conflicting properties.

Elsewhere Ibn al-'Arabī explains that the primary divine attribute designated by the name Lord is *iṣlāḥ*, which means to make whole, wholesome, and sound; to put in order; to ameliorate; to remedy; to conciliate and to establish peace. Hence the cosmos has need of the Lord so that it may reach its *maṣlaḥa* (a word from the same root), which can be translated as "(means to) wholesomeness." "The cosmos needs the Lord more than any other name, because it is a name for every means to wholesomeness" (II 442.20). The opposite of *iṣlāḥ* is *ifsād*, to corrupt. The fact that the basic attribute designated by Lord is "making wholesome" explains why the angels objected to God's plan to create Adam as vicegerent in the earth and why they said to Him, *What, wilt Thou place therein one who will work* corruption *and shed blood?* (2:30).

> The angels glorify only the praise of their Lord. The Lord is He who makes wholesome. Making wholesome applies only to corruption. God never mentioned that the angels glorify any name other than Lord. . . . Hence the angels knew that it was the name Lord that turned its attentiveness toward the cosmos, because that which dominates over the earth is the authority of caprice, and it is caprice that gives rise to the corruption of which the angels spoke.[2] . . . The angels knew what would happen because of their knowledge of the realities. And it did indeed happen as they had said. Their mistake was only that they hurried to pronounce these words without knowing God's wisdom in His act. (II 251.24)

In the chapter of the *Futūḥāt* devoted to the name Lord, the Shaykh explains in more detail how God in respect of being the Lord undertakes to establish the wholesomeness and best interest of the things in the cosmos. He looks at the fundamental purpose of each thing's existence, and He gives it the exact situation appropriate for its own nature in order to assure its own specific felicity. In each case, the thing exists for the purpose of praising and glorifying God, or to make manifest the divine names and attributes in the most fitting and appropriate way.

> If you look at the possible things in respect of their own essences, there is nothing that would determine the preferability of one of the two sides [that is, existence or nonexistence] over the other. The Lord looks upon the preferability of their existence and nonexistence, their coming into existence at an earlier time or a later time, their place and position, and then He establishes relationships between them and their times, their places, and their situations. He undertakes what is most wholesome for each possible thing and makes it appear within that. For He only makes it appear in order to glorify Him and to know Him with the knowledge that is appropriate for it in keeping with what its capacity can accept. There is nothing more.[3] This is why you will see some possible things coming at an earlier time than other possible things and some coming later, some being high and some being low. They undergo variations in diverse states and levels, such as rulership and dismissal, craftsmanship and trade, movement and rest, joining and separation, and other such things. Thus the possible things undergo change and fluctuation in the midst of other possible things, not in anything else. (IV 199.15)

Having discussed in his myth of origins how God chose the name Lord to put the cosmos in order, the Shaykh turns to the human situation in order to explain the ontological necessity of revelation, which brings about the wholesomeness of human beings and allows them to choose their own best interest. The idea of establishing wholesomeness keeps on recurring throughout the passage, reminding us that the basic point of the narrative is to illustrate how God keeps balance in creation in function of the name Lord, whether this takes place on the level of creation as a whole or on the level of the human situation within the cosmos. The Shaykh points out that wise thinkers, left to their own devices, are able to grasp the divine origin of the cosmos. Here his narrative is slightly reminiscent of *Ḥayy ibn Yaqẓān*, the famous philosophical tale written by his contemporary Andalusian Ibn Ṭufayl (d. 1185).[4] In the manner of many Muslim philosophers, Ibn Ṭufayl thought that the rational perception of philosophers could achieve the same level of knowledge as the revelation given to the prophets. Ibn al-'Arabī disagrees vehemently, as he makes clear throughout his works. In this particular passage, he says that true philosophers will acknowledge the superiority of the prophets and follow them, for they will recognize that the rational knowledge achieved by philosophy pertains only to God's incomparability. Knowledge of His similarity and of how this functions to bring about salvation and nearness to God is inaccessible to the unaided human reason. However, a sound rational faculty will recognize the truth of the prophetic message and accept it. Toward the end of the passage, Ibn al-'Arabī turns to criticizing the philosophers and theologians of his own time.

Interestingly, at the very end of the chapter, the Shaykh excludes from criticism the great philosopher Averroes (d. 1198). As mentioned in the introduction, Ibn al-'Arabī had met Averroes when he was perhaps fifteen, at which time Averroes would have been fifty-five; the present passage makes clear that Ibn al-'Arabī had a good opinion of him. In the West, Averroes was more influential than any other Muslim thinker except perhaps Avicenna. But the Shaykh portrays Averroes not as a skeptic who questioned the validity of revealed religion—as he has sometimes been described in Western sources—but rather as a great master of rational discourse who defended revelation. Already in the Shaykh's time Averroes was remembered more as a doctor of the Shariah than as a philosopher. In any case his philosophical works remained largely unstudied in the civilization that nurtured him, while Ibn al-'Arabī's teachings spread to every corner of the Islamic world.

In what follows, I translate Shariah (*sharī'a*) as "revealed religion." This term has long since entered the English language to mean the revealed law of Islam, or the individual, social, and ritual regulations of the religion. In this sense, the term is often contrasted with *ṭarīqa*, or the spiritual path, the body of teachings that is concerned with transformation of the soul and is codified in many forms of Sufism. Literally, the word *Shariah* means "road (leading to water)," and Ibn al-'Arabī frequently employs it in a broad sense to refer to all the teachings brought by a divine messenger, not simply the social and ritual regulations. He also employs it in the plural to refer to the religions brought by the prophets, or the divinely instituted paths for reaching the water of life. This then is the chapter:

Chapter 66

On the True Knowledge of the Mystery of
Revealed Religion,
Outwardly and Inwardly,
and On the Divine Name
That Brought It into Existence

God says, *Had there been in the earth angels walking at peace, We would have sent down upon them out of heaven an angel as messenger* [17:95]. He also says, *We never chastise, until We send forth a messenger* [17:15].

Know that *divine names* is an expression of a state given by the realities. So pay attention to what you will hear, and do not imagine manyness or an ontological gathering! What we will discuss in this chapter is only a hierarchy of intelligible realities that are many in respect of relationships, but not in respect of entified *wujūd*, for the Essence of the Real is one in respect of being the Essence.

We know in respect of our *wujūd*, our poverty, and our possibility, that there must be a Preponderator by whom we are supported. We also know that our *wujūd* must demand from that Support diverse relationships. The Lawgiver alludes to these relationships as the "most beautiful names." In respect of being the Speaker He named Himself by them at the level of the necessity of His divine *wujūd*, which cannot be shared by anyone, for He is One God, and there is no other God.

After this introduction concerning the origin of this matter and the production of effects and the giving of preponderance within the possible cosmos, I say:

The names gathered together in the presence of the Named. They gazed upon their own realities and meanings and sought the manifestation of their own properties in order that their entities might become distinct through their effects. For Creator—who is Ordainer—Knower, Governor, Differentiator, Originator, Form-giver, Provider, Life-giver, Slayer, Inheritor, Grateful, and all the rest of the divine names gazed upon their own essences. But they found nothing created, governed, differentiated, or nourished. They said, "What can be done so that the entities within which our own properties become manifest may become manifest that thereby our authority may become manifest?"

Hence the divine names—which are demanded by some of the realities of the cosmos after the manifestation of the entity of the cosmos—had recourse to the name Originator. They said to him, "Perhaps you can give existence to these entities so that our properties may become manifest and our authority established, for the presence within which we now dwell does not receive our effects."

Originator said, "That goes back to the name Powerful, for I am under his scope."

The root of this is as follows: In their state of nonexistence the possible things asked the divine names—an asking through their state of abasement and poverty—as follows: "Nonexistence has blinded us, so we are not able to perceive one another or to know what the Real requires you to do with us. If you were to make manifest our entities and clothe them in the robe of *wujūd*, you would be giving us blessings and we would undertake the appropriate veneration and reverence. Moreover, your ruling authority becomes genuine through our becoming manifest in actuality. Today you possess ruling authority over us only potentially and virtually. What we seek from you is what you should be seeking to an even greater degree from us."

The names replied, "What the possible things have said is true!" So they fell to seeking the same thing.

When the names had recourse to the name Powerful, he said, "I am under the scope of the name Desiring, so I cannot bring a single one of your entities into existence without his specification. The possible thing itself does not give me the ability to do that. First the command of Commander must come from his Lord. When he commands the thing to enter into engendered existence, saying to it 'Be!' then he gives me the ability from himself, and I undertake to bring it into existence and immediately give it engendered existence. So have recourse to the name Desiring. Perhaps he will give preponderance to and specify the side of *wujūd* over the side of nonexistence. Then I, Commander, and Speaker will join together and give you existence."

So the names had recourse to the name Desiring. They said to him, "We asked the name Powerful to bring our entities into existence, but he deferred the command to you. What do you decree?" Desiring said, "Powerful spoke the truth! But I have no news about the property of the name Knowing in respect to you. Does he or does he not have precedent knowledge that you will be given existence, so that we can specify it for you? I am under the scope of the name Knowing. Go to him and mention your situation to him."

So they went to the name Knowing and mentioned what the name Desiring had said. Knowing said, "Desiring spoke the truth! And I have precedent knowledge that you will be given existence. But courtesy must be observed. For we have a presence that watches over us, and that is the name God. So we must make ourselves present before Him, for he is the Presence of All-comprehensiveness."

All the names gathered together in the presence of God. He said, "What is on your mind?" They told him the story. He said, "I am the name that comprehends your realities and I denote the Named, who is an All-holy Essence described by perfection and incomparability. Stay here while I enter in upon the Object of my denotation." So he entered in upon the Object of his denotation and told It what the possible things had said and what the names were discussing. The Essence said, "Go out, and tell each one of the names to become connected to what its reality requires among the possible things. . . ."

So the name God went out, next to him the name Speaker, acting as his spokesman to the possible things and to the names. He mentioned to them what the Named had said. Knowing, Desiring, Speaking, and Powerful established their connections, and the first possible thing became outwardly manifest through the specification of Desiring and the property of Knowing.

Once the entities and the effects had become manifest in the engendered universe, some of them exercised authority and dominated over others in keeping with the names by which they were supported. This led to quarrel and dispute. Then the possible things said, "We fear lest our order be corrupted and we return to the nonexistence where we used to dwell." So they called upon the names through that which was cast to them by the names Knowing and Governing. They said, "O names! If your properties were to follow a known scale, a designated boundary, and a leader to which you all go back, that would preserve our *wujūd* for us as well as your effectivity within us for you. That would be more wholesome for both us and you. So have recourse to God! Perhaps He will present to you someone who will set a boundary at which you can stop. If not, we will be destroyed, and you will no longer have any effects!"

The names replied, "This is the right means of wholesomeness and the best opinion!" Hence they did what they were asked. They said, "The name Governor will communicate your situation." They informed Governor, and he said, "I will do so."

The name Governor entered, and then he emerged with the Real's command to the name "Lord." He said to him, "Do what wholesomeness demands so that the entities of the possible things may subsist." The name Lord took two viziers to help him in what he was commanded to do. One vizier was the name Governor, and the other was the name Differentiator. God says, *He* governs *the affair, He* differentiates *the signs; haply you will have certitude concerning the encounter with your* Lord [13:2], who is the "leader." So consider how exact is the Word of God, since it employs expressions that fit the state that is demanded by the actual situation!

The name Lord set down for them limits and established for them customs by which the wholesomeness of the kingdom might be established, and *to test them, which one of them is more beautiful in works* [11:7]. God made these limits and customs of two kinds: One kind is called "wise regulation." He cast it into the original dispositions of the souls of the great human beings. Hence they set down limits and established laws through a power that they found in their own souls. They did so in every city, place, and clime, in accordance with what was demanded by the constitution and nature of those areas, since they knew what wisdom demanded. Through that they preserved the possessions, lives, families, relatives, and kinship relationships of the people. They named it the "laws," a word that means "cause of good," since *nāmūs* in technical usage is the one through whom good comes, while *jāsūs* is employed for evil.

So these were the wise laws established by the rational thinkers as the result of an inspiration from God of which they were unaware for the sake of the wholesomeness, order, and arrangement of everyone in the world where there was no divinely revealed religion. The founders of these laws did not know that these affairs would bring about nearness to God, nor that they would yield a Garden or a Fire, nor [did they know] anything connected with the next world. They did not know that there is a next world and a sensory resurrection within natural bodies after death, or an abode within which there is food, drink, clothing, marriage, and joy, and another abode within which there is chastisement and pain. For the existence of all this is possible, its nonexistence is possible, and they had no proof of the preponderance of one of the possibilities over the other.

And monasticism they invented [57:27]. So their laws and their means to wholesomeness were built upon bringing about the subsistence of wholesomeness in this abode. Then individually, in their own souls, they came to know the divine sciences, such as *tawḥīd*, the glorification and veneration worthy of God's majesty, the attributes of incomparability, the lack of any likeness or similarity. Those who knew and understood this called it to the attention of those who did not. They urged people to accept the correct view. At the same time they let the people know that rational faculties are limited in respect of their reflective powers and cannot pass beyond certain bounds; that God effuses His knowledge into the hearts of certain of His servants, thereby teaching them *a knowledge from Him* [18:65], and that this did not seem unlikely in their eyes; and that God has deposited within the celestial world certain commands concerning which some knowledge can be gained by drawing conclusions from the existence of their effects in this elemental world. This is indicated by God's words, *He revealed to each heaven its command* [41:12].

They investigated the realities of their own souls. They saw that when the bodily form dies, nothing is lacking from any of its members. Hence they came to know that the body perceives and moves by means of something added to it. They investigated this added thing and they recognized their own souls. Then they saw that the soul gains knowledge after having been ignorant, so they understood that even though the soul is nobler than the body, it is accompanied by poverty and need. They ascended through rational consideration from one thing to another. Each time they reached something, they saw that it was in need of something else. Finally rational consideration took them to something that was in need of nothing, which had no likeness, which was similar to nothing, and to which nothing was similar. They stopped there and said: This is the First. It must be One in itself in respect of itself, and its Firstness and Unity must not accept a second, since there is nothing like it and nothing comparable to it. So they declared the unity of its *wujūd*. When they saw that the possible things in themselves had no reason to come into existence, they knew that this One had given them *wujūd*. Hence the possible things have need of the One and venerate it by negating from it everything by which their own essences are described. This is the furthest limit of the rational faculty.

While these rational thinkers were busy with their own affairs, there arose among them a person of their own kind whom they looked upon as having no position in knowledge. They did not believe that he was the possessor of sound reflection or correct rational consideration. He said to them, "I am God's messenger to you."

They said, "Let us be fair. Look at his claim itself. Does he claim what is possible, or what is impossible? Logical proofs have established for us that God possesses a divine effusion that He may give to whomsoever He wills, just as He has effused it upon the spirits of these celestial spheres and the intellects. All things share in possibility, so no possible thing is more worthy than others in respect of possibility. Hence we must consider the truthfulness or falsity of this claimant. We should not proceed to make either of these judgments without a proof, for that would be discourtesy, given our knowledge."

They said, "Do you have a proof for the truthfulness of what you claim?" So he brought them proofs and they considered his manner of proving and his proofs. They considered that this person had no reports that reflective thoughts could have reached by drawing conclusions, nor was any such thing known from him. So they came to know that He who *revealed to each heaven its command* [41:12] had revealed to each heaven the existence of this person and of what he brought. Hence they hurried to declare their faith in him and acknowledge his truthfulness. They came to know that God had given him knowledge of the sciences which He had deposited in the celestial world and which could not be reached by their reflective powers, and that He had given him a knowledge of Himself which they did not have.

They saw that this person descended in his knowledge of God to the level of the weak-minded common people, bestowing upon them what would make their rational faculties wholesome; and also to people of great rational faculty and sound consideration, giving them also that which would make their rational faculties wholesome. Hence they knew that this man possessed, through the divine effusion, something from beyond the stage of reason and that God had given him a knowledge of that effusion and a power over it that He had not given to them. They acknowledged his superiority over themselves, had faith in him, declared his truthfulness, and followed him. So he designated for them the acts that bring about nearness to God. He taught them about possible things created by God and hidden from them and about what would come to be among them from Him in the future. He told them about the resurrection, the gathering, the mustering, the Garden, and the Fire.

In this way messengers were sent according to the diversity of the times and the variety of the situations. Each of them confirmed the truth of the others. None of them differed whatsoever in the roots by which they were supported and of which they spoke, even if rulings differed. Revealed religions were sent down, and rulings came. The governing property belonged to the time and the situation, just as God has declared: *To every one of you We have appointed a right way and a revealed law* [5:48]. So the roots coincided, without disagreeing on anything.

The people distinguished between the prophetic regulations promulgated by God as revealed religion and the wise regulations established by the sages in accordance with their rational consideration. They understood that the [prophetic] command was more complete and that it came from God, without doubt. They accepted what they were told about the unseen things and had faith in the messengers. None of them resisted except him who did not counsel his own soul concerning his knowledge, but followed his caprice and sought leadership over his fellows. He was ignorant of his own soul and its measure and he was ignorant of his Lord.

Hence the root and the cause of the establishment of revealed religions in the cosmos was the search for the wholesomeness of the cosmos and for the knowledge of God of which reason is ignorant, because it does not receive it through its own reflection. In other words, reason cannot discover this knowledge independently in respect of its own consideration. Hence the revealed books came down with this knowledge, and the tongues of the messengers and prophets spoke about it. Then the rational thinkers came to know that there were certain things concerning the knowledge of God in which they were deficient and which the messengers completed for them.

I do not mean by "rational thinkers" those who nowadays speak about philosophy. I mean only those who followed the path of the prophets. In other words, they busied themselves with their own souls and with ascetic discipline, inner struggle, retreats, and preparing themselves for that which enters in upon the heart from the celestial world when the heart is purified, that which has been revealed to the high heavens. These are the ones I mean by "rational thinkers." As for those who busy themselves with chatter, talk [*kalām*], and debate, employing their reflective powers to analyze the component words that have issued from the first philosophers while remaining oblivious of the affair undertaken by those great men, the likes of these—who are among us today—have no worth in the eyes of any person of intelligence.[5] For they mock at religion, show contempt for God's servants, and have reverence only for those among themselves who stand in the same place. Their hearts have been overcome by love for this world and the search for position and leadership. So God has abased them, just as they have abased knowledge. He has scorned them and derided them, letting them have recourse to the doors of the ignorant—the kings and the rulers. So the kings and the rulers abase them.

The words of people like this are of no account. God has *sealed their hearts* [2:7] and *made them deaf and blinded their eyes* [47:23], despite the fact that among themselves they claim extravagantly to be the best of the world's inhabitants. Even the jurist—he who gives legal pronouncements in God's religion—is better than they in every respect, in spite of the paucity of his abstinence. After all, people who have faith, even though they acquire it only through following the authority of others, are better than those who consider themselves "rational thinkers." God forbid that any intelligent person have the attributes of such as these!

We have met few people who are true rational thinkers. These are they who have the greatest knowledge of God's messengers. They are among those who follow most carefully the examples [*sunan*] of the Messenger and are most concerned with preserving his examples. They know the veneration demanded by God's majesty, and they are aware of the knowledge of Himself that God singles out for His servants—the prophets and the friends of God who follow them—in respect of a special divine effusion. This effusion is outside the ordinary learning that is acquired through study and effort and cannot be reached by reason in respect of its own reflective power.

I have listened to the words of one of the great ones among them [i.e., Averroes]. He had seen the knowledge that God had opened up to me without rational consideration or reading, but through a retreat in which I had been alone with God, even though I had not been seeking. He said, "Praise belongs to God, that I should have lived in a time in which I saw *one whom God has given mercy from* Him, *and has taught him knowledge proceding from* Him [18:65]." *God singles out for his mercy whom He will, and God is of bounty abounding* [2:105]. (I 322-25)

9

Diversity of Belief

Like other Muslims, Ibn al-'Arabī views the Koran and the Sunnah of Muhammad as guidebooks that must be followed if human potential is to blossom. People enter the world possessing the *fiṭra*, which predisposes them toward *tawḥīd*, but they grow and develop in a manner that is largely determined by environmental and social factors. The soul unfolds as a matter of course, but not every path of unfoldment will lead to a full deployment of human possibilities. Although felicity is the ultimate destiny of every existent thing, people cannot count upon achieving it in the *barzakh* or during the fifty thousand-year-long day of resurrection, and the different modes of felicity are in effect infinite. Strictly "human" felicity, which leads to the vision of God's self-disclosure in its full splendor, depends upon the actualization of all the divine attributes latent in the original human nature. And this actualization in turn depends to some degree upon human effort to bring it about. Since people were created in God's form, they partake of the divine attribute of freedom. They are "forced"—by the fact of being free—to play a role in determining the extent to which the latent divine attributes come to be present in their souls. As the Shaykh puts it in a formulation that he often approximates, "The freely choosing human being is compelled to have free choice" (III 300.22). If people make choices that lead in the direction of disequilibrium and disharmony, they may forfeit the possibility of felicity in the next stages of existence.

Ibn al-'Arabī maintains that Koranic eschatological teachings include allusions to every conceivable mode of human equilibrium and disequilibrium, every perfection and imperfection, every actuality of the divine form, and every failure to achieve full humanity. He talks of 5,105 degrees of paradise, only twelve of which belong exclusively to Muslims (I 319.18). In his view, each level or degree of the posthumous worlds encompasses a broad range of possible human destinies. For him it is self-evident that followers of different religions experience things differently at death, even if all of them should have reached perfection and felicity, since the self-disclosure of God in the human form never repeats itself.

Few people doubt that perceptions of reality differ in some ways. Even persons of similar cultural backgrounds may diverge profoundly in psychological makeup, intellectual ability, and aesthetic sensitivity, all of which represent important dimensions of the soul. If this is true in the present world of concretions and sedimentations, where the essences and realities are largely veiled from sight, it is much more true in the subtle, imaginal realms that are experienced after death, where the nonmanifest realities are able to assume a far wider variety of forms.

If every posthumous state is different from every other, some must be closer to the Real and some farther away, some brighter and some darker, some better and some worse. Perhaps the eschatological teachings of the Semitic religions as usually understood put too much emphasis on an absolute distinction between paradise and hell, but certainly one basic insight is incontestable: People will experience the next stages of their existence in a manner profoundly influenced by the way in which they live their lives in the present world, and this in turn will be affected by the goals they set for themselves. The states after death are determined not only by "works," but also by the ideas and thoughts that bring works into existence. Hence beliefs about who we are, where we can go, and what we can become play a major role in determining the actual manner in which human potential unfolds.

The Roots of Belief

The Arabic word *i'tiqād*, which is typically translated as "belief," derives from the root *'.q.d*, which means to knit, knot, or tie; to join together, to convene, to make a contract. *I'tiqād* itself, the eighth verbal form from the root, means to become firmly knotted, tied, or established, literally or figuratively. As a technical term signifying belief, it suggests a knot tied in the heart that determines a person's view of reality. The Shaykh employs the word to refer to all the knottings that shape understanding—the whole range of cognitions, ideas, theories, doctrines, dogmas, prejudices, perceptions, feelings, and inclinations that allow people to make sense of the world. To be human is to have a perspective on self and other, even if one is unaware of one's underlying mind-set or is unable to articulate it. Beliefs lie at the root of every human thought and action. They determine the way people live their lives and experience their deaths. In short, "belief" is unavoidable, since it follows upon human existence.

The Shaykh usually poses questions of belief in terms of God, but this should not lead us to conclude that his discussions have no relevance for those who have no beliefs about God, or who reject the idea of God altogether. "God," after all, is *wujūd*, and *wujūd* embraces all of reality on whatever level it is envisaged. In respect to its manifestation, *wujūd* is named by every name in the cosmos. Thus every knowledge possessed by every knower—that is, every awareness of whatever it may be, every cognitive knotting—is in fact knowledge of God.

> There are none but knowers of God. However, some of the knowers know that they know God, and some of them do not know that they know God. The latter have knowledge of what they witness and examine, but they do not know that it is the Real. If you ask such a person, "Do you know God?" he will say that he does not. But if you ask him about what he witnesses, "Do you know what you witness in respect of the fact that it is the object of your witnessing?", he will say that he does. . . . So he is only ignorant of the fact that this [divine] name applies to that object of witnessing. (III 510.32)

Everyone has knowledge, beliefs, assumptions, and knottings about *wujūd*, because nothing else presents itself to us. Hence the Shaykh's explanations of the nature of belief apply also to the peculiar modes of belief that characterize the modern and postmodern worlds, that is, belief in all sorts of social and political goals, ideologies, and programs, not to mention the many other sorts of beliefs that have a more recognizably "religious" element to them.

If everyone has a belief, can we say that all beliefs are true? Most Muslim theologians would immediately say, "No, only belief in a true religion is a true belief." The Shaykh, however, would not be so precipitous. He would most likely say that the answer depends on what we mean by "true." If "true" means that a knotting corresponds to reality, then of course all beliefs are true, since each belief represents some aspect of reality, however limited and distorted that aspect might be. If a belief did not correspond to reality in some way, it would not exist. Each belief represents the subjective side of an existential state. The fact that someone holds a belief proves that the belief coincides in some manner with the way things are, whether or not the believer's mind establishes a real contact with what lies outside of itself. Hence, we can reach a preliminary conclusion that all beliefs are true, no matter what their content. There can be no error in existence, because everything that exists is demanded by the Real, which is *wujūd*.

> God is wise without qualification. It is He who has put things in their places. It is He who has *given each thing its creation* [20:50]. Hence, God has made no error in engendered existence in relation to its order. (II 267.33)

> People like us, who have an overview of all the stations and levels, distinguish from whence every individual speaks and discourses and recognize that each is correct in his own level and makes no errors. Indeed, there is absolutely no error in the cosmos. (II 541.23)

The idea that there are no errors and that all beliefs are true rises up logically from *waḥdat al-wujūd*. Each existent thing represents a particular self-disclosure of nondelimited *wujūd*. The cosmos in its indefinite spatial and temporal extension manifests the whole range of possibilities possessed by *wujūd*. Each thing is like a color brought into existence by the prism of *wujūd*'s infinite possibility. Through its own specific nature—its own special limitations that distinguish it from other colors—each color delimits and defines the invisible light, thereby making it visible. From one point of view, every entity veils or obscures *wujūd* by its own specific color and characteristics. From another point of view, it manifests *wujūd* by virtue of being found in the cosmos. The first point of view is that of incomparability or "Not He"; the second, that of similarity or "He."

In one of many passages in which the Shaykh explains the truth of all beliefs because of the oneness of *wujūd*, he alludes to the idea that all things in the universe—including the words that people speak—are words articulated within the Breath of the All-merciful. Hence all speech is the word of God, and all is true. However, the mode in which that speech is true often escapes the understanding of the observer.

> There is no speaker but God, and none who causes to speak but God. All that remains is the opening of the eye of understanding to God's causing to speak in respect to the fact that He only causes speech that is correct. Every speech in the cosmos derives either from wisdom or from [God's] decisive address.[1] So all speech is protected from error and slipping. However, speech has homesteads, loci, and playing fields within which it has a great expanse to roam. Its playing fields are so vast that the eyes of insights are unable to perceive their outer limits. (III 545.11)

The diversity of divine and human speech derives from the infinity of *wujūd*'s possible modes of manifestation. The divine names designate the various modes in which nondelimited *wujūd* delimits itself when it brings the universe into existence. God makes the full range of the names manifest through His self-disclosure in the cosmos, or through articulating the words of the All-merciful Breath. But at any given time and place, no single existent entity can manifest all the possible attributes of *wujūd* in their full deployment. Each existent thing represents a delimitation of nondelimited *wujūd* and hence manifests *wujūd*'s attributes only to a limited degree.

The infinite possibilities of self-disclosure possessed by nondelimited *wujūd* are known to *wujūd* itself for all eternity, because *God encompasses all things in knowledge* (65:12). Each entity, along with all its specific characteristics, represents a self-delimitation of nondelimited *wujūd*, determined by the nature of *wujūd* itself, and known by *wujūd* forever by virtue of its self-knowledge. Whether the entities are viewed as immutably fixed in God's knowledge or existing in the cosmos, each has a specific entification (*ta'ayyun*) or thingness (*shay'iyya*) or delimitation (*taqyīd*) that distinguishes it from every other entity.

The extent to which an existent entity allows the light of *wujūd* to shine forth, or its capacity to act as a locus of manifestation within which *wujūd* displays its properties, is known as the entity's "preparedness." Human beings, made in the image of the all-comprehensive divine name, possess the greatest preparedness for manifesting the properties of *wujūd* (even though the preparedness of each individual differs). The different capacity of each entity means that each delimits nondelimited *wujūd* in its own fashion. God is one and nondelimited, but His self-disclosures are infinitely diverse. "He who discloses Himself, in respect to what He is in Himself, is One in Entity, but the self-disclosures—I mean their forms—are diverse because of the preparednesses of the loci of self-disclosure" (I 287.19).

Each human individual represents a unique possibility of expression possessed by nondelimited *wujūd*. In the same way, each individual's knowledge represents a unique understanding of *wujūd*, an understanding that is determined by *wujūd*'s self-disclosure. Hence beliefs are determined by the ontological possibilities that make up the individual. Just as each person is a unique existent, so also each is a unique knower. Just as each person's existence represents a unique knot tied in nondelimited Reality, a unique word articulated within the Breath of the All-merciful, so also each person's belief represents a unique configuration of nondelimited Awareness. And all this goes back to the divine names. "Every observer of God is under the controlling property of one of God's names. That name discloses itself to him and gives to him a specific belief through its self-disclosure" (II 85.14).

The Two Commands

To say that all beliefs are true means that each of them expresses limitations that have been assumed by nondelimited *wujūd*. It also suggests that in the end all beliefs will lead to felicity for those who hold them. But God's self-disclosure to human beings is not the same as His self-disclosure to other creatures. If full and complete human felicity depends upon total actualization of the divine form, then failure to actualize the divine form demands distance from God in the next world, and, in its initial stages, this distance will be experienced as pain and chastisement.

Felicity depends upon divine guidance, and guidance entails commands and prohibitions. In other words, people must observe God's commandments in order to reach paradise. However, the Shaykh is quick to point out that the "God" who issues commands and prohibitions is not identical in every respect with the God who is envisaged as *wujūd*. God as *wujūd* demands delimited *wujūd* in every form it can take, but God as Guide urges people to follow the prophets and to avoid misguidance. Muslim theologians had long distinguished between these two perspectives by talking of God's "engendering command" (*al-amr al-takwīnī*) in contrast to His "prescriptive command" (*al-amr al-taklīfī*). Through the first command, God brings all creation into existence: *His only command when He desires a thing is to say to it "Be!" and it is* (36:82). Through the second, He sets down the instructions whereby people can achieve felicity. Hence the prescriptive command entails activities such as prayer, fasting, almsgiving, and the observance of moral constraints.

Through the engendering command, God bestows *wujūd* upon all things, thereby allowing them to be themselves. Through the prescriptive command, He calls human beings to felicity in the *barzakh* and beyond. The engendering command cannot be disobeyed, because it establishes the creature's existence in the cosmos. The prescriptive command can be rejected, whether partially or completely. Rejecting it leads to chastisement and distance from God, though the chastisement (*'adhāb*) will eventually turn sweet (*'adhib*).

The prescriptive command grows up out of certain specific attributes of *wujūd*—such as guidance and compassion—which focus upon eliminating the constraints and limitations that cause human suffering. In contrast, the engendering command arises from nondelimited *wujūd*, or God as such. Hence the prescriptive command is in fact embraced and determined by the engendering command. It is a specific form assumed by the engendering command for the purpose of accomplishing certain defined ends. From the point of view of the engendering command, there can be no disobedience. Disobedience to the prescriptive command always results from obedience to the engendering command.

The Shaykh explains why disobeying the prescriptive command may lead to wretchedness by referring to the implications of some of the qualities of *wujūd*. God is not only Guide, He is also Misguider (*muḍill*). Although not mentioned in the well-known lists of ninety-nine names, this name is implied by thirty-five Koranic verses in which God is the subject of the verb "to misguide." In certain circumstances, God's misguidance may dominate over His guidance, leading to disobedience in this world and wretchedness in the next.

Whether a given human being falls under the influence of the Guide or the Misguider goes back to the nature of *wujūd* itself. After all, what is it that determines the preparedness of the immutable entities, which are known by God for all eternity? Each entity in fact represents a possible self-disclosure of *wujūd*. To say that a person is misguided is to say that misguidance pertains to the reality of the person, the configuration of *wujūd* that determines the specific nature of the person.

To the objection that this means that God makes people sin and then punishes them for sinning, the Shaykh replies that the entities are immutable and God does not "make" (*ja'l*) them do anything. He simply gives them existence. If misguidance is the property of an entity, the entity will be misguided when it enters into existence. God shines the light of *wujūd* on the entities, and they come to exist as they are, doing what they do. God can no more change the entities than He can change His own Essence, *wujūd* itself. As Ibn al-'Arabī puts it, "God wills only the actual situation. His will in the things is that they be what they are" (III 356.30). Thus, when God manifests *wujūd* to the entity of the sun, it shines, and when He manifests *wujūd* to the entities of sinners, they sin, thereby displaying within themselves the properties of the name Misguider. Sinners are loci of manifestation for delimited possibilities of outward existence possessed by nondelimited *wujūd* in virtue of the fact that *wujūd* allows for dispersion, deviation, error, suffering, and wretchedness.

To ask why God misguides people is like asking why *wujūd* is *wujūd*, or why reality is reality. The answer is simply that reality is what it is, and it cannot be otherwise. To say that God is the Misguider is simply to assert that *wujūd* allows for the possibility of misguidance and wretchedness and that entities representing this possibility will have to exist. This is why the Shaykh insists that, in the last analysis, God misguides no one. Rather, people follow their own natures, which is to say that they manifest their own immutable entities. No one can blame the gardener when an apple tree fails to yield grapes, and no one should blame God when a sinner fails to do good works. The sinner can blame only his own reality. This, says the Shaykh, explains Satan's answer to those who will complain to him at the resurrection that he had misguided them: *Do not blame me, but blame yourselves* (14:22).[2]

Ibn al-'Arabī explains many of these points while discussing the meaning of the divine name Withholder (*al-māni'*). If God is pure mercy and unlimited munificence (*jūd*), why does He hold things back from His servants? There are, of course, several answers to this question, but in this particular context the Shaykh looks at the preparedness of the creatures. He says, in brief, that God does not hold back in His giving, but the servants receive the gift in keeping with their own natures. No one can complain about his own nature without denying his own reality.

> Once you recognize the receptacle, then you will know the Withholder and withholding. For the receptacles receive from God's nondelimited munificence in keeping with their preparednesses. They are like the garment and the washerman when the sun effuses its light. The garment becomes white, but the face of the washerman turns black—if it was white.

> The wise man says to the two of them, "The light is one, but the constitution of the washerman receives only blackness from the sun. The garment has a constitution that receives whiteness. Hence [O washerman,] your constitution held you back from receiving whiteness." And he says to the garment, "Your constitution held you back from receiving blackness."
>
> Each of these two can protest. [The garment can say:] "Nevertheless, the problem remains. Why did He not give me a constitution that receives blackness?" And the washerman can say, "Why did He not give me a constitution that receives whiteness?"
>
> We would reply as follows: "There must be garments and washermen in the cosmos. Hence there must be constitutions that receive whiteness and constitutions that receive blackness. So there must be the two of you—be whatever you are. For there must be all things within the cosmos. Hence there must be within it every constitution."
>
> The Real does not act according to the individual motives that He has brought into existence in His servants. He acts only in accordance with wisdom. That which wisdom requires is that which occurs in the cosmos. Its manifestation itself is identical with wisdom, for God's acts are not caused by wisdom; rather, they are wisdom itself. . . .
>
> Whenever you posit any locus for a specific constitution, it can be supposed that the locus will say, "This constitution has held me back." But this is a mistake, because the constitution itself is identical to what has become manifest. It is not something else. It is not correct for a thing to say about itself, "Why am I not something else?" (III 530.3)[3]

It perhaps needs to be reiterated that the Shaykh is not denying, in passages such as these, the reality of human freedom. His perspective on this specific discussion pertains to the engendering command and the omnipresence of *wujūd*, or God's utter incomparability with all things. But as soon as God's similarity is taken into account, human freedom once again presents itself. People possess a certain freedom because they are forms of God, and God is free. Hence they are forced to deal with their freedom and—to the extent that they are free—to accept responsibility for the choices that they make. If they could truly recognize that they have no freedom because God alone is free, this would mean utter surrender (*islām*) to the divine will. But such surrender is achieved only by the "universal servant" (*al-'abd al-kullī*)—one of the many terms that the Shaykh employs to refer to the perfect human being.[4] Long before reaching perfection, people are faced with the need to surrender to the prescriptive command and follow the path to salvation. Recognizing that they are forced to be free, they must freely make choices about how to act or not to act in everyday life.

Paths to God

The Koran refers to a number of paths, but it commands people to follow the "straight path." The Shaykh tells us that this cannot be the "straight path of God," where God is taken to mean nondelimited *wujūd*, because all things follow that path in any case, given that they all obey the engendering command. "The path of God is the general path upon which all things walk, and it takes them to God. It includes every divinely revealed religion and every construction of the rational faculty. It takes to God, and it embraces both wretched and felicitous" (III 410.24).

When it is said that all beliefs are true, this amounts to saying that all beliefs lead to God, or that all of them fall under the general rule established by the several Koranic verses that say that all things come from God and return to Him. But this tells us nothing about how people can achieve the full perfection of the divine form and avoid being veiled from the vision of their own *fiṭra* in the next world. Hence, from a human point of view, paths need to be judged by criteria that relate to human destiny. These criteria can only be those qualities of *wujūd* that help the human soul reach the fullness of the divine form.

One of the divine attributes that benefits human souls is blessing (*in'ām*). Because blessing is inherent to *wujūd*, God commands people to seek it out—not of course because He benefits, but because He is compassionate and He knows that they will benefit. Hence, in their daily prayers, Muslims are commanded to recite the *Fātiḥa*, the opening chapter of the Koran, and thereby to ask God to lead them on the straight path of the Blessing-giver: *Guide us on the straight path, **the path of those whom Thou hast blessed,** not of those against whom Thou art wrathful, nor of those who are misguided* (1:5-7). The Shaykh cites a number of Koranic verses to show that all the prophets brought this "straight path of the Blessing-giver" and that following it leads to felicity.

Ideally, however, Muslims should follow a third and still narrower path. This is the "Path of Muhammad" as set down in the guidance that was given exclusively to him, that is, the Koran. It leads to the specific form of mercy and felicity that God has singled out for the followers of Islam.[5] At the same time, because of the all-embracing nature of the Koranic revelation, it includes within itself the paths of all the previous prophets. As the Shaykh writes,

> Among the paths is the path of blessings. It is referred to in God's words, *To every one of you [messengers] We have appointed a right way and a revealed law* [5:48]. The Muhammadan leader chooses the path of Muhammad and leaves aside the other paths, even though he acknowledges them and has faith in them. However, he does not make himself a servant except through the path of Muhammad, nor does he have his followers make themselves servants except through it. He traces the attributes of all paths back to it, because Muhammad's revealed reli-

> gion is all-inclusive. Hence the property of all the revealed religions has been transferred to his revealed religion. His revealed religion embraces them, but they do not embrace it. (III 410.21)

In short, even though all paths lead to God, "The road of felicity is that set down by revealed religion, nothing else" (II 148.12). When faced with the reality of their own situation, people cannot simply take what God offers them in respect of His engendering command, because this may well lead them to wretchedness. Rather, they must take from the Nondelimited Real only what He delimits through the prescriptive command, which is His designated scale for weighing everything that has a bearing on felicity.

> God gives to His servants from Himself, and also on the hands of His messengers. As for what comes to you on the hand of the Messenger, take it without employing any scale. But as for what comes to you from the hand of God, take it with a scale. For God is identical to every giver, but He has forbidden you from taking every gift. Thus He says, *Whatever the Messenger gives you, take; whatever he forbids you, forgo* [59:7]. Thus your taking from the Messenger is more profitable for you and better able to actualize your felicity.
>
> Your taking from the Messenger is nondelimited, but your taking from God is delimited. The Messenger himself is delimited, but taking from him is nondelimited. God is not delimited by any delimitation, but taking from Him is delimited. So consider how wonderful this affair is! (IV 186.22)

Equilibrium

As the human soul develops, the qualities latent in the *fiṭra* gradually manifest themselves. Perfection is achieved when the latent divine form becomes the soul's actuality. But perfection, it needs to be remembered, does not imply some sort of static finality. It represents fully conscious participation in the dynamic and never-ending self-disclosure of *wujūd*. Perfect human beings participate with total presence and undistracted awareness in the process whereby the cosmos is reborn at each instant. Just as God's activity is continual and ever-renewed, so also perfect human beings enjoy a new growth and a more complete knowledge of *wujūd* from moment to moment. As the Shaykh writes, perfect human beings "never cease witnessing nearness [with the Real] continuously, since they never cease witnessing forms within themselves and outside themselves, and that is nothing but the Real's self-disclosure" (II 558.30).

Although perfection is the ideal human situation, it is rarely achieved in this world. Nevertheless, those who strive to the extent of their capacity (*wus'*) to manifest the divine attributes latent within themselves will achieve the vision of God's self-disclosure—the full awareness of the divine form within themselves—in paradise. That is why the inhabitants of the Garden experience what perfect human beings have already tasted in this life—God's constant and never-ending unveilings of Himself. At every instant God removes a new veil, displaying His face in greater beauty and glory. Paradise lasts forever because the unique Beloved never repeats His endless self-display. God draws the souls into greater and greater vision, knowledge, awareness, and bliss. These are the Koranic fountains and houris, the endlessly flowing rivers of milk, honey, water, and wine. "In the Gardens, at every instant there is a new creation and a new bliss, so that boredom will never occur. . . . With every glance that the inhabitants of the Gardens cast toward their kingdoms, they perceive things and forms that they had never seen before, and thus they increase in delight" (II 280.27).

Viewed from the context of the engendering command, the prescriptive command brings about the full development of human qualities, and these coincide with the deployment of certain possibilities of *wujūd* that cannot be actualized in any other way. The attributes brought into manifestation only by human beings include attractive and beautiful qualities such as generosity, mercy, compassion, and patience, but also repelling and wrathful attributes such as terrible punishment and vengeance. Without the revelations brought by the prophets, neither the highest nor the lowest human possibilities could be actualized, and these are the highest and lowest possibilities of manifest *wujūd* itself. Thus the prescriptive command serves the engendering command by bringing into existence a whole range of *wujūd*'s modalities that could not otherwise be actualized. Both paradise and hell depend upon revelation for their actual existence. As the Shaykh writes, "If not for the existence of the revealed religions, there would be no disbelief in God resulting in wretchedness" (II 248.3). So also, what are called "evil" and "Satan" are called such only because of the prescriptive command. "Prescription alone makes the entity of evil manifest from Satan" (IV 223.27).

The primary divine attributes that display their traces in the human form are life, knowledge, desire, power, and speech. Guidance is addressed to living beings who possess knowledge, choose among the objects of knowledge through desire, put their desire into effect through power, and understand the divine word while articulating their own situation through speech. Leaving aside other divine attributes that have a specifically moral dimension, we can see that these primary qualities are not possessed to the same degree by all human beings. It should also be obvious that equilibrium among these attributes contributes to human perfection.

Each of these five primary attributes supports the others. An imbalance that sets up an improper relationship among them will vitiate the usefulness of all. Even in a contemporary context, "knowledge without power" or "power without knowledge" are conditions well known to everyone. If the worth of increasing one's knowledge and power is universally acknowledged, what Islamic teachings add here is that human potential for growth and development is not limited by any conceivable bounds, given that every divine attribute can be actualized to an unlimited degree.

Full human perfection involves the actual, living presence of every attribute of *wujūd*. People need revelation to achieve this perfection because they are ignorant of their own divine form. Without too much instruction, they can understand the value of knowledge and power, but it is totally beyond their individual capacities to grasp the value of all the divine attributes and then to actualize each of them in proper balance with the others. Because the human *fiṭra* is defined by *wujūd*, and because *wujūd* is unknowable and nondelimited, people need revelation in order to understand their own selves.

Human imperfection grows up out of the failure to actualize the correct balance among the divine attributes found in the original human disposition. The correct balance of attributes is rooted in mercy's precedence over wrath. Mercy pertains to *wujūd*'s essential nature, while wrath comes into play in relation to certain specific characteristics of delimited *wujūd*. Hence all things are embraced by mercy (Koran 7:156), but only some things are touched by wrath.

Mercy is closely connected to those attributes that pertain to the achievement of nearness to God, such as knowledge, illumination, union, unity, and equilibrium. In contrast, wrath is bound up with the limiting characteristics of created things, such as distance, separation, ignorance, multiplicity, dispersion, differentiation, and deviation. To the extent that people are dominated by attributes of wrath, they remain far from God and hence far from mercy and felicity. Only by seeking out God's mercy and forgiveness are they able to ascend to the realm of union, unity, balance, and joy.

Wrath plays a necessary role in the cosmic harmony, but it remains subordinate to mercy. In the same way, the delimited *wujūd* of the cosmos remains subordinate to the nondelimited *wujūd* of God. Without delimitation, there could be no cosmos—without wrath, the Breath of the All-merciful could not articulate the words of its vocabulary. Only through every creaturely possibility can the full disclosure of the properties of the divine attributes be achieved. And all of this creative activity, through *wujūd*'s delimitation, is an expression of the precedent divine mercy—that is, of the inherent fullness and overflowingness of *wujūd*.

Mercy's precedence over wrath becomes manifest even in the midst of distance and misguidance, for without these two, nearness and guidance have no meaning. In the same way, without sins, the divine attributes of pardon and forgiveness could not become manifest. In other words, sins are necessitated by God's attribute of forgiveness. The Shaykh likes to quote the following hadith as a scriptural source for this teaching: "By Him in whose hand my soul is, if you had not sinned, God would have removed you and brought a people who do sin, then ask God's pardon and are forgiven."[6] Through these words, the Shaykh says, "The Prophet let us know that everything that happens in the cosmos occurs only to make manifest the property of a divine name" (II 96.12). In case his point is not completely clear, I quote an anecdote he narrates concerning one of the faithful who complained to a friend of God about the corruption of the times. The friend replied, "What business have you with God's servants? Do not interfere between the Master and His slave! Mercy, forgiveness, and beneficence are seeking them [sinners]. Do you desire that the properties of the Divinity should remain ineffectual? Busy yourself with yourself and pay no heed to such things!" (II 177.11).

The Marks of Belief

Revelation is a self-delimitation of nondelimited *wujūd* with a view toward human perfection and felicity. To reject the possibility of attaining to the perfection of the human state is to delay the arrival of felicity for an unimaginably long period of time, if not "forever." To accept the possibility of reaching perfection is to acknowledge the truth brought by revelation and to commit oneself to its demands (*īmān* or "faith") and to put this commitment into practice (*islām* or "submission"). To the extent that individuals weigh their thoughts and actions in the scales provided by the prophets, they will be led to the actualization of the potentialities of human nature, which are determined and defined by the full range of the divine attributes, latent within their *fiṭra* by virtue of their having been created in God's form.

The degree to which conformity to the prophetic scales will be actualized depends to a large degree upon belief, the knotting of cognitive reality that people experience through their existence in this world. To the extent that people believe in God as He is in Himself, they will be led to the precedent mercy that is pure and nondelimited *wujūd*. When belief conforms to the instructions given by the prophets, the divine names that define the object of belief will be those of guidance and mercy. Hence the belief will draw believers in the direction of unity, harmony, and equilibrium. But if believers reject the proffered guidance and instead follow the myriad paths set down by the Misguider, the divine names ruling over the situation will be names of wrath that result in disequilibrium, dispersion, disintegration, and wretchedness.

Perfect human beings are transparent before every self-disclosure of *wujūd*. In contrast, all other created things have delimited capacities that impose upon *wujūd* specific knottings and colorings that result in distinct beliefs. All beliefs demand delimited and defined standpoints, and these exclude other standpoints. To the extent that people cling to their beliefs, they cause conflict with the beliefs of others. This is especially obvious in the modern world, where beliefs about the nature of things that were once shared by most people have gradually been undermined, giving rise to radically diverse personal and political beliefs that are constantly causing conflict on every level of society.

Delimited beliefs rise up out of the limited degree to which people have actualized their own *fiṭra*, and this in turn goes back to the capacity or preparedness of the immutable entity, known eternally by God. Individual preparedness allows people to be receptive toward the properties of *wujūd*'s names to a certain specific degree, no more and no less. Just as preparedness delimits *wujūd*, so also it delimits knowledge. Preparedness allows people to understand what they understand. Hence all knowledge is constricted by the subject, which is to say that within the infinite possible configurations of *wujūd*, the subject knows only itself: "You judge your object of knowledge only in terms of yourself. Hence you know only yourself" (III 161.25).

If people know only themselves, they also believe only in themselves, for their beliefs are determined and defined by their own conceptual limitations. When they gaze upon existence, they constrict and construe it in their own individual terms. "Neither your heart nor your eye ever witnesses anything but the form of your own belief concerning God" (*Fuṣūṣ* 121). Or, more succinctly, "No one has ever seen anything except his own belief" (III 132.29). As a result, people devote themselves to nothing but their own fabrications. "The creatures are bound to worship only what they believe about the Real, so they worship nothing but a created thing. . . . There are none but idol-worshipers" (IV 386.17).

In a chapter in which he discusses the significance of the Koranic prayer, *I entrust my affair to God* (40:44), Ibn al-'Arabī points out that the ability of human beings to entrust their affairs to others grows up out of a divine attribute, and that attribute is God's entrusting His affair to the creatures when He "makes religious prescriptions for them and He commands them and prohibits them." Moreover, God entrusts to the creatures the ability to understand something about Him and to speak about what they understand. He lets them speak of *wujūd* in accordance with their own capacities. On the human level, the diversity of creaturely voices appears in the diversity of utterances (*maqālāt*) about *wujūd*, the doctrines posited by the myriad groups of thinkers and believers of every type.

> God entrusts His affair to them in speech. Hence their utterances about Him become diverse. Then God explains to them His actual situation on the tongue of His messengers so that He will have an argument against those who contradict His speech and who say about Him things that oppose what He has said about Himself. Once the utterances are diverse, He discloses Himself to the possessor of each utterance in accordance with or in the form of his utterance. The reason for this is that He has entrusted His affair to them, for He has bestowed upon them rational faculties and powers of reflection. (IV 100.8)

God assumes the form of every belief because the belief itself is nothing but the self-disclosure of *wujūd*. People create the objects of their own belief by imposing conceptual limitations upon *wujūd*. "God receives the form of every belief. Were this not so, He would not be a god. When a listener hears the divine report that God exists, he has faith in it in accordance with his own conception. Hence he only has faith in that to which he has given conceptual form. God exists within every conceptualization, just as He exists in the exact contrary of that conceptualization" (IV 133.30).

The God in which everyone has faith is *wujūd* as it discloses itself to each individual. Since each self-disclosure of God is unique, each belief is unique. And since the object of each belief is unique, the lord that is worshiped by each individual differs from the lord of every other individual. This helps explain one of the meanings of the famous prophetic saying, "He who knows himself knows His Lord." By knowing oneself, one comes to know God as He discloses Himself within oneself. It is the self-disclosing God—not the independent Essence, *wujūd* in itself—which determines belief, or rather, which corresponds to the capacity of the individual for understanding, a capacity that in turn is determined by the individual's immutable entity. "Since you do not know Him except through yourself, your knowledge of Him necessarily depends upon your knowledge of yourself. So your existence depends upon His *wujūd*, while knowledge of His lordship over you depends upon knowledge of yourself. So He possesses the root in *wujūd*, and your property is that of the branch in *wujūd*. But you are the root in knowledge of Him, and He has the property of the branch in knowledge" (III 495.10).

To say that the creature is a branch of *wujūd* but the root of knowledge is to say that human knowledge of God is determined by human capacity to know Him. "God discloses Himself to the created thing only in the form of the created thing" (IV 110.7). That divine self-disclosure is the person's Lord, because it determines his destiny in this world and in every world to come, for all eternity. It is also the "mark" that people will recognize on the day of resurrection, for, as noted already, a hadith tells us that God will disclose Himself to the people gathered at the resurrection in a series of forms. They will continue to deny Him until He shows them a mark that they will recognize. That mark is their belief concerning their Lord.

> Every believer has a Lord in his heart that he has brought into existence, so he believes in Him. Such are the People of the Mark on the day of resurrection. They worship nothing but what they themselves have carved.[7] That is why, when God discloses Himself in other than that mark, they are confounded. They know what they believe, but what they believe does not know them, for they have brought it into existence. The general rule here is that the artifact does not know the artisan, and the building does not know the builder. (IV 391.12)

> The divine effusion is vast, because He is vast in bestowal. There is no shortcoming on His part. But you have nothing of Him except what your essence accepts. Hence your own essence keeps the Vast away from you and places you in the midst of constraint. The measure in which His governance occurs within you is your "Lord." It is He that you serve and He alone that you recognize. This is the mark within which He will transmute Himself to you on the day of resurrection, by unveiling Himself. In this world, this mark is unseen for most people. Every human being knows it from himself, but he does not know that it is what he knows. (IV 62.23)

What distinguishes perfect human beings from others is that they recognize God in every self-disclosure. They have imposed no limits upon God that would lead them to deny some self-disclosures and acknowledge others.

Nondelimited Belief

In Himself, God cannot be constrained by any belief. He is able to assume the form of every belief precisely because He is incomparable with every belief. He is "far exalted above entering under delimitation or being tied down to one form rather than another" (II 85.21). Adequate knowledge of God as He is in Himself demands seeing Him as disclosed in every belief and nondelimited by belief. As a result, the "gnostics" (*'ārifūn*)—those perfect human beings who have perfected their knowledge of God's self-disclosures in the universe and in themselves—recognize the truth of every belief and understand that every tying, every knotting, every restriction, is a delimitation of nondelimited *wujūd*. Standing in the Station of No Station, they acknowledge the rights of every station and every belief, for each corresponds to one of the infinitely variegated self-disclosures of God. In effect, the gnostics recognize that the whole of existence represents the dance of possibilities, the self-manifestation of the Nondelimited in the forms of the endless multitudes of delimited entities. Each thing is exactly what it must be; every belief demonstrates the scope of the believer's preparedness at the moment of belief. All things walk on the Path of God. Everything obeys the engendering command, and each person possesses a belief that will take him or her to God, the end of all paths.

Belief, as knotting, delimits the object of belief and thereby restricts the share of the believer in the vision of *wujūd*. From this point of view, all beliefs are false. Nevertheless, each belief corresponds to a divine self-disclosure. Since God's mercy is all-inclusive, He accepts all beliefs. Every god worshiped by every believer will eventually bring about the believer's felicity, even if this demands being veiled from God. "Were it not for His self-disclosure in the forms of the gods, no happy souls would take pleasure in Him" (IV

332.11). In discussing "the diversity of beliefs concerning God, whether among the people of divinely revealed religions or others," the Shaykh writes,

> If God were to take people to account for error, He would take every possessor of a belief to account. Every believer has delimited his Lord with his reason and consideration and has thereby restricted Him. But nothing is worthy of God except nondelimitation. *In His hand is the dominion of each thing* [23:88], so He delimits, but He does not become delimited. Nevertheless, God pardons everyone.
>
> When God wants someone to attain the truth and give it its full due, He bestows upon him knowledge of His breadth and vastness and that He is witnessed in the belief of every believer. He cannot be absent from the belief of the believer, for He has bound the belief to him, and *He is witness over everything* [22:17]. Hence the possessor of this knowledge sees God constantly in every form and does not deny Him when the delimiters deny Him. Nevertheless, God pardons all the leaders of religion who delimit Him with incomparability or similarity. (III 309.30)

Self-disclosure never repeats itself. Every moment of existence represents a new self-disclosure and a new knotting. The divine attribute of freedom allows people to have a certain effect upon their own preparedness for knowledge and hence on their reception of the divine showings. Hence the Shaykh encourages seekers to expand their own beliefs in order to have a greater "share" (*ḥaẓẓ*) in the vision of the Real in the next world. For, he says, "Vision [of the Real] in the next world follows upon beliefs in this world" (II 85.1).[8]

Each divine attribute in the human form can be compared to one of the colors of the rainbow. Each human individual embraces the whole visible and invisible spectrum, since each is created in the form of all the divine attributes. By having specific identities at this time and that place, individuals manifest certain hues rather than others and have little control over their situations. But they are free to select many of the colors that they bring into manifestation; by choosing to do one thing rather than another, they accept responsibility for the color that will display itself. Within the parameters of their own possibilities, they can choose to move toward pure Light, which is free of color's limitations while embracing all its perfections; or they can aim at one specific color rather than another.

For the Shaykh, beliefs are so many colors that people impose upon colorless light by their own delimited existences. To the extent that freedom is involved in what they believe, their beliefs are so many colored eyeglasses that they choose to wear. The color they set their hearts upon—the knots they tie in their souls—determines their share of *wujūd* and of actualized *fiṭra*. Choosing delimitation fixes their situation within the configuration of reality, both epistemologically and ontologically, and therefore also eschatologically.

But choosing nondelimitation opens them up to the Real.

Having actualized the Station of No Station, perfect human beings recognize that all beliefs are true and all lead to God. Through experiencing the unveiling of the divine self-disclosures, they understand the legitimacy of every belief and the wisdom behind every knot tied in the fabric of Reality, every possibility of ontological and epistemological delimitation represented by human subjects. By accepting each knot for what it is, they learn what it has to teach, and by not allowing themselves to be limited and defined by it, they allow for the untying of every knot. Only by standing in all stations of human possibility and not being defined by any of them can they achieve the Station of No Station. Then they know concretely the implications of every divine name. They recognize what each demands in the cosmos and among human beings, because they find it in themselves.

> The People of Unveiling have been given an all-inclusive overview of all religions, creeds, sects, and doctrines concerning God. They are not ignorant of any of these. Adherents follow creeds, sects conform to specific laws, and doctrines are held concerning God or something in the engendered universe. Some of these contradict, some diverge, and some are similar. In every case the Possessor of Unveiling knows from where the doctrine, the creed, or the sect is taken, and he ascribes it to its place. He offers an excuse for everyone who holds a doctrine and does not declare him in error. He does not consider the doctrine to be vain, for God *did not create the heaven and the earth and what is between them for unreality* [38:27] and He did not create the human being *in vain* [23:115]. On the contrary, He created him alone to be in His form.
>
> Hence everyone in engendered existence is ignorant of the whole and knows the part, except only the perfect human being. For God *taught him the names, all of them* [2:31] and gave him the all-comprehensive words, and thereby his form became perfect. So the perfect human being brings together the form of the Real and the form of the cosmos. He is a *barzakh* between the Real and the cosmos. He is a mirror that God has set up, within which the Real sees His form and creation sees its form. He who actualizes this level has actualized a level of perfection more perfect than which nothing is found in possible existence. The form of the Real is seen within him because all the divine names are ascribed to him. (III 398.11)

Since perfect human beings understand the truth and legitimacy of every belief, they do not deny any of God's self-disclosures in the next world. Embracing every possibility of manifestation found in *wujūd*, they coincide with the whole cosmos. In contrast, those who have not reached perfection embrace only a limited portion of cosmic possibility, so they will recognize God at the resurrection only when He conforms Himself to their limitations.

> The perfect human being witnesses God in the manifest domain inasmuch as He is in the cosmos, and he witnesses Him in the nonmanifest domain inasmuch as He is concealed. Hence the perfect human being's vision is diverse, though God's Entity is one.
>
> This is why some people will deny Him on the resurrection when He discloses Himself, whereas the perfect human being will not deny Him. Not every human being has achieved perfection. He will be denied only by the animal human being, because he is a part of the cosmos. When He discloses Himself to the animal human being in the mark and undergoes transmutation within it, then he will recognize Him, because he recognizes Him only as delimited. (IV 246.12)

The understanding of perfect human beings that all beliefs are true is intimately connected to their vision with the "eye of the heart" that all existent things are controlled by the engendering command. In no way does their acceptance of all beliefs negate their acknowledgment that everyone is called to follow the prescriptive command, which sets down the immediate path to felicity. This is why Ibn al-ʿArabī writes, "It is incumbent upon you to practice the worship of God brought by the Shariah and tradition [*al-samʿ*]" (III 311.23). He explains that the person who sees things as they truly are "travels on the path of felicity that is not preceded by any wretchedness, for this path is easy, bright, exemplary, pure, unstained, and without any crookedness or deviation. As for the other path, its final outcome is felicity, but along the way are found deserts, perils, vicious predators, and harmful serpents. Hence no created thing reaches the end of this second path without suffering those terrors" (III 418.12).

In short, perfect human beings accept the truth of every belief, yet they walk on the Path of the Blessing-giver, or more specifically, the Path of Muhammad, since these paths provide the means to integration and unity, or a fuller share of the vision of God. They "believe" in all religions and all constructions of the human mind, but they have "faith" only in God as He has revealed Himself to humankind through a particular prophet. Hence their practice is based upon prophetic practice, and more specifically, on the practice of Muhammad, whose way is viewed as embracing the ways of all prophets.

The Circle of Religious Diversity

To bring this chapter to a close, I quote a section of the *Futūḥāt* that deals with the ontological roots of religious diversity. Ibn al-ʿArabī is commenting on the various Koranic verses that affirm that God has sent a great number of prophets and established many ways to return to Him. He understands this to mean that just as *wujūd* never repeats itself in its cosmic self-disclosure, so also it never repeats itself when it sets down ways of guidance. The revealed religions are diverse because they cannot possibly not be diverse. They all point to a single *wujūd*, but each is a providential specification of that *wujūd* with a view toward human felicity.

For the Shaykh, the mercy that takes precedence over wrath demands both religious diversity and human felicity through that diversity. Since human dispositions are diverse, divine dispensations must also be diverse to take into account the diversity of these dispositions. In the introduction a passage was quoted in which the Shaykh says that God "has brought about the existence of everything in the cosmos in a constitution not possessed by anything else," and as a result, "everyone will end up with mercy." No attempt was made there to explain this view of things. By now it should be clear what the Shaykh has in mind, and the following passage will help make it doubly clear. But perhaps one more quotation that illustrates the Shaykh's way of thinking on these matters is not out of order. He is in the process of explaining a general principle: When someone makes a claim, he has to support himself with a clear proof. This principle applies to God's messengers just as much as it applies to other human beings. If God does not provide a given messenger with proofs strong enough to convince everyone, this means that many who deny the messengers will suffer no punishment as a result. They will be punished only if they are convinced by the proof, but then, out of obstinacy or spite or envy or some other blameworthy character trait, they refuse to accept the message. Thus, when God says, *We never chastise, until We send forth a messenger* (17:15), this means that those who do not have the capacity or the opportunity to understand the message will not be punished for ignoring it. For Ibn al-'Arabī this is yet another indication of God's grand mercy to His servants. His text is as follows:

> God says, *We never chastise, until We send forth a messenger.* Note that He did not say, "until We send forth a person." Hence the *message* of the one who is sent must be established for the one to whom it is directed. There must be clear and manifest proofs established for each person to whom the messenger is sent, for many a sign [*āya*] has within it obscurity or equivocality such that some people do not perceive what it proves. The clarity of the proof must be such that it establishes the person's messengerhood for each person to whom he is sent. Only then, if the person refuses it, will he be taken to account. Hence, this verse has within it a tremendous mercy, because of the diversity of human dispositions that lead to a diversity of views. He who knows the all-inclusiveness of the divine mercy,

which, God reports, *embraces all things* [7:156], knows that God did this only because of mercy toward His servants. (III 469.25)

The Shaykh calls Chapter 48 of the *Futūḥāt* "On the True Knowledge of 'This came to be only because of that,' or, The Affirmation of Causes and Occasions." At the end of the chapter, he provides the accompanying diagram as an example of one sort of causality. Elsewhere he remarks that he employs diagrams "so that the possessor of imagination may gain nearness to knowledge, since, despite his rational faculty, the human being never departs from his imaginal faculty" (III 398.24). In what follows, I translate the Shaykh's explanations of the diagram's captions.

Note that the term *divine relationships* is roughly synonymous with *divine names. Abrogation* as employed here refers to a prophet's replacing the ruling of a preexistent revealed law with a new ruling. For example, wine is permissible in the law revealed to Christ, but forbidden in the Shariah revealed to Muhammad.

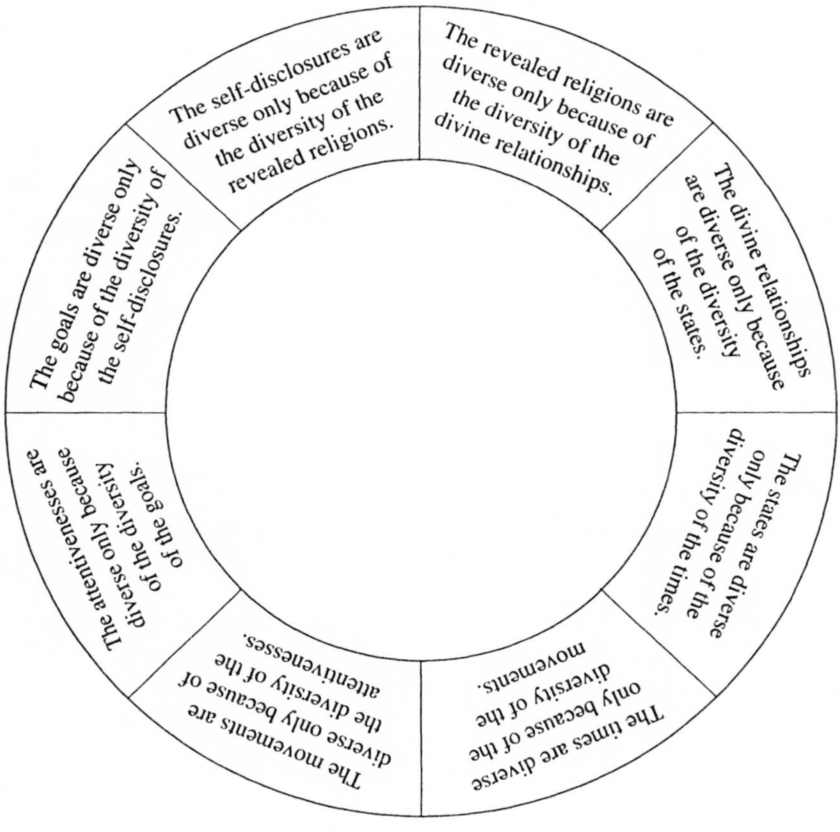

The revealed religions are diverse only because of the diversity of the divine relationships.

If the divine relationship demanded that a particular thing be lawful in the revealed law, or if the relationship demanded that something be forbidden, then divine rulings could not change, but it is established that rulings do change. And if divine rulings could not change, then God's words would be incorrect: *To every one of you [messengers] We have appointed a right way and a revealed law* [5:48]. But every community does in fact have a right way and a revealed law brought to it by its prophet and messenger. So abrogation [of rulings] does take place.

We know for certain that God's relationship to Muhammad in what He revealed to him as religion is different from His relationship to any other prophet. Were this not so and were the relationship one in every respect—that is, the relationship that demands revelation of the specific law—then the revealed religions would be one in every respect.

If you ask: Why then are the divine relationships diverse? We will reply,

The divine relationships are diverse only because of the diversity of the states.

One person has the state of illness. He calls out, "O Cure-giver, O Healer!" Another is hungry and calls out, "O Provider!" Still another is drowning and calls out, "O Helper!" Hence the relationships are diverse because of the diversity of the states. This is indicated by God's words, *Each day He is upon some task. . . . We shall attend to you at leisure, O mankind and jinn!* [55:29-31].[9] It is also indicated by the Prophet's words while describing his Lord with the scales in His hand: "He lets down and lifts up." Because of the state of the Scales, God is called "Uplifter" and "Downletter." In the same way these various relationships become manifest in the diversity of the states of the creatures.

The states are diverse only because of the diversity of the times.

The cause of the diverse states of the creatures is the diverse times in which they dwell. Their state in the time of spring differs from their state in the time of summer, their state in the time of summer differs from their state in the time of autumn, their state in the time of autumn differs from their state in the time of winter, and their state in the time of winter differs from their state in the time of spring.

One of those who is learned in the way in which the times act upon natural bodies says that you should expose yourself to the air in the time of spring, because it does to your bodies what it does to your trees. And you should protect yourselves from the air of winter, because it also does to your bodies what it does to your trees. And God has stated explicitly that we are among the growing things of the earth, for He says, *God has made you grow out of the earth as growing things* [71:17]. . . .

The times are diverse only because of the diversity of the movements.

I mean by *movements* the movements of the celestial spheres, for these movements give rise to night and day and delineate the years, months, and seasons. All this is what is known as the "times."

The movements are diverse only because of the diversity of the attentivenesses.

I mean by *attentivenesses* God's turning His attention toward the movements to bring them into existence. God says, *Our only speech to a thing, when We desire it, [is to say to it "Be!" and it is]* [16:40]. If the attentiveness toward the movements were single, the movements would not become diverse, but they are diverse. This proves that the attentiveness that moves the moon in its sphere is different from that which moves the sun in its sphere or those which move the other planets and spheres. Were this not the case, the speed or slowness of all of them would be the same. God says, *Each of them floats in a sphere* [21:33]. Each movement has a divine attentiveness, that is, a specific divine connection to it in respect of the fact that He is the Desiring.

The attentivenesses are diverse only because of the diversity of the goals.

If the goal of the attentiveness that causes the moon's movement were the same as the goal of that which causes the sun's movement, no effect would become distinct from any other effect. But the effects are diverse, without doubt. Hence the attentivenesses are diverse because of the difference in goals. Thus God's attentiveness with good pleasure toward Zayd is different from His attentiveness with wrath toward 'Amr, for His goal is to chastise 'Amr and to give bliss to Zayd. So the goals are diverse.

The goals are diverse only because of the diversity of the self-disclosures.

Were God's self-disclosures one in every respect, He could have no more than a single goal. But the diversity of goals has been established, so every specific goal must have a specific self-disclosure that is different from every other self-disclosure. For the divine Vastness demands that nothing be repeated in existence. It is this fact upon which a group of the Sufis depend, even though *The people are in confusion as to a new creation* [50:15]. Shaykh Abū Ṭālib al-Makkī, author of *Heart's Food*, and other men of God have said, "God never discloses Himself in a single form to two individuals, nor in a single form twice." That is why effects are diverse in the cosmos. These have been alluded to as "good pleasure" and "wrath."

The self-disclosures are diverse only because of the diversity of the revealed religions.

Each revealed religion is a path that takes to God, and these paths are diverse. Hence the self-disclosures must be diverse, just as divine gifts are diverse. Do you not see what happens when He discloses Himself to this community at the resurrection, while within it are hypocrites? Moreover, people's views of the revealed law are diverse. Each possessor of independent judgment [*mujtahid*] has his own specific law that is a path to God. That is why the schools of law are diverse, even though each is revealed law, within a single revealed religion. And God has established this for us on the tongue of His messenger.

So the self-disclosures are diverse, without doubt. Each group has believed something concerning God. If God discloses Himself to them in other than that something, they will deny Him. But when He discloses Himself in the mark that they have established for God in themselves, they will acknowledge Him. Thus, for example, when God discloses Himself to the Ash'arite in the form of the belief of his opponent, whose knotting concerning God is opposed to his, or, when He manifests Himself to his opponent in the form of the Ash'arite's belief, each of the two groups will deny Him.[10] And so it is with all groups.

Then, when God discloses Himself to each group in keeping with the form of their belief concerning Him—and that is the "mark" mentioned by Muslim in his *Ṣaḥīḥ*, quoting from the Prophet—then they will acknowledge that He is their Lord. But He is He, none other than He, so the self-disclosures are diverse because of the diversity of the revealed religions.

As for our words, "The revealed religions are diverse only because of the diversity of divine relationships," that has already been discussed. Thus the circle is closed (I 265-266).

10

The Divine Roots of Religion

Islamic thought begins with what can be known for certain. This can only be the reality of God, as expressed in the first Shahadah: "There is no god but God." In general, this certainty is seen as outweighing every other consideration, not least the claims of the ego to objective knowledge. Only the Real is clear and sure. Everything else is vague, opaque, and unreal.

Like most other Muslim thinkers, Ibn al-'Arabī considers the first Shahadah a self-evident principle of universal validity. In contrast, the second Shahadah, "Muhammad is the Messenger of God," pertains to the domain of teachings specific to Islam, and hence it needs to be discussed with reference to a specific historical context.

As a truth universally recognizable and always available to human experience, the first Shahadah is considered the fundamental message of the 124,000 prophets from Adam down to Muhammad. In other words, it pertains to the very substance of what it means to be human. Its recognition and acceptance can be said to belong to the human *fiṭra.* In terms of the first Shahadah, the function of the prophets is simply to "remind" (*dhikr*) people of what they already know. Teachings specific to each prophet belong to a realm analogous to that announced by the second Shahadah.

The first Shahadah teaches that all divine attributes belong in an absolute and unmixed sense to God alone, who is true *wujūd.* Like other divine attributes, knowledge cannot be found in pure form outside the Real. Hence human knowledge is always imperfect, especially human knowledge about God. "None knows God but God." Human beings can and do have knowledge of God, but only to the extent that He chooses to reveal Himself. *They encompass nothing of His knowledge save such as He wills* (2:254). The initiative always pertains to the side of the Real.

Human knowledge of the Real takes the two basic forms of declaring incomparability and asserting similarity. God is incomparable inasmuch as He is totally different from all things and similar inasmuch as He discloses Himself through the cosmos and makes Himself known through lesser realities. Everything in the universe—all God's signs—say something about the qualities of the Real through their modes of existence. To look at God in respect of either incomparability or similarity is misleading and incomplete; accurate knowledge of the Real demands that God be declared both incomparable and similar at one and the same time.

Gods of Belief

Ibn al-'Arabī employs many arguments and analogies to bring home the implications of the first Shahadah for understanding the nature of *wujūd*. As we have seen, one of his basic points is that everything other than real *wujūd* is neither completely real nor completely unreal. Rather, all things stand in an intermediate domain, a *barzakh* or isthmus. The universal isthmus or Supreme Barzakh is the whole cosmos; on one side stands the ocean of the Real, utterly unknowable in itself. On the other stands the ocean of nonexistence, also unknowable, because there is nothing to be known. In between is found everything that can be known or experienced, the whole cosmos in all its unimaginable temporal and spatial expanse. And just as the cosmos in its entirety is a *barzakh*, so also each thing and each event is a *barzakh* between other things and other events. Everything in the universe is "imagination"—God and not-God, real and unreal, existent and nonexistent, itself and not itself, He/not He, it/not it.

Since everything is a *barzakh*, there are no completely distinct and discrete qualities or things; all are ambiguous. The exact status of things is always open to question. Inasmuch as the Real is incomparable with everything else, He is the one and only reality, so things have no reality and do not truly exist. Inasmuch as the Real is similar to all things, His attributes and reality are present within them. Without the presence of the Real in things, they could not be found. There would be no life, knowledge, power, or desire—no reality, no existence, no cosmos.

Every created thing is a self-disclosure of the Real, but never the Real Himself, who remains forever incomparable, inexpressible, undisclosed, and nondelimited. Delimitation is a characteristic of the creatures, or the letters and words articulated within the All-merciful Breath. The limitations of things separate them out from nondelimited and absolute reality. When the Real discloses His qualities, the act of disclosure delimits and defines what is disclosed; when God speaks, He articulates His nondelimited awareness.

From a slightly different point of view, we can say that the divine self-disclosure is colored by the receptacle. As the famous ninth-century Sufi Junayd put it, "The water takes on the color of the cup." Rūmī asks, "If you pour the ocean into a jug, how much will it hold?" Ibn al-'Arabī makes the point repeatedly in all sorts of formulations. For example,

> The Real becomes manifest to His servants in the measure of their knowledge of Him. (III 215.32)

> The servant sees nothing of the Real save his own form. (III 254.21)

> The human being—whoever he may be—is not able to go beyond knowledge of himself in his knowledge of the other. (III 274.1)

> You are the one who becomes manifest to yourself, and this gives you nothing of Him. . . . You do not know other than yourself. (IV 421.34)

The domains of ontology and epistemology are inseparable. Reality is experienced by knowers, and knowledge is supported by reality. And just as experienced reality is utterly ambiguous, at once real and unreal, so also perceptions and understandings of things are always marked by uncertainty and intermediateness. The Shaykh frequently refers to this underlying indefiniteness of knowledge by pointing out that people give meaning and orientation to their lives in terms of gods that they themselves create through their own beliefs. The gods of belief, like all other experienced reality, dwell in the domain of He/not He. Inasmuch as they are He, they designate God, but inasmuch as they are Not He, they designate a diversity of perspectives and views.

> Although the Real is One, beliefs present Him in various guises. They take Him apart and put Him together, they give Him form and they fabricate Him. But in Himself, He does not change, and in Himself, He does not undergo transmutation. However, the organ of sight sees Him so. Hence location constricts Him, and fluctuation from entity to entity limits Him. Hence, none becomes bewildered by Him except the discerning, and no one understands this admonition except him who combines the assertion of similarity with the declaration of incomparability. (IV 393.6)

Everything experiences the Real's self-disclosures. In the last analysis, these self-disclosures define the modes in which things exist and know. Hence a person's experience of reality is constrained and confined by God's self-revelation. The points of reference around which people build their lives are determined by their limited experience of the Real. As noted in the previous chapter, people's imperfect understanding of things is called *i'tiqād*, a word that means literally "to tie a knot" but which is the standard theological term for "belief." People have diverse beliefs because each person represents a distinct knotting of nondelimited Reality. This subjective knotting is the mirror image of the objective reality embodied within and experienced by the knower. "God is known through every knotting. Although the beliefs are totally diverse, their aim is one. He is a receptacle for everything that you tie Him to and every knotting you make concerning Him. And within that He will disclose Himself on the day of resurrection, for it is the mark which is between you and Him" (IV 416.29).

Each self-disclosure of the Real ties a knot in the fabric of existence, distinct from every other knot. Each articulates a word in the Breath of the All-merciful, distinct from every other word. Every human being represents a unique knot or word, a unique self-disclosure and belief. It is true that beliefs, like things in general, tend to be similar and can be put into categories. Nevertheless, no two individuals have exactly the same belief, for each individual represents a self-disclosure of reality that can never be repeated.

Both the universe and human individuals live in constant change. The axiom "Self-disclosure never repeats itself" applies both to the spatial and to the temporal configuration of reality. At each instant the Real renews the self-disclosure that is the universe, which is to say that at each moment all knots are undone and then retied. Human beings, however, do not play a totally passive role. Given the presence within them of a certain freedom because of a special relationship with the Real, they can exert an effect upon the direction of their changing beliefs. Every bodily and cognitive act paves the way for changing perceptions of reality, changing beliefs, and transformation of the soul.

Each human being follows the authority of his or her own belief, and this gives rise to an indefinite variety of often contradictory gods. "The god of each believer is constricted by his proofs" (IV 435.11). But this does not imply that these gods are false. People worship what they understand as real, and this understanding is rooted in both the self-manifesting Real and the degree to which a person experiences the Real. "The doctrines are diverse because of the diversity of the views of those who view Him. Every viewer worships and believes only what he himself has brought into existence in his own heart. He brings into existence in his heart nothing but a created thing. That is not the Real God. Yet in that doctrinal form He discloses Himself to him" (IV 211.30).

In the last analysis, the God who is worshiped is none other than a manifestation of the divine mercy that takes precedence over wrath, and hence the innate human ignorance of God becomes an excuse that people can offer to God on the day of resurrection, an excuse rooted in God's own mercy. After explaining that the people of the Fire will eventually end up in mercy, Ibn al-ʻArabī writes,

> God's mercy takes precedence over His wrath, and the ruling property belongs to God. As for everything other than God, that is a fabrication. The gods of beliefs are fabricated. Absolutely no one worships God as He is in Himself. Everyone worships Him inasmuch as He has been fabricated within the worshiper's self. So understand this secret! It is extremely subtle. Through it God establishes the excuses of His servants, those concerning whom He says, *They have not measured God with His true measure* [6:91]. Thus all people—both those who declare His incomparability and those who do not—share in this fabrication. Everyone who has a knotting concerning God has a fabrication. (IV 229.12)

Everyone serves God on the basis of God's self-disclosures, so all beliefs are rooted in reality and all are true. However, all beliefs do not have the same effect on human becoming, and this provides an important criterion for discerning among them.

Rational Investigation

God is similar inasmuch as He discloses Himself through the articulations of the Breath of the All-merciful. From the point of view of human subjectivity, God's similarity is perceived through the faculty of imagination. To speak of similarity is to speak of imagination as both the objective configuration of reality and the subjective perception of reality. Objectively, imagination refers to the intermediate status of all things; subjectively, it refers to the perception of the images or intermediate forms that make up the cosmos, images and forms that are words articulated within the All-merciful Breath.

Human understanding has a second, complementary dimension known as reason (*'aql*). The rational faculty has the (relative) ability to see beyond images.[1] If imagination's proper function is to recognize the Real within the images of Its self-disclosure, reason's function is to recognize that the images can never be the Real. As the Shaykh frequently reminds us, reason knows innately that *Nothing is like Him* (42:11).

Language about the Real tends in two fundamental directions that coincide with incomparability and similarity, or reason and imagination. As the Shaykh puts it, "Through reason one knows but does not see, while through unveiling one sees but does not know" (IV 411.14). Rational, discursive language predominates in intellectual disciplines such as theology and philosophy, while visionary language predominates in myth and expressions of unveiling. Theology and philosophy tend to negate qualities from the Real and differentiate Him from experienced reality, thereby asserting His incomparability. Myth and unveiling tend to present us with positive knowledge of the Real's qualities, thereby asserting His similarity. As for revelation, it combines the two perspectives: "Reason has nothing but the attribute of incomparability, while transmitted knowledge [i.e., that provided by revelation] has the like of that along with the attribute of similarity" (IV 357.24).

In combining the two perspectives of incomparability and similarity, revelation provides knowledge closest to the truth of God. For both reason and imagination delimit God, the one by making Him incomparable and the other by making Him similar. But in fact, God is neither incomparable nor similar. It is precisely His nondelimitation by any attributes that allows Him to be perceived in both modes.

> The most difficult knowledge of God is the affirmation of nondelimitation in knowing Him, but not in the respect that He is a God. In respect of the fact that He is an Essence, or in respect of Himself, nondelimitation concerning Him consists of the incapacity to know Him. He is neither known, nor unknown; rather, He makes incapable.
>
> In respect of the fact that He is a God, the most beautiful names delimit Him, and the level [of Divinity] delimits Him. The meaning of "delimiting Him" is the demand that the object over which He is a God [*ma'lūh*][2] demands the incomparability that is worthy of Him, but incomparability is a delimitation.
>
> Knowledge of Him in respect of the fact that He is a God is established by revealed religion and by reason. Concerning Him reason asserts incomparability specifically, and thereby it delimits Him by it. Revealed religion declares both His incomparability and His similarity. Hence revealed religion is closer than reason to asserting God's nondelimitation. (IV 423.11)

Ibn al-'Arabī's distinctions among the types of knowledge acquired by reason and imagination provide a scheme whereby it is possible to discern between different ontic and epistemic stresses found in the nature of things. It should not be supposed that he means to draw sharp lines differentiating one side from the other. All things are *barzakhs*. Language cannot express the perspective of incomparability without some input from similarity, and vice versa. Imagination never functions in total isolation from reason, nor can reason work without some help from imagination. What differentiates the Shaykh in these discussions from most other Muslim authorities is his constant awareness of the creative tension between incomparability and similarity, or reason and unveiling, and his assertion that real understanding of the Real demands a delicate balance between the two. The fact that he insists that revealed religion in general and the Shariah in particular provide the only fully reliable source of the proper balance between reason and imagination places him squarely in the mainstream of Islamic thought.

Names and Knottings

For Ibn al-'Arabī, as for most other Muslim theologians, each name of God expresses the Real, and each expression is different from every other expression. From the viewpoint of the Real's similarity, differentiation among the names pertains to the Real's self-disclosures in the cosmos: Each name designates a specific cosmic quality different from every other quality; each is a *barzakh* between the Real and the cosmos. From the standpoint of incomparability, the Real is utterly beyond differentiation; every name designates the same incomparable and unknowable Reality.[3]

The divine names designate what might be called "universal knottings" within Reality itself. Each refers to a specific divine attribute that reverberates throughout the cosmos, different from every other attribute. Each attribute has specific implications for the things within which it becomes manifest as well as for our understanding of the things, since each designates a relationship in terms of which the connection between the absolutely Real and the relatively real can be grasped (in a relative way, of course).

To look at reality from the position of incomparability is to stress that everything in the cosmos dwells in distance, separation, and otherness from the Real. God is transcendent, far, inaccessible, magnificent, majestic, severe, wrathful. He is an aloof king who does not deign to look upon the petty affairs of creatures made out of dust, a strict and authoritarian father who issues commandments and expects to be obeyed.

To look at reality from the standpoint of similarity is to stress that all things participate in nearness, union, and sameness. God is present, near, loving, forgiving, beautiful, gentle, merciful. He is a concerned and caring mother who desires to help the creatures in every possible way. Incomparability demands distance, inaccessibility, and estrangement, while similarity demands nearness, accessibility, and mutual love. Ultimately the divine nearness means sameness—human reality, inasmuch as it is real, can only be the self-disclosure of the divine Reality. The human *fiṭra* is *wujūd*. "Not He" is constantly undergoing annihilation and "He" subsists.

To dwell in otherness is to live in distance, multiplicity, difference, dispersion, separation, discreteness, disequilibrium, instability, unreality, and suffering. To dwell in sameness is to live in nearness, unity, union, equilibrium, balance, permanence, reality, and joy. The latter qualities pertain to the fundamental nature of the Real, while the former pertain to the cosmos inasmuch as it is distinct from the Real.

Asserting God's incomparability grows up from the perception of difference and unreality, while asserting His similarity grows up from perceiving sameness and reality. In terms of the Real, similarity takes precedence, because, from the Real's standpoint, there are no "others," there is no "distance"—*God is with you wherever you are* (57:4). But, as the Shaykh likes to remind us, this does not mean that we are with God wherever He is. Nevertheless, if Islamic teachings tend to stress incomparability (the otherness that we experience now), the purpose of these teachings is to establish similarity (the sameness from which we arose and to which we will return).

Mythically, the priority of similarity and nearness over incomparability and distance is commonly expressed by citing the hadith of God's precedent mercy. This hadith indicates that attributes like wrath, severity, majesty, justice, and distance serve the purposes of the more fundamental attributes, which are mercy, gentleness, beauty, bounty, and nearness.

The precedence of mercy over wrath has clear implications for human understanding. Imagination perceives the Real's similarity, while reason grasps His incomparability. Hence imagination erases difference and unites, while reason discerns and separates. When people are left to their rational faculties, they tend to separate the Real from the cosmos and themselves. This leads to a loss of the vision of the divine presence in all things. To the extent that they stress incomparability, they abstract the Real from His manifestations and perceive reality as disjointed and disconnected. In contrast, imagination allows them to establish links and overcome difference. However, excessive stress upon similarity leads to an identification of the Real with His manifestations and a loss of the vision of unity, centrality, and equilibrium. Knowledge of the Real as He is in Himself demands a balance of the perspectives of reason and imagination, a vision with "both eyes."

According to the Shaykh, only reason can grasp the first Shahadah, which demands incomparability and difference, and only imagination can bridge the gap between the Real and the unreal, since it alone grasps similarity. But God's mercy takes precedence over His wrath, so His similarity and sameness are more fundamental to reality than His incomparability and difference. It follows that reason, which perceives difference, must in some sense be subservient to imagination, which perceives sameness. If incomparability is a necessary starting point, it has to be oriented toward establishing the precedent and more basic attribute, which is similarity. Here we begin to see the essential role played by revelation in general and the second Shahadah in particular, which make assertions about the Real's self-disclosures and explain how it is possible to intensify one's similarity with the Real.

The Divine Form

Everything in the universe is a "sign" of God, since all things reflect the Real in some manner, on pain of nonexistence. But human beings are signs of God as God, since they alone are given a share of every attribute of the Real. This is proven, for example, by the fact that they have the potential to know everything—as the Koran puts it, *God taught Adam all the names* (2:31). Their fundamental cognitive (and ontological) archetype is God himself, not any specific attribute of God. The fullness of human actuality brings all divine attributes into play, those of majesty as well as those of beauty, but, as in God, the attributes are ranked according to a specific hierarchy, with the names of mercy taking precedence over the names of wrath, the names of similarity being more fundamental than the names of incomparability.

Islam, like other postaxial religions, is oriented primarily toward salvation. Felicity, which is the condition of those who enter paradise, is identified with nearness to God, while wretchedness is experienced in distance from Him. To be near to God is to recognize and actualize the qualities of the Real as one's own. To be distant is to fail to actualize the divine form. To achieve nearness is to live in the divine similarity. To remain in distance is to be dominated by the attributes of incomparability. If people are to achieve felicity, their imagination must dominate over their reason, though it must conform to reason's guidance.

The human being begins as a potentially total form of God. Perfection is achieved when the potential becomes actual. This human embodiment of divine attributes is known as "goodness" and "virtue" and is studied in the science of ethics. In the last analysis, to be humanly good is to participate in the divine goodness, the only real goodness. But since ethics goes back to divine qualities, and divine qualities are unknowable in their incomparability, reason cannot be the final arbiter of human goodness. Revelation must intervene to show the way to actualize the divine attributes in proper proportion (or to explain the underlying nature and purpose of ethical activity).

All and Nothing

The Real is a coincidence of opposites that possesses fully and absolutely every real quality. To the extent that things are real, they manifest the Real's attributes. From this point of view, all reality found in the unreal things of the cosmos is God's reality. In other words, God is "all," but not in a pantheistic sense, because God's incomparability demands that He remain infinitely beyond every limitation that defines the things.

When human perfection is viewed in relation to God as All, it is understood as the full actualization of the qualities of the Real. In Koranic language, the perfected human being is known as God's "vicegerent."

But God is not only all; He is also "nothing." In other words, viewed in respect of incomparability, the Real is no thing as opposed to any other thing, since the Real transcends all things and all attributes. God possesses all qualities, so He cannot be defined by any of them to the exclusion of any other. Hence He has no specific reality other than to be Reality as such, without any delimitation. Reality as such is not a thing as opposed to other things, but the source of all things. Hence the Real is no thing, nothing.

When human perfection is viewed in relation to God as incomparable, it demands the abandonment of individual existence. Individual existence is configured through the limitations that derive from the fact that each person is a knot tied in *wujūd*, or a word articulated within God's Breath. Each thing imposes restrictions and constraints upon reality by being what it is. Nothing can give up what it is without ceasing to be what it is, with the sole exception of human beings: They alone become what they are by giving up what they are.

All things other than human beings are defined by their specific attributes. Human beings are defined by being the form of God. God's form, like God himself, represents no specific attributes, since it is the self-disclosure of *wujūd* as such. The *fiṭra* of other creatures is defined by specific and delimited attributes of *wujūd*, whereas the human *fiṭra* manifests *wujūd*'s nondelimitation. The true meaning of existing as something other than a human being is to be defined by a specific limitation and to dwell in a "known station," but the true meaning of existing as a human being is to abandon all limitations and to enter the unknown station. Nonhuman things have no choice but to remain what they are, but human beings can be truly human only by choosing to become nothing. In Koranic language, this utter nothingness is known as being God's "servant."

Logically, being a servant (nothing) precedes being a vicegerent (everything). In order to be everything, human beings must abandon their own attributes. Abandoning attributes means to return everything positive and good to its rightful owner—the Real. Being a servant is to embody the reality of God's incomparability, the fact that God alone is real and nothing else has any reality. The servant actualizes his utter servitude, emptiness, poverty, and nonexistence. In contrast, being a vicegerent is to embody the reality of God's similarity. Once human beings are emptied of their own limitations, God discloses Himself fully within them, since they alone are made in His form. "The servant necessarily becomes manifest in the form of the Real when he makes manifest his servanthood, which is activity in conformity with what God has prescribed" (IV 104.3).

The Shaykh often refers to the realization of full human perfection as the "Station of No Station." The human being who actualizes the divine form ceases to be this or that and stands with the Real in every station while not being constrained by any specific station. Hence the perfected human being is "no thing," just as God is no thing. As the Shaykh puts it, "The most all-inclusive specification is that a person not be distinguished by a station whereby he is distinguished" (IV 76.31).

Prophecy and Guidance

God's mercy takes precedence over His wrath. In other words, God's similarity is more fundamental than His incomparability, even though people begin with the perception of incomparability. The priority of mercy expresses the inherent nature of *wujūd*. It demands that God's activity be oriented toward the good of all things. In more practical terms, the precedence of mercy demands that God take human felicity into account. Felicity means not only nearness to God, but also the proper situation of a thing without which it can only be miserable. In this sense of the word, all things have their own felicities. For a thing to be happy is for it to be allowed to be what it is in accordance with what its own *fiṭra* demands.

Human beings stand apart from other creatures because full perfection and felicity are achieved not through being but through not-being. Perfection demands giving up the limitations and constraints that make them this or that. But this freedom from constraint can only be reached freely. God cannot impose freedom on human beings, because imposition contradicts freedom. Nor can He impose felicity upon them without depriving them of their humanity, because full human perfection demands standing in the Station of No Station, not the station of felicity. Given that God's primary motivation arises from His predominant attributes—mercy, compassion, love, gentleness—His goal is to provide human beings the best means to actualize fullness and freedom. More specifically, God as Guide shows people the way to reach felicity, and He does this by sending messages by means of prophets.

Knowledge provided by revelation is oriented toward the overcoming of difference. Hence it is rooted in God's similarity, tends to take mythical form, and is more easily grasped by imagination than by reason, because imagination perceives God in terms of similar attributes. Revelation provides a map that leads to felicity. When Muslims utter the second Shahadah, "Muhammad is the messenger of God," they commit themselves to follow the Path of Muhammad, rather than the general Path of the Blessing-giver, not to mention the myriad other paths that fill the cosmos.

The first Shahadah, in contrast to the second, expresses the underlying nature of reality and is innate to human nature. The prophets do not provide people with knowledge of the first Shahadah but simply remind them that they already possess it. The first Shahadah is grasped by reason, and this helps explain why human beings are defined as "rational" animals. But the specifically prophetic and eschatological knowledge pertains to myth and the imaginal realm rather than to rational discourse, to similarity rather than to incomparability. That is why the Shaykh tells us in his Myth of Origins that the sages were able to understand God's incomparability without external help, but they had to wait for the coming of the prophets in order to understand the path to salvation.

The positive qualities present in cosmic existence merge with *wujūd*. In one respect these qualities are similar and can be known, and in another respect they are incomparable and unknowable. God in Himself is inexpressible, while everything other than God is an expression. Expression demands difference, delimitation, otherness, knotting. Revelation represents God's self-expression out of mercy and gentleness with a view toward guidance. It delineates and describes Reality in modes that are capable of being grasped by beings tied in knots. It brings about the possibility of dissolving difference, delimitation, and otherness. It is governed by attributes of similarity, that is, the precedent attributes of the Real. It is an active expression of nearness, configuring a clear pattern within the ambiguity of existence and oriented toward felicity. It ties knots that are conducive to ultimate happiness. And it provides the means to untie the knots that prevent people from being all and nothing.

Guidance is oriented toward the actualization of sameness with the Real, or union with God. But authorities like Ibn al-'Arabī do not understand concepts such as "union" in an absolute sense, since there can be no absolutes outside the Absolute. What such concepts imply is that the proper course of human becoming—the course that leads to felicity and fulfillment—moves from relative distance to relative nearness, relative darkness to relative light, relative unreality to relative reality, relative separation to relative union, relative otherness to relative identity. Nevertheless, normal language and the demands of human psychology and felicity eliminate the adjective "relative." And this is justified by Reality itself, since the difference between the fullest achievement of human possibilities and its least achievement is significant enough to warrant the use of absolute terms.

The Shaykh brings out the implications of the never-ending and never-repeating self-disclosures of the Real explicitly: Created beings, human or otherwise, can never reach the Real as such, nor can they ever be completely separate from the Real. Hence they can never come to a halt. The veils standing between the absolutely Real and the relatively real are infinite and will never be totally lifted; or rather, they will be lifted continuously for all eternity. To experience *wujūd* is to live in the never-ending flux of continual creation, the everlasting affirmation of difference and sameness, incomparability and similarity. But the modes of experiencing God's continual self-disclosures differ infinitely. Divine guidance assures that the experience of self-disclosure takes place in a manner that is harmonious with and congenial to the being that experiences it, whereas misguidance and error mean that peace and harmony will not necessarily be experienced in the next stages of existence.

Providential Limitations

Generally speaking, expressions of Islamic religiosity focus on the implications of God as Guide, not God as God. Only certain forms of Sufism and philosophy make knowledge of the (relatively) unqualified Real a goal of human life. Otherwise, the demands of general human welfare take precedence over the need for some human beings to achieve the Station of No Station. In other words, the vast majority of expressions of Islam make no attempt to take into account the naked, unqualified truth of the first Shahadah. Rather, the religious teachings focus on the second Shahadah and color the first Shahadah appropriately.

For Muslims, guidance takes the concrete form of the Koran and the Sunnah of the Prophet. Other modes of guidance, other revealed religions, are affirmed in the Koran and generally recognized, but these are never stressed and usually explained away. In effect, "Muhammad is the Messenger of God" becomes an absolute point of reference, determining how "There is no god but God" will be interpreted. And this is not a position to be condemned, because it is demanded by the implications of God as Guide for this community as a whole. People in any case will worship the gods of their beliefs; the Guide provides the only means for them to escape (to some degree) from their own limitations. The revealed knots are providential, because they help untie the knots that keep people from felicity.

The stress of a given religious community on a specific self-revelation of the Guide brings into existence its hard edges. God's guidance provides a (relative) divine justification for focusing on a single manifestation of the unqualified and nondelimited Real and ignoring others. But to make absolute claims for a revelation that by nature can only be one of many brings about a certain imbalance and distortion that modern-day observers quickly sense. It skews reality in a way analogous to what happens when the ego lays claim to uniqueness and fails to "love its neighbor as itself."

The divine quality of guidance orients human beings toward mercy, compassion, harmony, love, and unity. In its outer realms, guidance is concerned with regulating activity. Regulated activity demands difference and conflict with unregulated activity, or with activity regulated by other self-revelations of the Guide. In its more inner realms, however, guidance brings about conformity with the Real, which is one, and hence it correlates with peace, love, and harmony. The internal logic of revealed religions fosters a movement from the outside to the inside, from dispersion to unity, from separation to union, from wrath to mercy, from disdain to love. The demands of externality, which correlates with incomparability and distance, are relativized by the demands of the precedent attributes, which correlate with the internal, the similar, the near.

Guidance leads to the center, the Real. Those human beings who have actualized the Real's attributes in perfect harmony and equilibrium stand in the Station of No Station, free of domination by any specific attributes. As Ibn al-'Arabī's disciple Qūnawī puts it, they have become "the point at the center of the circle of *wujūd*" (*nuqṭa wasaṭ dā'irat al-wujūd*). Perfect human beings, having realized the divine form, put all things in their proper places and recognize the legitimacy of everything that exists. At the same time, they observe the rights of the individual divine names. They give God as Guide His due. This means that perfect human embodiments of the Real will recognize both the necessity of error for the equilibrium of reality as a whole and the need to avoid it for the sake of human felicity. "Muhammad is the messenger of God" retains all its rights, even though, when seen from the perspective of "There is no god but God," it has specific implications that do not coincide with a broader based view of Reality. In the terms employed in the previous chapter, this is to say that the prescriptive command must be followed even if the engendering command demands the existence of every sort of error and misguidance.

Fully actualized human beings, free of all limitations, choose freely to enter back into limitation and expression with a view toward guidance. "The perfect human being stands in the station of the name 'God' among the divine names. He is nondelimited, but he speaks only in a mode that is delimited by the situation" (IV 194.14). Even though perfect human beings stand in the Station of No Station, they adopt the station of guidance for the good of those who need it. This is simply the implication of the nature of things, for "God's mercy takes precedence over His wrath," oneness overcomes manyness, guidance is more real than error, and compassionate human beings give of themselves in order to deliver lost souls from ignorance and suffering.

Appreciating Knots

Any methodology can be nothing but a knot in terms of which reality is construed. In the name of objectivity or other norms, certain assumptions are made about experienced reality. Modern methodologies are often considered to have achieved a superior view of things because of their critical approach, but the belief that one's approach is "critical" already represents a particularly intractable knot. As the Shaykh would point out, the gods of critical belief have no privileged place in the pantheon. God is also the Critic, no doubt, but God as the Guide has a far greater claim to human loyalty. Were the Critic a revealed divine name, it would be allied with names such as Differentiating, Just, Severe, and Wrathful. Hence it would fall into the category of names that demand difference and incomparability. But the Real demands the predominance of undifferentiation over differentiation, bounty over justice, gentleness over severity, and mercy over wrath. One ignores this fact at one's peril. In this sort of context, the Shaykh likes to quote the *ḥadīth qudsī* in which the Real says, "I am with My servant's opinion of Me, so let him have a good opinion of Me."

Ibn al-'Arabī's approach provides a predisposition toward the study of religion that is also a knot, no doubt. Nevertheless, by recognizing the existence of knots and appreciating their value, and by acknowledging the position (perhaps never attainable) of untying all knots, this approach may provide certain insights unavailable to other points of view.

By taking up the Shaykh's standpoint, one is predisposed to deal with religious diversity as follows: Religion appears among human beings because the Real as Guide desires to bring about human wholeness and felicity. But manifestations of the Guide can never embrace the total truth—the Real as such, which lies beyond expression and form. Hence each religion has its own specific mode of expression that is necessarily different from other modes of expression.

Each revealed religion establishes a unique imaginal world, conceived of by the divine imagination—the Breath of the All-merciful—with the specific aim of allowing human beings to overcome distance and establish nearness, or to move from disequilibrium to harmony, from the many to the One, from the unreal to the Real, from dispersion to Unity, from ignorance to knowledge, from forgetfulness to wakefulness. The goal is felicity, which is inseparable from the precedent attributes of the Real. Reason plays a fundamental role, because it alone allows people not to fall into the error of *shirk*, of associating the Real's self-disclosures with the Real Itself. Reason alone allows people to understand that the Real is situated beyond every image. Pushed too far, however, reason destroys the imaginal coherence of the revealed worldview. Hence, for the sake of human felicity, it must be held back by the bounds established through the revealed forms.

The specific imaginal forms that guidance assumes in a given religion will be determined by the cultural and linguistic receptacles as much as by the specific self-disclosure of the Guide—the prophet, avatara, buddha, sage—who initiates the religion. In the last analysis, these two sides of reality are inseparable: The cultural and linguistic receptacles, like the revelations, are self-disclosures of the Real. "The water assumes the color of its cup," but the cup is nothing but frozen water.

Each religion explains in its own terms the goal of human existence by differentiating between what human beings are now and what they should be. The description of the present situation correlates with the expression of incomparability, distance, and difference. Human beings dwell in imperfection and suffering, because in some way they are cut off from the Real. The description of what people must become correlates with the expression of similarity. They must establish harmony with the precedent attributes of the Real.

Each religion sets down practical instructions to bring about greater harmony with the Real. In concrete terms, this means that each religion has a variety of means to transform thought, activity, attitudes, and whatever it is that makes up a human being. Revelation overthrows or revalorizes the preexistent gods of belief by providing new perspectives on reality and untying knots. Nevertheless, it establishes gods of belief that help people orient themselves toward felicity. But felicity itself is open-ended, which is to say that there is no upper limit on what it implies. As full forms of the Real, human beings can eliminate—with the Real's guidance—all the constraints and knots that make them this and not that. Many religions have the means to dissolve their own myths and gods, since full human perfection demands the Station of No Station, while revealed myths and gods, as imaginal apparitions, are themselves knots (though providentially so).

In short, Ibn al-'Arabī maintains that one should recognize and appreciate both the perspective of eliminating gods and knots and that of affirming gods and tying knots. I know of no advice to the student of religion better than the following:

> Beware of becoming delimited by a specific knotting and disbelieving in everything else, lest great good escape you. . . . Be in yourself a matter for the forms of all beliefs, for God is wider and more tremendous than that He should be constricted by one knotting rather than another. (*Fuṣūṣ* 113)

> He who counsels his own soul should investigate, during his life in this world, all doctrines concerning God. He should learn from whence each possessor of a doctrine affirms the validity of his doctrine. Once its validity has been affirmed for him in the specific mode in which it is correct for him who holds it, then he should support it in the case of him who believes in it. (II 85.11)

Notes

Introduction

1. Given the sophistication of Ibn al-'Arabī's works, scholars tend to overlook the popular radiance of his personality and teachings. See Chodkiewicz, "Diffusion of Ibn 'Arabī's Doctrine," pp. 36-57.

2. On Ibn al-'Arabī's meeting with Averroes, mentioned in most accounts of the former's life, see Corbin, *Creative Imagination in the Ṣūfism of Ibn 'Arabī*, pp. 41-42; and Addas, *Quest for the Red Sulphur*, pp. 34-38.

3. To quote the name of a section from Seyyed Hossein Nasr's chapter on Ibn al-'Arabī in *Three Muslim Sages*.

4. See, for example, S. H. Nasr's essay, "Islam and the Encounter of Religions," in his *Sufi Essays*. Nasr defends and even represents the Sufi form of Islam, and his Gifford lectures, *Knowledge and the Sacred*, show how a contemporary Sufi is able to find God's mercy in all traditional religions. Also noteworthy are the works of Frithjof Schuon, who writes with intellectual rigor from within a perspective that is often recognizably Sufi. His *Transcendent Unity of Religions* sets the tone for his many books.

5. All quotations from Ibn al-'Arabī are from *al-Futūḥāt al-makkiyya* unless otherwise indicated. Roman numerals indicate the volume number, and Arabic numerals refer to the page and line numbers.

6. Judith A. Berling, "Is Conversation about Religion Possible?" *Journal of the American Academy of Religion* 61 (1993): 3.

7. As Eliade puts it, "Nonreligious man has been formed by opposing his predecessor, by attempting to 'empty' himself of all religion and all transhuman meaning" (*Sacred and the Profane*, p. 204).

8. "Diffusion of Ibn 'Arabī's Doctrine," p. 51.

9. For an extended discussion of the meaning of this title, its historical context, and the passages in which Ibn al-'Arabī lays claim to it, see Chodkiewicz, *Seal of the Saints*.

10. For this vision, see Addas, *Quest for the Red Sulphur*, Chapter 3.

11. For the universe as God's dream, see Chittick, *Sufi Path of Knowledge*, especially pp. 120-21. From here on this book will be referred to as SPK.

12. The original versions of the chapters appeared (or will appear) as follows: 1. "Higenshō kara Genshōsekai e: Ibun Arabī no 'Sonzaisseiron,'" in *Isurāmu Shisō* II, edited by T. Izutsu (Tokyo: Iwanami, 1988), pp. 85-108; English version as "Ebno'l-'Arabi's Doctrine of the Oneness of Being," *Sufi* 4 (1989-90): 6-14. 2. "Microcosm, Macrocosm, and Perfect Man," in *Man the Macrocosm: Proceedings of the Fourth Annual Symposium of the Muhyiddin Ibn 'Arabi Society*, March 1987, pp. 10-15. 3. "Ethical Standards and the Vision of Oneness: The Case of Ibn al-'Arabī," in *Mystics of the Book: Themes, Topics and Typologies*, edited by R. A. Herrera (New York: Peter Lang, 1993), pp. 361-76. 4. "Between the Yes and the No: Ibn al-'Arabī on Innate Mystical Consciousness," in *The Innate Capacity*, edited by Robert Forman, forthcoming. 5. "The World of Imagination and Poetic Imagery According to Ibn al-'Arabī," *Temenos* 10 (1989): 99-119. 6. "Meetings with Imaginal Men," in *Proceedings of the Fourth Annual U.S.A. Symposium on Ibn 'Arabi*, forthcoming. 7. "Death and the World of Imagination: Ibn al-'Arabī's Eschatology," *The Muslim World* 78 (1988): 51-82. 8. "From the *Meccan Openings*: The Myth of the Origin of Religion and the Law," *The World and I* 3/1 (January 1988): 655-65. 9. Combination of a. "Belief and Transformation: The Sufi Teachings of Ibn al-'Arabī," *The American Theosophist* 74/5 (1986): 181-92. b. "A Sufi Approach to Religious Diversity: Ibn al-'Arabī on the Metaphysics of Revelation," in *The Religion of the Heart*, edited by S. H. Nasr and W. Stoddart (Washington: Foundation for Traditional Studies, 1991), pp. 50-90. 10. "Appreciating Knots: An Islamic Approach to Religious Diversity," in *Interreligious Models and Criteria*, edited by J. Kellenberger (London: Macmillan, 1993), pp. 3-20.

13. See also the selections from the *Futūḥāt* translated in Chodkiewicz et al., *Meccan Illuminations*.

Chapter 1. Oneness of Being

1. Many of Ibn al-'Arabī's important students, beginning with his most influential disciple, Ṣadr al-Dīn Qūnawī (d. 1274), tried to bring the intellectual expression of Sufism into harmony with Peripatetic philosophy. The primary concern of the philosophers was *wujūd* or "existence." Thus the term *waḥdat al-wujūd*—built from the word *waḥda* (derived from the same root as *tawḥīd*, the "assertion of unity" that is taken as the first principle of Islam) and from a second word that delineates the central concern of philosophy—alerts us to the fact that we are dealing with a synthesis of the religious and philosophical traditions. In attempting to trace the history of this expression, I found that Qūnawī uses it on at least two occasions in his works, while his disciple Sa'īd al-Dīn

Farghānī (d. 1296) employs it many times. But neither uses the term in the technical sense that it gained in later centuries. At the same time, certain relatively peripheral members of Ibn al-'Arabī's school, such as Ibn Sab'īn (d. 1270), writing in Arabic, and 'Azīz al-Dīn Nasafī (d. before 1300), writing in Persian, were employing the term *waḥdat al-wujūd* to allude to the worldview of the sages and Sufis. Then the Hanbalite jurist Ibn Taymiyya (d. 1328), well-known for his attacks on all schools of Islamic intellectuality, seized upon the term as a synonym for the well-known heresies of *ittiḥād* ("unificationism") and *ḥulūl* ("incarnationism"). From Ibn Taymiyya's time onward, the term *waḥdat al-wujūd* was used more and more commonly to refer to the overall perspective of Ibn al-'Arabī and his followers. For jurists like Ibn Taymiyya it was a term of blame, synonymous with "unbelief" and "heresy," but many Muslim intellectuals accepted *waḥdat al-wujūd* as a synonym for *tawḥīd* in philosophical and Sufi language. See Chittick, "Rūmī and *Waḥdat al-wujūd*."

2. For detailed discussions of the meaning of *wujūd* in Ibn al-'Arabī's thought, see SPK, pp. 3, 6, 80-81, 133, 212, 226-27 and passim.

3. Throughout this book quotations from the Koran are printed in italics, with chapter and verse indicated in parentheses in the text and in brackets in quoted material.

4. On divine roots and supports, see SPK, pp. 37-38. For a fine analysis of the scriptural foundation of Ibn al-'Arabī's writings, see Chodkiewicz, *Ocean Without Shore*.

5. It can be objected to my exposition here and elsewhere in this book that if God is truly "unknowable," then *tanzīh* does not represent the perspective of unknowability, because through *tanzīh* we "know" God in negative terms. This is true enough, and Ibn al-'Arabī is perfectly aware of it, but usually he does not bother refining the discussion to this extent, because the opposition between incomparability and similarity is sufficient for the context. In a number of passages, he refers to the fact that in respect of the Essence itself, God cannot be known or discussed. That leaves us with two points of view that can be discussed: the first acknowledges that God can be known negatively; the second, that He can be known positively. See, for example, II 257.22, translated in SPK, p. 172. In a similar vein, he qualifies the perspective of incomparability as follows: "The name Nonmanifest belongs to Him, not to us. We have nothing in our hands of it save *Nothing is like Him* [42:11] in certain plausible senses of the verse. However, the attributes of incomparability have a certain connection with the name Nonmanifest. Although declaring incomparability involves a certain assertion of delimitation, nothing more than this is possible, for this is the utmost limit of the understanding that our preparedness gives to us" (III 440.16).

6. The word for dream interpretation is *ta'bīr*, which comes from a root meaning, "to pass over, to cross, to ford." The interpreter crosses over from the formal content of the dream to its hidden meaning. The Koran issues the commandment, *So interpret, O possessors of eyes!* (59:2) in one instance, the context having to to with how God shaped certain events that took place during the Prophet's stay in Medina. The word the Koran employs here is *i'tibār*, from the same root as *ta'bīr*. In its most basic sense, *i'tibār* means "to undergo a (mental) crossing (from one thing to

another thing)." Koran translators render the word in ways that bring it closer to ordinary English: "Take example" (Palmer), "Learn a lesson" (Pickthall), "Learn from their examples" (Dawood), "Take heed" (Arberry). But here Ibn al-'Arabī reads the word as being synonymous with *ta'bīr*, and the Arabic language certainly allows this reading.

7. For the passage in its context, see SPK, p. 118.

Chapter 2. Microcosm, Macrocosm, and Perfect Man

1. For some of the names, see SPK, Chapter 8; Ḥakīm, *al-Mu'jam al-ṣūfī*, p. 158.

2. Allusion to the words of Satan to his followers when they enter the chastisement of hell: *Do not blame me, but blame yourselves* (14:22).

Chapter 3. Ethics and Antinomianism

1. In the last analysis, the laws of *wujūd* cannot be contravened by a *mawjūd*, an existent thing. In Chapter 9, we will look more closely at the difference between *wujūd* itself, which cannot be contradicted, and certain specific attributes of *wujūd*—such as guidance—which focus on delivering human beings from limitation and suffering and which can be contravened, at least in the short term.

2. See SPK, pp. 304-9.

Chapter 4. Self-Knowledge and the Original Human Disposition

1. The root meaning of the term *ḥanīf* is to incline toward or away from something, while the term itself is understood to mean someone who inclines toward the right way. The Koran uses it in twelve verses, and these determine the way Muslims have understood it. It is taken to signify the faith of Abraham and those who continued to follow him in the Arab milieu, even after most people had become polytheists. Thus the Prophet is said to have been *ḥanīf* before he was made a prophet. See the article "Ḥanīf," in *Encyclopedia of Islam* (new edition).

2. Compare his discussion in II 616.91, quoted in SPK, p. 195.

3. This saying should not be understood as a blanket criticism of the three mentioned religions, especially in the Koranic context, which, as noted in the introduction, mentions various religions in both positive and negative lights. In the majority of cases in which the Koran makes negative statements, the objects of criticism are specified as certain people among the followers of the religion in question, not all followers.

4. On this double significance of the word *dhikr*, which arguably sums up Islamic teachings better than any other word, see Chittick, "Dhikr."

5. For the image of sun and clouds in this context, see II 616.26, translated in SPK, p. 195.

6. This is not to suggest that clay is negative or evil. The point is simply that clay represents an opposite extreme from spirit . Muslim thinkers, Ibn al-'Arabī in particular, were well aware of the many virtues of clay, earth, and water. See Murata, *Tao of Islam*, pp. 136-41 and passim.

7. I provide basic definitions for this second set of terms in SPK, Chapter 13 and passim. Ibn al-'Arabī also discusses numerous "states" (*aḥwāl*) and "stations" (*maqāmāt*), which represent various psychological and spiritual modalities in which people experience *wujūd*. Likewise, he discusses the faculties of mind, the nature of thoughts, techniques of meditation and concentration, and so on.

8. On God's two hands and their relationship with these two groups of names as expounded by Ibn al-'Arabī and his commentators, see Murata, *Tao of Islam*, Chapter 3.

9. For some of Ibn al-'Arabī's basic teachings on witnessing, see SPK, pp. 225-28 and passim.

10. For a detailed study of the Shaykh's spiritual ascents, see the passages translated into English and explained by J. W. Morris in Chodkiewicz et al., *Meccan Illuminations*, pp. 351ff.; also Morris, "Spiritual Ascension."

11. Ibn al-'Arabī's disciple Ṣadr al-Dīn Qūnawī recounts a similar visionary experience and explains how he saw that the person who reaches this stage has no immutable entity. Since the immutable entity denotes the fixed and delimited reality of a specific thing—as opposed to the nondelimited reality of *wujūd*—this is to say that such a human being attains to the vision of the human archetype, which is God Himself. Qūnawī's own words are as follows: "I saw in this tremendous locus of witnessing, when the Real allowed me to witness it, that its possessor has no immutable entity and no reality. This is the situation of him who is in His form. Everything other than this witnesser and his Lord possesses an immutable entity that is clothed in *wujūd*" (*al-Nafaḥāt al-ilāhiyya*, p. 305).

Chapter 5. Revelation and Poetic Imagery

1. The expression *naẓar 'aqlī* can be translated as "rational speculation" or simply "reason" and was a primary concern of the theologians. Nicholson may have thought that this is the sort of *naẓar* that Ibn al-'Arabī had in mind. But he should have known that the Shaykh is highly critical of the rational approach of Muslim theologians.

2. It is important to make a distinction between the positive meaning given to *ta'wīl* by many Muslim thinkers, Shi'ites in particular, and the negative sense it assumes

in the eyes of Ibn al-'Arabī, especially because one of the greatest authorities on these issues, Henry Corbin, failed to make this distinction. See SPK, pp. 199ff.

3. For the Shaykh's understanding of the importance of courtesy and its connection with wisdom, see SPK, pp. 174-79.

4. The feminine gender of nouns had far-reaching implications for the Shaykh's meditations on the masculine and feminine dimensions of God and the cosmos, as he brings out in the final chapter of the *Fuṣūṣ al-ḥikam*. For a careful study of relevant passages from this chapter and the commentary literature, see Murata, *Tao of Islam*, pp. 188-202.

5. The world created from the remainder of Adam's clay is a visionary, imaginal world experienced by the gnostics. The "Market of the Garden," mentioned in the hadith literature, is a market in paradise wherein are displayed beautiful forms; when one of the felicitous desires a form on display, he enters into it. More will be said about this in Chapter 7. Spirits of light are angels, while spirits of fire are jinn; the "bodies" of both appear in the imaginal world.

6. The Koran refers to Joseph's dream interpretation in 12:46-49. By deriving the last two examples of Joseph's knowledge from sayings of Muhammad, Ibn al-'Arabī seems to be alluding to a certain permanence of symbolic forms in the imaginal world.

7. The name of the woman who is celebrated in the *Tarjumān al-ashwāq*—playing a similar role to Dante's Beatrice—was Niẓām or "harmonious arrangement." From Ibn al-'Arabī's perspective, the fact that this quality pertains to the sphere of Joseph and poetry surely had something to do with the destiny that led her to be given the name and to inspire the Shaykh's poetical imagination.

Chapter 6. Meetings with Imaginal Men

1. Ibn al-'Arabī maintains that "Everything the human being perceives in dreams derives from that which was apprehended by the imagination through the senses in the state of wakefulness. [The contents of dreams are] of two kinds: In one kind, the form of the thing was perceived in the sensory realm; in the other kind, the parts of the form perceived in the dream were perceived in the sensory realm. There is no doubt about this" (II 375.10).

2. These three are mentioned along with the Real as the source of imaginal apparitions in II 333.33. In a typical passage, the Shaykh speaks of the kinship of these three kinds of spirit: "The angels are spirits blown into lights, the jinn are spirits blown into winds [*rīḥ*], and humankind are spirits blown into bodily forms [*shabaḥ*]" (I 132.20). On the question of the appearance of a human being "in any of the forms of the children of Adam like himself, or in the form of animals, plants, or minerals," see *Futūḥāt*, Chapter 311, translated into English in Chodkiewicz et al., *Meccan Illuminations*, pp. 287ff.

3. See SPK, pp. 336-37.

4. The term *secondary causes* (*asbāb*) refers to everything other than God that acts as a cause for something else. In other words, it refers to everything in the cosmos, beginning with the First Intellect, since there is nothing that is not the cause of something else. The term is roughly equivalent to "things" (*ashyā'*) or "entities" (*a'yān*). See SPK, pp. 44-46 and passim.

5. See SPK, p. 387, note 17.

6. Allusion to Koran 15:18: *We have set in heaven constellations and decked them out fair to the beholders, and guarded them from every accursed satan, excepting such as listens by stealth.*

7. This word, derived from the Greek *sêmeia*, is often translated as "letter magic," but it has a far wider application, as can be seen by looking at the instances in which Ibn al-'Arabī uses it. See Chodkiewicz et al., *Meccan Illuminations*, passim.

8. See SPK, p. 117.

9. Cf. ibid., p. 404, note 24.

10. See Addas, *Quest for the Red Sulphur*, Chapter 5.

11. For a translation of the whole passage, see ibid., pp. 174-75.

12. For a fuller (but not complete) translation of this passage, see ibid., pp. 215-16.

Chapter 7. Death and the Afterlife

1. See SPK, pp. 73-76.

2. See Ghazālī, *Precious Pearl*, pp. 30, 34, 36, 49, 50, 53, 60, 87; Tabrīzī, *Mishkat al-masabih*, pp. 340, 448-49, 490-91, 1176.

3. On the development of the soul, cf. Murata, *Tao of Islam*, Chapters 8-10.

4. Quoted in Chittick, *Faith and Practice of Islam*, p. 99. The three Sufi texts translated in this work along with the notes provide many examples of how the Shaykh's teachings on the afterlife were understood and applied by the next generation of scholars.

5. For diagrams that Ibn al-'Arabī provides to summarize his teachings, see Chittick, "Ibn 'Arabī and His School," pp. 75-79.

6. See Murata, *Tao of Islam*, Chapter 5.

7. Particular spirits (*al-arwāḥ al-juz'iyya*) are contrasted with universal spirits, which include the Intellect, the Soul, and human spirits. The latter are all disengaged (*mujarrad*) and therefore exist beyond the level of nature as defined here. On "natural bodies," see I 261.5; II 335.10.

8. He often distinguishes these from *ajsām* by calling them *ajsād*. See I 133.13, 307.8; III 186.28, 389.13.

9. I 294.27; compare II 184.1, 244.33. On the location of paradise and hell, see I 123.9, 169.9, 299.20; II 440.1; III 442.8. On the fact that the next world is natural rather than elemental, see I 276.24; II 184.1. On the elemental nature of hell, see III 244.33.

10. It would appear that the natural but nonelemental corporeal bodies that dwell *below* the eighth sphere, such as the lower angels and the mental faculties, manifest both mercy and wrath.

11. In the present context, I can only mention a small number of his arguments. His basic contention is nothing new in Islamic thought, given that even a majority of the Kalām authorities were forced to conclude the same thing (cf. Smith and Haddad, *Islamic Understanding of Death and Resurrection*, p. 95).

12. Ibn al-'Arabī refers to the sinners (*mujrimūn*) as "the people of the Fire, those who are its inhabitants" (*ahl al-nār alladhīna hum ahluhā*) in order to distinguish them from others who enter the Fire for a time and then are removed from it. He divides the *mujrimūn* into four distinct and well-defined groups: the proud (*al-mutakabbirūn*), the associators (*al-mushrikūn*), the atheists (*al-mu'aṭṭila*), and the hypocrites (*al-munāfiqūn*), and discusses the traditional basis for considering only these four as permanent inhabitants of hell. See *Futūḥāt*, Chapter 61, "Fī marātib ahl al-nār" (I 301-4; compare I 314.27).

13. On the meaning of *ahwā'*, plural of *hawā*, see SPK, p. 137.

14. Compare III 389.21, quoted in SPK, p. 291.

15. Compare II 486.2; III 328.27, 433.5.

16. The Shaykh often refers to fifty thousand years as the length of the day of resurrection and provides various reasons for doing so, but in one passage he adds that he is not certain about this length, because God has not unveiled this specific knowledge to him (III 383.10).

17. On felicity as the "agreeable," see II 327.34, 486.4; III 387.23.

18. See SPK, Chapter 12 and passim.

Chapter 8. A Myth of Origins

1. Few scholars have paid much attention to Ibn al-'Arabī's criticisms of other religions. One exception is Mahmoud al-Ghorab in his article, "Muhyiddin Ibn al-'Arabi Amidst Religions (*adyān*) and Schools of Thought (*madhāhib*)," in Hirtenstein and Tiernan, *Muhyiddin Ibn 'Arabi*, pp. 200-227. Most of this material relates to the Shaykh's criticisms of various positions taken by Muslim scholars, but some of it makes reference to critical remarks directed against Jews and Christians. However, al-Ghorab

does not take into account the general principles that underlie Ibn al-ʻArabī's teachings on these matters—principles that I will be concerned to bring out in these final chapters. The Shaykh never denies the relative validity of limited perspectives, including even the schools of thought that he criticizes. What he does deny is that any specific position can embrace the position of no positions, or the Station of No Station, which is available only through divine bestowal and unveiling.

2. Ibn al-ʻArabī has in mind the connection between caprice and corruption established by the verse, *Were the Real to follow their caprices, the heavens and the earth and whosoever is in them had surely been corrupted* (23:71). On caprice as a technical term in his vocabulary, see SPK, index; compare Chittick, *Faith and Practice of Islam*, index.

3. Here the Shaykh is alluding to a Koranic verse that he frequently comments on: *I created jinn and humankind only to worship Me* (51:56).

4. See the translation by L. E. Goodman, *Ibn Tufayl's Hayy Ibn Yaqzān*.

5. The "great men" among the early philosophers include Plato, whom Ibn al-ʻArabī calls the "divine Plato." See SPK, p. 203. His criticisms pertain not only to certain of his contemporaries among philosophers, but also to the theologians or proponents of Kalām, to whom he has just alluded. Later in this same passage he places these philosophers and theologians even lower on the human scale than jurists, whom he criticizes vehemently in several passages in his works. See, for example, SPK, p. 202.

Chapter 9. Diversity of Belief

1. Allusion to Koran 38:20, words that speak of the prophet David: *We strengthened his kingdom, and We gave him wisdom and the decisive address.*

2. See SPK, pp. 297-301.

3. For more on the role of receptivity in determining the nature of the divine self-disclosure, see SPK, pp. 91-93.

4. See SPK, p. 371.

5. On these three paths, see SPK, pp. 301-3.

6. The hadith is found in Muslim (Tabrīzī, *Mishkat al-masabih*, p. 494).

7. Here the Shaykh is alluding to the words of Abraham quoted in the Koran, *Do you worship what you yourselves carve, while God created you and what you do?* (37:95-96).

8. Speaking of the beatific vision granted to the friends of God in paradise, the Shaykh points out that its scope depends upon the variety of beliefs concerning God that they are able to encompass in this world. See SPK, pp. 354-56; see also James Morris's English translation of a relevant part of Chapter 73 of the *Futūḥāt* in Chodkiewicz et al., *Meccan Illuminations*, pp. 176-84.

9. On the relationship of the divine "tasks" to the continual and constant re-creation of the cosmos, see SPK, pp. 98ff.

10. The "opponent" of the Ash'arite theologian is the follower of the Mu'tazilite school.

Chapter 10. The Divine Roots of Religion

1. In other words, we can set up a meaningful opposition between reason and imagination for purposes of discussion, even though reason cannot escape completely from imagination's hold. As Ibn al-'Arabī remarks, "The locus of beliefs is the imagination. . . . The human being never stays safe from imagination. . . . The rational faculty cannot escape his humanity" (IV 420.30, translated in SPK, p. 339).

2. The *ma'lūh* (or "divine thrall," as I have translated the term elsewhere) is demanded by conceiving of *wujūd* as a God. In a similar way, "Lord" demands "vassal," "Creator" demands "creature," "Knower" demands "object of knowledge," and so on. See SPK, pp. 60-61 and passim.

3. Cf. SPK, "The Two Denotations of the Names," pp. 36-37.

Bibliography

Addas, Claude. *Quest for the Red Sulphur: The Life of Ibn 'Arabī.* Cambridge, England: The Islamic Texts Society, 1993.

Asin Palacios, Miguel. *El Islam cristianizado.* Madrid, 1931. French translation as *L'Islam christianisé: Etude sur le Soufisme d'Ibn 'Arabī de Murcie.* Paris: Guy Trédaniel, 1982.

Austin, R. W. J. *Ibn al'Arabī: The Bezels of Wisdom.* Ramsey, N.J.: Paulist Press, 1981.

Burckhardt, Titus. *Muhyi-d-Dīn ibn 'Arabī: La sagesse des prophètes* [partial translation of the *Fuṣūṣ al-ḥikam*]. Paris: Albin Michel, 1955. English translation as *The Wisdom of the Prophets.* Gloucestershire: Beshara Publications, 1975.

———. *Mystical Astrology According to Ibn 'Arabī.* Gloucestershire: Beshara Publications, 1977.

Chittick, William C. "Dhikr." In *Encyclopedia of Religion.* New York: Macmillan, 1987, vol. 4, pp. 341-44.

———. "'Your Sight Today Is Piercing': Death and the Afterlife in Islam." In H. Obayashi (ed.), *Death and Afterlife: Perspectives of World Religions.* New York: Greenwood Press, 1992, pp. 125-39.

———. "Eschatology." In S. H. Nasr (ed.). *Islamic Spirituality: Foundations.* New York: Crossroad, 1987, pp. 378-409.

———. *Faith and Practice of Islam: Three Thirteenth Century Sufi Texts.* Albany: SUNY Press, 1992.

———. "Ibn 'Arabī and His School." In S. H. Nasr (ed.). *Islamic Spirituality: Manifestations.* New York: Crossroad, 1991, pp. 49-79.

———. "Rūmī and *Waḥdat al-wujūd.*" In A. Banani and G. Sabagh (eds.). *The Heritage of Rumi.* Cambridge: Cambridge University Press, forthcoming.

———. *The Sufi Path of Knowledge: Ibn al-'Arabī's Metaphysics of Imagination.* Albany: SUNY Press, 1989.

Chodkiewicz, Michel. "The Diffusion of Ibn 'Arabī's Doctrine." *Journal of the Muhyiddin Ibn 'Arabi Society* 9 (1991): 36-57.

———. *An Ocean Without Shore: Ibn Arabi, the Book, and the Law.* Albany: SUNY Press, 1993.

———. *The Seal of the Saints.* Cambridge, England: The Islamic Texts Society, 1993.

Chodkiewicz, Michel, et al. *Les illuminations de la Mecque/The Meccan Illuminations: Textes choisis/Selected Texts.* Paris: Sindbad, 1988.

Corbin, Henry. *Creative Imagination in the Ṣūfism of Ibn 'Arabī.* Princeton: Princeton University Press, 1969.

Eliade, Mircea. *The Sacred and the Profane: The Nature of Religion.* New York: Harper and Row, 1961.

Ghazālī, al-. *The Precious Pearl (al-Durra al-Fākhira).* Translated by J. I. Smith. Missoula: Scholars Press, 1981.

Goodman, L. E. *Ibn Tufayl's Hayy Ibn Yaqzān.* 2d ed. Los Angeles: Gee Tee Bee, 1983.

Ḥakīm, Su'ād al-. *al-Mu'jam al-ṣūfī.* Beirut: Dandara, 1981.

Hick, John. *An Interpretation of Religion.* New Haven: Yale University Press, 1989.

Hirtenstein, S., and M. Notcutt (eds.). *Muhyiddin Ibn 'Arabi: A Commemorative Volume.* London: Element Books, 1993.

Ibn al-'Arabī. *Dhakhā'ir al-a'lāq.* Edited by M. 'Abd al-Raḥmān al-Kurdī. Cairo, 1968.

———. *Fuṣūṣ al-ḥikam.* Edited by A. 'Afīfī. Beirut: Dār al-Kutub al-'Arabī, 1946.

———. *al-Futūḥāt al-makkiyya.* Cairo, 1911. Reprinted Beirut: Dār Ṣādir, n.d. Critical edition by O. Yahia. Cairo: al-Hay'at al-Miṣriyyat al-'Āmma li'l-Kitāb, 1972- .

———. *Mawāqi' al-nujūm.* Cairo: Maktaba Muḥammad 'Alī Ṣabīḥ, 1965.

———. *Risāla Lā yu'awwal 'alayhi.* In *Rasā'il Ibn 'Arabī.* Hyderabad-Deccan: The Dāiratu'l-Ma'ārifi'l-Osmania, 1948.

———. *Tarjumān al-ashwāq.* See Nicholson.

Ibn Sawdakīn. *Wasā'il al-sā'il.* Edited in M. Profitlich, *Die Terminologies Ibn 'Arabīs im "Kitāb wasā'il al-sā'il" des Ibn Saudakīn.* Freiburg im Breisgau: Klaus Schwarz Verlag, 1973.

Izutsu, Toshihiko. *Sufism and Taoism.* Los Angeles: University of California Press, 1983.

Jandī, Mu'ayyid al-Dīn. *Nafḥat al-rūḥ*. Edited by N. Māyil Harawī. Tehran: Mawlā, 1362/1983.

Morris, James. "The Spiritual Ascension: Ibn 'Arabī and the Mi'rāj." *Journal of the American Oriental Society* 107 (1987): 629-52; 108 (1988): 63-77.

Murata, Sachiko. *The Tao of Islam: A Sourcebook on Gender Relationships in Islamic Thought*. Albany: SUNY Press, 1992.

Nasr, Seyyed Hossein. "Islam and the Encounter of Religions." In the same author's *Sufi Essays*. London: George Allen and Unwin, 1972, pp. 123-51.

———. *Knowledge and the Sacred*. New York: Crossroad, 1981.

———. *Three Muslim Sages*. Cambridge: Harvard University Press, 1964.

Nicholson, R. A. *The Tarjumān al-Ashwāq: A Collection of Mystical Odes by Muḥyi'ddīn ibn al-'Arabī*. London: Theosophical Publishing House, 1978.

Nyberg, H. S. *Kleinere Schriften des Ibn al-'Arabī*. Leiden: E. J. Brill, 1919.

Qūnawī, Ṣadr al-Dīn. *al-Nafaḥāt al-ilāhiyya*. Tehran: Aḥmad Shīrāzī, 1316/1898.

Schuon, Frithjof. *The Transcendent Unity of Religions*. London: Faber and Faber, 1953.

Smith, J. I., and Y. Y. Haddad. *The Islamic Understanding of Death and Resurrection*. Albany: SUNY Press, 1981.

Tabrīzī. *Mishkat al-masabih*. Translated by James Robson. Lahore: Muhammad Ashraf, 1963-65.

Index of Sources

Chapter 66
I 322-25: 130-36
Chapter 71
I 638.32: 93
Chapter 72
I 755.7: 83
Chapter 73
II 15.27: 93
II 49.24: 8
II 58.7: 75
II 67.28: 34
II 69.27: 36
II 85.1: 153
II 85.11: 176
II 85.14: 141
II 85.21 152
II 96.12: 149
II 96.33: 37
II 98.21: 81
II 116.7: 124
II 132.25: 60
II 133.19: 63
Chapter 76
II 148.12: 146
Chapter 92
II 177.11: 149
Chapter 99
II 183.22: 109
Chapter 149
II 241.28: 47
Chapter 152
II 248.3: 147
Chapter 154
II 251.24: 127
Chapter 161
II 261.9: 92
Chapter 165
II 267.33: 139
Chapter 167
II 275.13: 81
II 280.27: 147
Chapter 176
II 295.30: 100
II 296.10: 100
II 296.27: 100
Chapter 177
II 307.21: 72
II 311.2: 12
II 313.6: 103
II 313.17: 28
Chapter 178
II 331.12: 86
II 333.28: 85
II 333.31: 85
II 335.18: 116
Chapter 188
II 375.10: 182
II 375.32: 75
II 379.3: 54
Chapter 198
II 438.23: 45
II 442.20: 127
II 466.23: 61
Chapter 206
II 485.20: 79
II 485.33: 103
Chapter 220
II 512.27: 60
II 512.30: 60
Chapter 221
II 515.24: 62
Chapter 227
II 525.2: 7
Chapter 241
II 541.23: 140
Chapter 256
II 556.14: 76
Chapter 260
II 558.30: 146
Chapter 278
II 605.13: 10
Chapter 283
II 622.22: 87
Chapter 284
II 628.4: 109
Chapter 299
II 690.30: 51
Chapter 311
III 43.19: 89
III 44.12: 87
Chapter 312
III 47.26: 98
Chapter 320
III 77.24: 35

Index of Koranic Verses

Index of Hadiths and Sayings

Index of Names and Terms